D0908775

The Undersea Discoveries
of Jacques-Yves Cousteau

DIVING FOR SUNKEN TREASURE

In the same series

THE SHARK: Splendid Savage of the Sea
(by Jacques-Yves Cousteau and Philippe Cousteau)

LIFE AND DEATH IN A CORAL SEA
(by Jacques-Yves Cousteau with Philippe Diolé)

The Undersea Discoveries
of Jacques-Yves Cousteau

DIVING
FOR
SUNKEN TREASURE

Jacques-Yves Cousteau
and Philippe Diolé

Translated from the French by J. F. Bernard

Doubleday & Company, Inc.
Garden City, New York 1971

Translated from the French by J. F. Bernard
Library of Congress Catalog Card Number 76-158349
Copyright © 1971 by Jacques-Yves Cousteau
All Rights Reserved
Printed in the Federal Republic of Germany
First Edition in the United States of America

Contents

1 IN THE GRAVEYARD OF SHIPS   11

July 18, 1968. A Half-Turn. A Warehouse of Treasures. Corsairs
of the Caribbean. A Challenge. Preliminary Reconnaissance.
Ghost Ships. 20° 43' North. The Secrets of Coral. A Garden of
Marvels.

2 A RIVER OF GOLD ACROSS THE OCEAN SEA   31

Candles, Commerce, and Colonies. The Golden Mule Train.
Wealth and Poverty. Departure. The King's Quintal. Shipboard
Mass. The Veracruz Convoy. Toward Europe. The Perils of Navi-
gation. Shipboard Life. Pastimes. The King's Debts.

3 THE SUNKEN SHIP   58

Monday, July 15. A Cannon. The Explanation. Gold Fever. The
Fantastic World of Coral. A Secret Ballot. Dynamite. In the
Heart of the Silver Bank. The Treasure Committee. Bad
Weather. An Accident. A Predicament. Where is the Rest of the
Ship? A Preliminary Balance Sheet. Reinforcements Arrive.

4 BLOOD AND GOLD 85

In Search of El Dorado. The Conquistadors. The Ancestor of the Dollar. Pirates of the Caribbean. Elizabeth I and Philip II. Ambush at Panama.

5 THE TREASURE-HUNTER'S PANOPLY 104

Our Noisy Monster. Didi's Shopping List. Final Preparations. Work Begins Again. The Pieces Begin to Fall into Place. The Bearskin. The Loch Ness Monster. An Accident.

6 GALLEONS IN PERIL 125

David and Goliath. Knives and Halberds. The Pirates' Den. The Mastery of the Seas. The Agony of the King. Nuestra Señora de la Concepción. The Hurricane.

7 THE EXCAVATION 145

St. Francis. A Lover of Coral. A Souvenir of Archimedes.

8 THE GREAT TREASURE 168

A Boston Carpenter. A Survivor Wrecking. A Secret Missions. The Treasure. The Division of Spoils. Honors.

9 STRANGE CARGO 191

Ten Tons of Coral. A Feast in the Sky and in the Water. A Hurricane Warning. Thirty or Forty Hurricanes. The Rising Ground-Level. The Stem. A Load of Ceramics. The Ship's Pharmacy. A Visit from Sharks.

10 MARITIME DISASTERS 213

A Franco-Spanish Fleet. The Opulent Caribbean. New Commercial Routes. Luxury in the New World. A Pitiful Fleet. Porcelain from China. A Hurricane Breaks. The Seafaring Dutch. The Company of the Indies.

11   FINALLY: A DATE   233

A Century Too Soon. A Large Cannon. A Find. More Bottles.
Two Sites. The Second Work Area. On the New Site. The Last
Dive. The Division of Spoils.

12   A LESSON FROM THE SEA   253

APPENDIX I   259

America Before Columbus

APPENDIX II   265

The Conquistadors and the Conquest

APPENDIX III   271

Sailing Ships

GLOSSARY   279

INDEX   299

PHOTO CREDITS

Except for those listed below, the photographs reproduced in this work were taken by Jean-Jérôme Carcopino, Bernard Chauvellin, Ron Church, Raymond Coll, Michel Deloire, François Dorado, Frédéric Dumas, Guy Richard, Ludwig Sillner and Guy Ventouillac.

Several of the photographs taken on the surface belong to the private collections of members of the *Calypso*'s team.

Iconography by Marie-Noëlle Favier.

Thanks to the following sources for the photographs listed:
Bibliothèque Nationale, Paris: 13, 15, 16, 17, 43, 149, 151.
Giraudon, Paris: 23, 25, 40, 42, 51.
Louros-Giraudon, Paris: 12.
Rickfot-Giraudon, Paris: 101.
Musée de la Marine, Paris, 50, 69, 150, 156, 159.
Musée de l'Homme, Paris: 39.
Bulloz, Paris: 24.
Roger Viollet: 41, 153.
Bibliothèque du Fort de Montrouge, Paris: 72.
Office National du Tourisme Espagnol, Paris: 74.
British Museum, London: 108, 109.
Parke-Bernet, New York: 126.
Archives Flammarion: 155.
Mariners Mirror, London: 160.
Claude Arthaud and François Hebert-Stevens (*l'Art des Conquistadors*, Arthaud): 46.
Photo of the *Vasa* by Anders Franzen (Nordstedt   Bonnier, Stockholm): 164.
Drawings by Pierre Lepetit: 10, 31, 34, 86, 91, 92, 118.
Map by Gustave Tocqueville.

Spanish possessions in the West Indies.

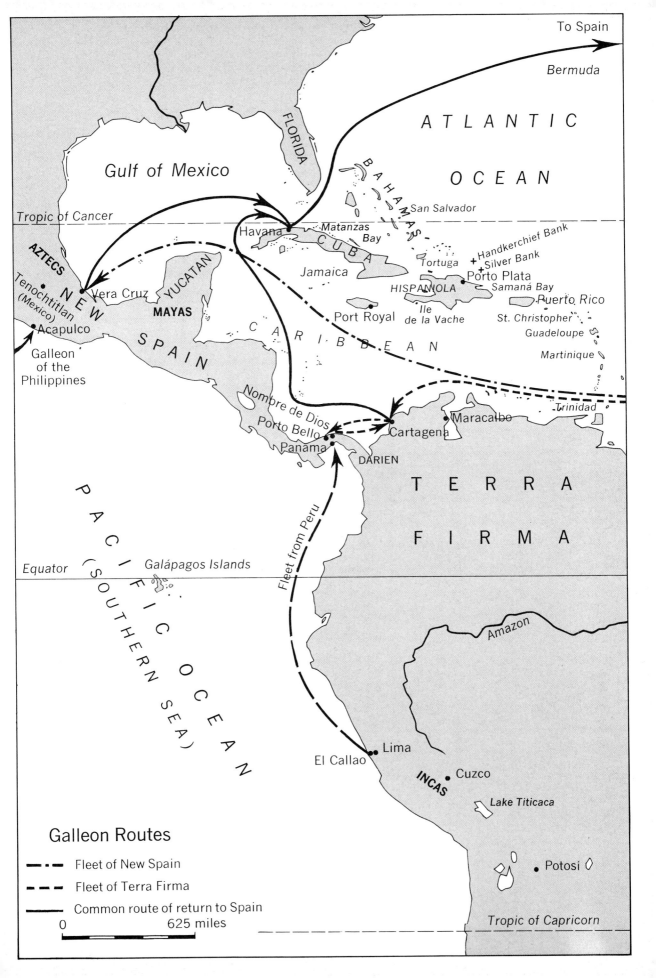

To Spain

Bermuda

ATLANTIC

OCEAN

Gulf of Mexico

FLORIDA

Tropic of Cancer

BAHAMAS

San Salvador

Havana

*Matanzas
Bay*

CUBA

Jamaica

Tortuga

+ *Handkerchief Bank*
+ *Silver Bank*

Porto Plata

Samaná Bay

HISPANIOLA

AZTECS

NEW

Vera Cruz

YUCATAN

Tenochtitlan
(Mexico)

Acapulco

MAYAS

SPAIN

Port Royal

*Ile
de la Vache*

CARIBBEAN

Puerto Rico

St. Christopher

Guadeloupe

Martinique

Galleon
of the
Philippines

Nombre de Dios

Porto Bello

Panama

Maracaibo

Cartagena

DARIEN

Trinidad

TERRA

FIRMA

PACIFIC

Equator

Galápagos Islands

Fleet from Peru

Amazon

(SOUTHERN

OCEAN

SEA)

El Callao

Lima

INCAS

Cuzco

Lake Titicaca

Potosí

Tropic of Capricorn

Galleon Routes

—·— Fleet of New Spain

– – – Fleet of Terra Firma

——— Common route of return to Spain

0 _____ 625 miles

ONE

In the Graveyard of Ships

July 18, 1968. At eight-thirty in the morning, the *Calypso* is cruising northward at reduced speed. There are a few stray clouds in the sky, and the sea is a
tranquil blue-green, rippled only occasionally by a breeze. The water is like
crystal, and we can see the bottom fifty feet below. Around us, peaks of coral
glint white and gold in the sun, some of them thrusting up above the surface
and others lying barely below it, like the bait of some alluring snare set by
Neptune to trap the unwary mariner. We know from our voyages in the Red
Sea, to the archipelagos of Far San and Suakin, that these coral formations,
splendid though they be, represent a deadly peril. Everyone aboard is on the
alert. One careless moment, one slip — and the *Calypso* will find her hull
ripped open by the sword-sharp coral.

This sea, the Caribbean, is a coral sea like other coral seas. It is equally
beautiful, and equally dangerous, but not very different from others that we
have known elsewhere. Coral is found in every sea throughout the world. The
area it covers is approximately twenty times that of Europe or the United
States. It is a world unto itself, with its own laws and its own life-styles. And it
is a world which the *Calypso* has painstakingly explored. We are in the Caribbean now to continue that exploration at another latitude, and for a somewhat different purpose. We intend to penetrate into the interior of one of the
most treacherous coral reefs of the Caribbean, the famous Silver Bank, which
is situated to the northeast of the island of Hispaniola.

A glance at the depth finder's despairing gymnastics is enough to tell me

Left: Aboard the *Calypso*, Captain Cousteau suits up for a dive into the Silver Bank.

that we are in the midst of the Bank now. The *Calypso* is surrounded by a forest of vertical pillars rising from the bottom to within eight or ten feet of the surface. They are everywhere, mazes of coral with towers and walls of sufficient mass to slash our hull if we should make one mistake. We continue cautiously on our way; and, for the first time in the Caribbean, we have men stationed on our *portique,* or watchtower. This watchtower is actually no tower at all, but a raised platform of lightweight metal that I had built over the *Calypso*'s foredeck. It houses our radar, with enough room left over for five or six members of our crew to keep watch for reefs and shallows. When the water is blue, as it is today, and when the sun is shining, from the portique one can easily spot the coral reefs and pinnacles and make out the clear paths of sandy bottom by means of which we hope to reach the interior of the Bank. Our navigation in coral waters, therefore, depends largely upon guidance from the men on watch. I originally got the idea for the portique from one of the adventure stories of Henri de Monfreid, in which the captain of an Arab smuggling ship always managed to escape by sailing through reefs where no one dared follow. His secret: to send a boy up to the crow's nest to see where the reefs were passable. In addition to my friends watching from this platform, there are two crew members perched on the stem of the ship, watching the bottom directly in front of us and ready to signal if we seem to be in danger of ramming a coral reef. The success of these measures, obviously, depends upon favorable conditions. If the water were less calm and waves were breaking on the reefs, our men would be able to see nothing, and it would be impossible to navigate safely.

On this occasion, the sea is kind, and we are making headway, however slowly. Nonetheless, I can sense a certain amount of tension aboard, a condition that always exists when we are making a difficult passage. Now the tension is not due so much to the perils of navigation among coral reefs as it is to the difficult nature of the *Calypso*'s new mission. And everyone aboard knows it and is wondering, Will we fail, or will we succeed? Waiting for us within the Silver Bank is the answer to that question. And we are gambling that the answer will be Yes. It is a human gamble; perhaps too human. For we are on the track of a fortune in gold.

A Half-Turn

Next to me, his eyes never leaving the depth finder, stands Remy de Haenen, the man who inspired the present voyage of the *Calypso*. When he speaks, it is only to urge me on to greater daring in steering among the reefs. It is easy to see that he was trained as an aviator, and not as a seaman. Now, only a few moments later, I order the *Calypso* to halt and announce that we will have to make a semicircular detour. Remy seems on the point of weeping with frustration. Still, there are limits to one's audacity when dealing with reefs. We seem to be facing a dead end in the coral maze, and we can see peaks surrounding us like sentinels, level with the surface of the motionless blue sea. From the *Calypso*, we can see sandy bottom in the distance; but between it and us is a forest of mauve-colored branches, passable only to the many-hued tropical fish whose home it is.

To turn the *Calypso* is not easy. For a moment, it seems that I have waited too long to make a decision, and that we are too deep within the Bank to be able to extricate ourselves. Even De Haenen is now silent. But, by making delicately balanced use of our two engines, we manage very slowly to turn without striking coral, and to begin withdrawing, as Jean-Paul Bassaget — who is standing watch at the bow — and the team on the portique, shout instructions. De Haenen's face is still a study in impatience, but he says not a word. I would very likely not hear him if he did. The whole of my attention is concentrated on the ticklish task at hand. We must now proceed at minimum speed — but not too slowly, or the *Calypso* will not respond to the rudder. Already we have come dangerously close to one of those steely peaks of coral.

As soon as we are free of that apparently endless labyrinth, I order the anchor to be dropped about three hundred yards away from the nearest reef. De Haenen is in despair, thinking that I have decided to abandon the attempt. I reassure him: we will lay at anchor while I try to work out another approach to the heart of the Silver Bank.

Now I can understand why, since the time of Columbus, the Bank has had such a terrible reputation among seamen. It is nothing more than a field of murderous reefs. Even the *Calypso*, which has spent a good part of its career playing hide-and-seek among the coral, seems to have met its match.

The Silver Bank, even though it has been known for centuries and even though mariners have always done their utmost to avoid it, is the graveyard of many ships. So fearsome was its reputation that the captains and pilots of the galleons that carried gold from the New World to Spain had a special term to designate the complex of surface-level reefs at the Bank: *abreojos* — the eye opener.

As though the difficulties presented by the Bank are not enough in themselves, it happens that we have chosen a particularly bad time of the year for our expedition. In the Caribbean, the month of July is not a very favorable

Our first dives at the Silver Bank disclose wonders of marine life that will remain a source of astonishment to us.

one for navigation. July is the beginning of the hurricane season, the time that gives birth to those giant storms that regularly sweep across the Gulf of Mexico, ravage Florida and the Gulf coast, and sometimes end up far along the Atlantic seaboard. These same hurricanes forced the sailing ships of the sixteenth and seventeenth centuries toward the Bank, and many galleons were lost because their pilots — whose skills and instruments were primitive — made serious errors in setting their courses. For us, it will take an effort of the imagination to put ourselves in the same state of mind as the mariners who sailed such ships and to take into account the conditions of navigation at that time.

A Warehouse of Treasures

It is estimated that, during the period from the sixteenth to the eighteenth centuries, approximately fifty ships were carried, by wind and wave, onto the reefs of the Silver Bank and were lost. Per square mile, the Bank contains more sunken ships than any other spot on earth; and there is also more sunken treasure here than anywhere else. There is not a diver, not an adventurer, not a hunter after fame and fortune, who has not, at some time, dreamed of striking it rich in the Silver Bank. Historians and economists tell us that a good part — perhaps as much as six hundred million dollars' worth — of the vast treasure of gold and silver, precious stones and works of art, taken by the Spaniards from the New World, was lost in shipwrecks and now lies buried in tons of limestone and encrusted in coral.

The appeal of this storehouse of treasure for the men of the *Calypso* is rather strange. We are, none of us, particularly money-mad. If we were, we would never have chosen to live the kind of life we do aboard the *Calypso*; a rather primitive life devoid of luxury and comfort and devoted exclusively to the sea. The fact is that my companions and I have heard so much from our

Part of the fantastic marine vista seen by our divers on their first visit to the Silver Bank. In the foreground are sponges of different shapes.

American friends about the fabulous wealth of the Silver Bank, listened to so many tales of gold pieces washed up onto the Florida beaches, read so many marvelous books by American divers on the shipwrecks along the East coast, that we were, so to speak, possessed by a demon — by the demon, not of gold, but of discovery. Moreover, there had been so much exaggeration, so many myths, regarding sunken treasure in the Silver Bank that our curiosity had been aroused, and we were determined to find out the truth of the matter. In a word, we could no longer resist the temptation to pursue the high adventure of a treasure hunt.

The moving spirit behind our adventure is Remy de Haenen. Now that we are at anchor, he has surrendered his post at the depth finder and is perched on the observation deck. I can see him there, scanning the horizon through his field glasses, attempting to pick out, among the masses of coral, the pathway to wealth and to the sunken galleon that is the object of our quest.

From his Nordic ancestors, Remy de Haenen, a modern adventurer, has inherited a determination to wrench from the sea all that he can of wealth and good fortune. And, as though his Dutch seaman's temperament were not incentive enough, he has also been subject to the influence of the Bretons, for his family resided, for a long time, on the Island of Bréhat in the Cotes-du-Nord, near Paimpol, off the northwest coast of France.

Remy is only fifty years old, but he has the brown and wrinkled face of a man exposed, over a long period of time, to the sun of the tropics and the winds of the sea. Even though he was born in London, Remy has lived in the Caribbean for many years — with everything which that fact implies concerning his spirit of daring and love of adventure. He and his family live on the little island of St. Barthélemy, which lies between Guadeloupe and Puerto Rico. On the island, Remy de Haenen is both the mayor and the innkeeper. But, above all, he is a pilot, and his Cessna serves as a means of communication with, and transportation to, the island of St. Martin and Puerto Rico and Guadeloupe.

The story of our treasure hunt in the Caribbean started one night on an island of the French West Indies, while Remy was spinning me tales of "his" sunken ships. There are men who have a compulsion to gamble, and men who have a compulsion to search for hidden treasure; and Remy, as I discovered that night, is one of the latter. I know several men like Remy, men of various

Right: Divers picking their way through a forest of sea fans.

ages and conditions; but I do not know one who has ever found the fortune that he desired and sought so passionately. Perhaps it is just as well that this is so. For men of this kind, the excitement and the uncertainty of the quest is more important than the treasure itself. They are a strange breed, the last in a long line of seafaring adventurers; and perhaps the last true poets of the sea.

Remy knew of a ship, he said, that contained a treasure worth no less than five million francs (about $1,250,000). He did not succeed in infecting me either with the virus of his compulsion or with his fever for gold. But I did suggest that he come aboard the *Calypso* and guide us to the site of this fabulous shipwreck.

Remy has spent many years exploring the Silver Bank, by both plane and boat. He has even drawn up a map showing all the sunken ships in the area; and he has dived to many of these wrecks — for, in addition to his other skills, he is an excellent diver. The ship that Remy was thinking of was one of

those hidden among the coral of the Bank; the ship that he lusted after above all others — the famous galleon called *Nuestra Señora de la Concepción*. Remy had never seen *Nuestra Señora;* but he had devoted considerable effort to establishing its location. He had not only searched for it from the air, in his Cessna, but had ransacked the archives of London and Madrid for clues. He was certain that the wreck of *Nuestra Señora de la Concepción* — lay at the foot of "a reef in the shape of a half-moon." For a long time, De Haenen had searched for that half-moon reef from his airplane; and now he was certain that he knew where it was.

Everything that De Haenen said about *Nuestra Señora* and its location seemed to fit in with what was known about the ship. It had indeed been wrecked and sunk on a crescent-shaped reef. No doubt, it was by now covered with the limestone secretion of marine fauna, but we are able to determine its approximate latitude and longitude. In fact, the ship had already been visited by English "wrackers" — seventeenth-century salvage operators — and notably by William Phips, who removed considerable wealth from the carcass, and who was one of the luckiest treasure hunters ever to walk the bottom of the sea. Given the limited means of his era, however, Phips had been forced to leave more than he took of the immense cargo. No doubt, his salvage operation would work to our benefit. He had certainly uncovered part of the hull; and he had left an estimate of the treasure left behind by himself and his crew, in the form of an inventory based upon the information available in his time. The remainder of that treasure of *Nuestra Señora* presents an almost irresistible temptation for wrackers of the twentieth century.

Corsairs of the Caribbean

Remy de Haenen talked at length as he and I sat in the pure tropical night, near a thicket of hibiscus and bougainvillea, beside the shimmering sea — and overlooking a hidden bay in which pirates of bygone days had found a hiding place. Our surroundings were a factor of which Remy knew how to take advantage. He would never have had so many adventures, and would not have so many friends, if he did not possess, in full measure, the gift of conjuring up images capable of charming his audience and taking on the appearance of truth. That night, he spoke of stately galleons, loaded with gold; of pirate captains navigating their small craft with unearthly skill; of pearls and emeralds stained with blood, won in an hour of combat and lost again in a moment of passion. From his store of information, flavored by his storyteller's wit, he expounded on the Caribbean, on that sea which has witnessed so much of human drama and which, with its rum, its sun, its vanished civilizations, its love of flowers and its taste for blood, has infected the world with a fever of desire for the Caribbean.

Did I succumb that night to the spell of Castilian ducats and golden doubloons? I have asked myself that question; I am, by nature, a sceptic. I am not a gambler, in any sense of the term; and I have never been attracted by the thought of "trying my luck." On the other hand, I am most strongly attracted by any marine undertaking which I have not yet had the opportunity to attempt. And Remy de Haenen was offering the chance for something entirely new.

I do not mean that the men of the *Calypso* have had no experience in archaeology. Far from it. We spent five years working at an underwater archaeological "dig"; the Roman wreck of Marcus Sestius, at the Grand Conglouée, near Marseille. On that occasion, our enemies had been the sea, the *mistral*,* the depth at which we were working, and the problems of bringing up thousands of amphora — the tall, two-handed earthenware jars of the ancients. The results, however, were infinitely rewarding. We discovered not only precious vessels, but also information of great importance on life in the Mediterranean area, and on the trade and navigation routes between Greece, Italy and Gaul, in the third century before Christ.

What Remy de Haenen was now suggesting, however, was something quite different: an expedition to a sunken ship no more than three centuries old, and one the history of which is relatively well known. We would be going from Antiquity to the Renaissance, from the Mediterranean to the Caribbean, from a merchant ship of Rome to a galleon of Spain. And, in the back of my mind, there was the romantic attraction of the history of piracy, the ghosts of great mariners, and the whole adventure of the New World and of the complex relations with Europe. It seemed that the expedition was worth while, if for no other reason than the possibility of shedding some light on a chapter of human history — a chapter that is not yet ended, but continues still to be written in the revolutions, and in the aspirations, of Latin America.

A Challenge

There were all these things. And there was also coral. Coral was the true problem, and I was aware of it from the very beginning, from the moment

---

*A cold, dry, violent northwest wind that blows through the southern provinces of France.

The *Calypso*, after trying to make its way into the heart of the Silver Bank, has anchored at the edge of the underwater plateau.

that De Haenen began to weave his spell. I could see, in my mind's eye, a ship crushed under tons of it, and perhaps haunted by sharks. It would surely be overrun, disfigured, and made unintelligible by an encrustation of Acroporas, whips, brain coral, and staghorn coral. In short, it would be a vision — but untranslatable into reality, and therefore useless. And it was precisely this that intrigued me. No one has ever dug out a sunken ship trapped in coral. And it is not hard to understand why, for it is an enormous, almost an impossible, undertaking.

I have traveled thousands of miles aboard the *Calypso* across the coral seas of the world — the Red Sea, the Indian Ocean, the Caribbean, the Pa-

Above left: Coral life, in its exuberant growth, has covered all traces of sunken ships with an enormous blanket of limestone.

Below left: The coral wall at the foot of which lies our sunken ship.

cific. Everywhere, my friends and I have dived, both in scuba equipment and in minisubs. We have returned to the same places after intervals of several years, and we have been able to observe and to study the growth of coral. In the Red Sea, for example, we saw what had happened to our undersea houses at Shab Rumi after four years: everything was covered with coral. In ten years, it is safe to say, coral will have wiped out the last trace of our presence there. We have seen sunken ships of iron in the Suakin Islands and in the Indian Ocean. Although they were hardly more than twenty to fifty years old, they had already been entirely taken over by marine life. Some of them were covered by "blindmen's canes," like the "white-haired wreck" that I described in an earlier work.* Others resembled nothing so much as rock gardens, or Japanese gardens. What would *Nuestra Señora de la Concepción* look like after several centuries at the bottom of the sea, in the world of the Madreporas? The answer to that question seemed to me to be worth discovering.

Having arrived at a decision, it remained to work out a realistic schedule. The *Calypso* had not visited its home port of Monaco for more than three years. We have always been too busy to take advantage of the opportunity for such a trip. We pride ourselves on the fact that the ship is always available — and always busy. It was therefore necessary to work the *Nuestra Señora* expedition into our Caribbean itinerary — which meant that there would have to be a slight delay before we could begin.

That same night, De Haenen and I arrived at a basic agreement only to the effect that the expedition would take place. Then I left to join the men of the *Calypso* who were then studying the habits of sea turtles in the Indian Ocean.

Preliminary Reconnaissance

One of the most remarkable things in the life my friends and I lead is that there always comes a moment when plans are translated into action by the arrival of the *Calypso* and the intervention of twenty-nine men. Then, an idea which existed only in our minds begins to take on reality. This is one of those moments. The *Calypso* is now at the Silver Bank.

Before we can really begin digging, there is preliminary work to be done. And, in this, we can count on the help of Remy de Haenen, who is now as excited as a hunter the night before the season's opening. Remy and Michel

*Life and Death in a Coral Sea, by J.-Y. Cousteau with Philippe Diolé. New York, Doubleday, 1971.

Deloire, our cameraman, have already made a final air reconnaissance of the Bank, and have filmed the entire devilish configuration of it; for there is no reliable marine chart of the area. On two occasions, Remy and Michel flew over the Bank from Puerto Rico, while the *Calypso* was cruising in the vicinity. Their pictures will complement the color photographs that De Haenen took, from his own plane, last year. Moreover, these reconnaissance flights allowed us to establish, beyond a doubt, that there really was a half-moon reef within the Silver Bank — in fact, that there were several. Remy, however, decided that there was only one such that corresponded both to the supposed latitude of the *Nuestra Señora* and to the data that he had gathered from archives and libraries. And now it was up to us to find that particular reef.

From the results of the reconnaissance flights, coupled with the photographs and information supplied by Remy, I am able to formulate a clear picture of the Bank's shape, and to prepare a chart showing its approximate extent and its winding contours. The Silver Bank, thus charted, appears as the greatest open-water concentration of coral in the entire Caribbean. It is an immense plateau of over a thousand miles, lying under approximately seventy-five feet of water; and this plateau rises sharply from the ocean floor which lies at a depth of more than three thousand feet. At its northern end, there is an almost impenetrable reef barrier forty kilometers long. It is this barrier that we are attempting to cross. And it is on this barrier that so many ships of the Spanish gold fleet met their end. The great galleons, difficult to maneuver, overloaded with the plundered wealth of the New World, tossed about by storms or led astray by their pilots, were doomed as soon as they entered these shallow waters.

Ghost Ships

In the Caribbean, coral takes on less massive forms than in the Red Sea or in the Indian Ocean. Coral formations here are more sharply defined, more branched. To hunters for sunken treasure, these formations all tend to look like the remains of sunken ships. We noticed this yesterday, even before arriving at the Silver Bank, when we halted the *Calypso* and dived to investigate a coral complex not far from Puerto Rico called the Bank of the Nativity. It seemed that every coral branch must enclose a piece of Spanish rigging, and that every column must conceal a stump of galleon mast.

Despite the problems that such circumstances forecast for our quest of *Nuestra Señora de la Concepción*, Remy de Haenen's eyes still blaze with the certainty that, thanks to the *Calypso*, his life's dream is about to be realized. Yesterday's dive was the first chance he had to see our divers in action and to appreciate the possibilities offered by the *Calypso* and by our equipment. And since then, his confidence (and his impatience) have reached a peak.

Although Remy's impatience continues unabated, his confidence has been somewhat shaken by this morning's failure to penetrate the barrier reef on the northern edge of the Silver Bank. The *Calypso*'s crew and I, however, have been made phlegmatic by years of dealing with reefs. If one method does not work we try another. In this case, the thing to do is to send our small boats — our *Zodiac* and launch — to reconnoiter the area. These light craft can go almost anywhere among the coral without danger, and the information they will bring back will supply the data we need to decide what we must do. Remy himself, Jean-Paul Bassaget, Raymond Coll, and Marcel Forcherie take the launch and start out immediately. Then, after the second sitting for breakfast, Bernard Delemotte and Jean-Clair Riant set out in the *Zodiac*. Remy's launch will investigate the reefs to the north of the Bank while the *Zodiac* explores the immediate vicinity of the *Calypso*.

About two o'clock in the afternoon, Remy de Haenen calls on the radio, asking that we send him "a pick hammer and two edging tools." It must be a joke. A pick hammer would indeed be very useful; but there is not a single one aboard the *Calypso*. Nonetheless, I contact the *Zodiac* by radio and ask Delemotte to return to the ship. A few minutes later, the *Zodiac* is alongside the *Calypso* and takes on Michel Deloire — as well as a good supply of picks and crowbars for Remy.

The two boats return at sundown, and their crews come aboard the *Calypso* with their faces wreathed in smiles. Remy is once more in a frenzy of enthusiasm, and he reports his findings: a piece of rigging from an old sailing ship, corroded and encrusted with coral; and also an old oaken plank. Moreover, the divers have seen something — a mysterious object imprisoned in the reef. It may be, they think, a *brimbale*; that is, a very old hand pump. All this, obviously, is interpreted as a good omen — so much so that, having observed that disappointment often follows a good beginning, I try, not very successfully, to dampen their enthusiasm.

We film these first "treasures" as they are brought aboard the *Calypso*. It may be that they will be important in identifying the wreck from which they came. For the moment, however, we know nothing for sure. And once more I caution my friends against expecting too much.

Right: To a diver, every piece of coral looks like a part of the sunken galleon.

20° 43' North

Tonight, after dinner, there is a showing of the aerial views taken last year by Remy from his Cessna. From these transparencies, we trace out an overlay map, showing the part of the reef that was explored this afternoon by the divers. Next, we send our launch out to the spot where the divers saw the wreck, following the launch all the way by radar. This enables us to establish the position of the wreck in relation to the *Calypso*. Since the *Calypso* is at 20° 41' north, we are able to deduce that the wreck's latitude is 20° 42' north. William Phips gave the position of the wreck whose treasure he salvaged as 20° 43' north. There is, therefore, one minute of difference in the position of his wreck and ours — a negligible discrepancy. It is possible that we have indeed located the fabulous *Nuestra Señora* that Phips described in 1687. And it is equally possible that we are entirely off base. The pieces of metal and wood that the divers have brought back do not necessarily prove that there is a sunken ship at 20° 42' north; or, if there is a ship, that it dates from the proper century.

According to our calculations, the place where these things were found is about three thousand yards from the *Calypso*'s anchorage-three thousand yards of virtually impassable coral reefs. And, tomorrow, if it turns out that there is indeed a sunken ship at that spot, and a ship of the appropriate century, then it will be necessary, if we are going to do any digging at all, somehow to get the *Calypso* to that spot. Which means that we will have to move into the very middle of the Silver Bank. The best we can hope for is that a hurricane will not come along at that time. If one does, there is a very good chance that the *Calypso* will suffer the same fate as *Nuestra Señora de la Concepción*.

The Secrets of Coral

This morning, I noted that there were several coral tables roughly in the shape of crescents — Remy de Haenen's "half-moon reefs." These crescents are level reefs, usually twenty or thirty yards long. The edges of these coral tables are covered with higher formations; and, on the bottom surrounding them there are forests of coral "trees" and other formations — some of them of enormous size. And these formations, as I have said, bear a surprising resemblance to the hulls of sunken sailing ships whose masts and yards have been covered with calcium.

Coral has peculiar growth patterns. For no apparent reason, it multiplies limitlessly in one place, and may leave another spot, only a short distance

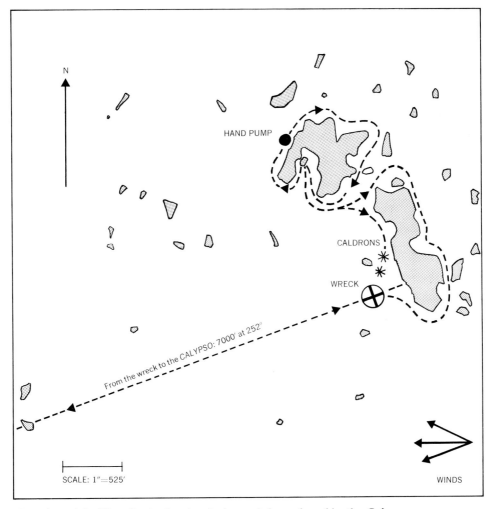

N

HAND PUMP

CALDRONS

WRECK

From the wreck to the CALYPSO: 7000' at 252°

SCALE: 1"=525'

WINDS

Overview of the Silver Bank, showing the buoyed channel used by the *Calypso*.

away, completely untouched. It is likely that *Nuestra Señora*, sunken as it must be in a gangue of calcium, is one of the places in which coral abounds. In the sea, stationary life-forms need, above all, a place to which to attach themselves. So vital is this need that they sometimes attach themselves, for lack of something better, to one another. A sunken ship is an ideal perch for them, with its masts and cabins, its massive framework and holds. In addition, coral needs oxygen. It often happens in the sea that a flat bottom is poor in oxygen — while a ship, with its crevices and angles and planes, is rich in that element. A sunken ship, therefore, is an oasis, and coral finds it an exceptional place in which to live. It therefore develops and grows in a way that is equally exceptional. And that is why I am afraid that *Nuestra Señora de la Concepción* is buried under layer upon layer of coral. All that coral will have to be removed — an enormous undertaking. I have not yet spoken to our team about this. After all, I may be wrong. We may find the wooden hull free of any growth at all; and we may find timbers that will prove to be archaeological keys in our search.

Much of this night is spent with Claude Caillart, Christian Bonnici and Yves Omer, working out a plan of action for the next day. The confidence of my friends in the existence of a treasure is so great that I have decided to proceed exactly as though I were equally certain. After all, for most of them this will be the adventure of a lifetime.

Obviously, the first thing we must do is to decide on an area in which to begin our work. Then we will have to remove whatever coral exists in that area; and the coral itself will have to be examined closely for any kind of historic relic that it may contain, precious or not. A single one of the Acroporas that we have seen on the bottom is capable of enclosing several gold or silver ingots, or of having swallowed an emerald necklace whole. We will therefore have to cut out the coral in blocks, raise the blocks onto the *Calypso*'s deck, and then break open the blocks to see if they contain anything of value. As a matter of general principle, it is decided that every piece of coral of a certain size will have to be broken apart, with hammers, aboard the *Calypso*. A herculean job is waiting for us.

A Garden of Marvels

July 14 — Bastille Day — dawns bright and unclouded, and, after a quick breakfast, several divers and I take to the water in high spirits. What we see, however, dampens my mood. Spread before us is a true garden of marvels, a fairyland of coral in every conceivable shape and color. And it is this marine paradise that we must destroy in order to explore a sunken hulk that may or may not be *Nuestra Señora de la Concepción*. It is not the amount of work entailed that troubles me, but the thought that we, with our picks, are going to demolish these exquisite forms, forms that have taken centuries to attain their present size and beauty. For these coral formations are extremely complex groupings of uncounted numbers of stationary animals, all existing together in a precarious and subtle biological equilibrium. The very fact of their existence is a miracle of nature. The slightest change in the water's temperature or salinity, even an unusually heavy rainfall, is capable of turning the Silver Bank into a lifeless desert.

The area around the *Calypso* is not composed exclusively of coral, of course; but coral is its principal component element, as we can see in swimming far above the bottom. There are vast fields of staghorn, delicate Acro-

Bernard Delemotte searches for the remains of a sunken galleon among the multiformed fauna that cover the bottom of the sea.

porian formations, leafy discs of fungia, huge lumps of Porites coral. But, in the midst of this living mass of calcium, there are other animal colonies of every form: sponges, like candles or chalices, whose flesh has a pulpy feel to it; stinging coral, capable of inflicting painful wounds; sea anemones with venemous tentacles; and, above all, lying at the foot of the cliff, a forest of mauve and yellow sea fans, their long branches bent over like ostrich plumes and waving gently as the swimmer passes through them.

This garden of marvels is also inhabited by larger creatures. A sizable grouper, who lives in a grotto in the coral wall, is already used to us and watches us calmly, unblinkingly. Snappers and mackerel swim past in well-ordered schools, while a friendly Platax tries to strike up an acquaintance. These fishes, of course, have nothing to fear from us. But I am conscience-stricken at the thought of what Project Sunken Treasure will do to the lovely coral that is their home. Should I discuss this with my comrade? With De Haenen? I should have thought of all this before rushing into this wild-goose chase for sunken treasure. It is too late to turn back now. Tomorrow, we must begin work; and the first step will be to turn our picks against the living coral.

Certainly, I will not allow any indiscriminate destruction. We will have to know beforehand what we are looking for and what we may find. In the sea, in the fields both of biology and of archaeology, one finds only what one already knows. In this instance, we must know the shape, the significance, and the nature of the sunken vessel that we are seeking. In other words, we must have before our minds the events of three centuries ago in the Caribbean.

TWO

A River of Gold Across the Ocean Sea

The galleons of His Most Catholic Majesty, Charles V, Holy Roman Emperor, King of Spain, rode at anchor at Porto Bello. Porto Bello, however, despite the name chosen for it by Columbus himself, was not a port. Rather it was a deep and relatively sheltered cove on the Isthmus of Darien; and even the ships of Spain were compelled to drop anchor in open water. To Porto Bello came all the wealth of the Incas, on muleback from Peru. The settlement itself comprised only a few hovels and barracks scattered along the shore. And beyond it, the dense tropical forest pressed in on three sides.

Dawn was breaking, but already the foremast hoists were hauling aboard the last of the fleet's cargo, while longboats made quick journeys between shore and the three vessels at anchor: the *Santa Ana*, the *Nuestra Señora del Rosario*, and a ship of six hundred tons, the *Margarita*. Around these galleons were clustered smaller ships: merchant vessels that would travel in convoy with the Fleet of Terra Firma as it returned to Spain on its annual journey to and from the New World. The flag of the Captain General of the Fleet, Don Francisco Rodriguez, was aboard the *Santa Ana*; and on the *Margarita*, sailed the fleet's admiral, Don Gaspar de Vargas.

The ships and galleons of the fleet were already loaded to their waterlines, but still one could hear the soldiers on shore, shouting to the Indians to make them work faster at loading the longboats, and the cries of the Indians as the shouts were reinforced by occasional blows. With this was mingled the laughter and songs of drunken men. For the night before the fleet's departure was always celebrated by much drinking, by games of chance in which fortunes were won and lost, and by as much wenching as the limited facilities of Porto Bello would allow. The only women available were indentured girls from Europe and Indian slaves; and over these there were constant fights with sword and dagger. This final night ashore was but the culmination of three weeks of collective frenzy in Porto Bello. The wealth that had been torn from Peru and transported to that town was intended for use in sustaining the grandeur of the Most Catholic Majesty of Spain: it would allow him to continue his fight against the infidels and heretics. In the meantime, the Spaniards of the port and the Fleet could see no harm in a bit of merrymaking.

During most of the year, Porto Bello was almost deserted. for the three weeks of the fleet's visit, however, it lived and breathed. There was literally silver in the streets — for the ingots were stacked on the ground, in the open air — and an air of festive bartering lent color to the crude shacks and barracks as the Spaniards exchanged European weapons, clothing, and tools for corn, cacao, indigo, and logwood. Then, as soon as the fleet sailed away, Porto Bello would fall once more into its customary isolation.

Candles, Commerce, and Colonies

On this occasion, the *flota* had brought comparatively little from Spain in the way of goods to barter. There were a few items of bedclothing, a few doublets, some boots. Of wine and weapons — swords, pikes, and shields — there was a fair amount. But, above all, there were candles; candles by the thousands for the Spanish colonists. All of this was stacked up on the ground among the huts of Porto Bello, and guards were posted to prevent pilferage. Even so, the greater part of these goods were stolen by colonists who had nothing to exchange, and who were desperately in need of clothing and boots. For these supplies, slender as they were, were their sole source of the necessities for survival. The colonists were not allowed to manufacture anything for themselves, or to trade with — or even to steal from — the French, English, and Dutch smugglers who plied their trade in the area; for the king of Spain had created a monopoly for himself of all trade and traffic in the West Indies. He had even forbidden the colonists to engage in trade on the smallest and most informal scale, or to practice even the humblest trades anywhere in the colonies of Spain. It was forbidden to weave or to sew clothing, or make shoes, or fashion cooking utensils, or plant cereals. And when it was discovered that a few enterprising colonists had planted vines for the purpose of making their own wine, the vines were uprooted and the miscreants punished. Even the clothing of the Indians was imported from Spain. The most unfortunate aspect of this situation was that, if the colonists were to have shoes and clothing, it was necessary for Spain to manufacture enough of these items and to transport them across the Atlantic; and Spain did not have nearly enough ships to satisfy even the most elemental needs of its subjects in the New World, who therefore went barefoot and ragged in that vast land from which tons of gold and silver were taken each year.

The Golden Mule Train

This year, for once, the gold and silver had arrived in time. This was always difficult, since its arrival had to be timed to coincide with the arrival of the ships. The danger of pirates attacking the port made it impossible, or at least unwise, for the Spaniards to store treasure there. As soon as a few of the galleons from Spain had landed in the New World, at Cartagena, urgent messages had been sent out, by courier, to Panama, Guayaquil, and Lima, so that the Fleet of the Pacific might hear the news. Then, from Arica, Autofagasta, Coquimbo, and Valparaiso, ships had assembled at Callao, the port of Lima. In their holds was the treasure of a continent, gold and precious stones from those distant and fabled lands that comprised the empire of the Inca, conquered by Pizarro, from which Spain had already taken so much. Loaded with this wealth, the galleons of the Southern Sea — known to later ages as the Pacific — had sailed for Panama, in a voyage lasting three weeks. On the shores of Panama, the gold and jewels, now firmly tied into leather sacks, and the silver, which had been melted down into large ingots called "tortas", were loaded onto mules. The mule train, heavily guarded, took twenty-two days to cross the Isthmus of Darien. Along the way, there were Indian attacks to fight off; and, even more difficult, a trail to be cut through the dense tropical forest. For no matter how carefully the Spaniards performed this task one year, they arrived in Panama the next year to find all evidence of their earlier presence obliterated by the plants which sprang up almost overnight to replace those that had been cut down.

More deadly than the Indians, too, were the fevers of the jungle — dysentery, malaria, yellow fever — which annually decimated the Spaniards who tried to gain a foothold on this continent. And against these killers, the notions of hygiene were too alien, and the science of medicine too primitive, to be of any help. The way that the Spaniards lived in these equatorial climates contributed, no doubt, to the high mortality rate; for they lived as they would have in Madrid or Seville. They ate and drank virtually anything that could be swallowed; and they sweated like demons within the breastplates and morions which, in Central and South America, were like miniature furnaces. It would have been considered unworthy of a Spaniard to disembark on the shores of the New World in anything less than embroidered vests, silken breeches, and silver-buckled shoes. Their ornate and embroidered suits, their plumed hats, and their shirts of finest silk or linen bedecked with lace could no more survive the jungle and the dampness than the splendid *hidalgos* who wore them so uncomfortably could live at peace with the snakes, the poisoned arrows and the rains of the jungle.

Wealth and Poverty

The physical misery of the Spaniards in the New World, the dangers they encountered and the deaths they risked in so many forms, was in striking contrast to the king's ransom in gold and silver that they moved from one side of the Americas to the other, and which they loaded into boats to be taken to Spain.

The sacks of coins, the bars of silver, the golden ingots in the shape of discs were stored, aboard ship, in a special place in the deepest part of the ship, a hole surrounded by iron bars in which ten men stood guard around the clock. There was only one means of entry — and that was by passing through the captain general's quarters.

The king's officials had counted the sacks containing the treasure. Then, they had opened them and weighed the glittering discs within: pieces of eight, stamped with a cross and bearing the word *Potosi* — the Peruvian mine from which this treasure had come. For the precious metals had been stamped with the king's sign of ownership before being brought to Porto Bello, at one of the royal mints scattered throughout the Caribbean. The first one to be built was probably that in Hispaniola, and it was followed by others — in Lima, two in Mexico, and in Santa Fe de Bogata. No less careful attention was given the great quantity of pearls (*margaritas*, the Spaniards called them) that had, appropriately enough, been stored aboard the *Margarita*.

Right: Titian's portrait of Charles V, the man who founded "an empire on which the sun never set." (The Prado, Madrid.)

Departure

Now, all was in readiness for departure, and already the men left on shore at Porto Bello could hear the sound of singing from the ships. These, however, were not the tribal songs with which the Spaniards had amused themselves ashore, but religious chants. For the subjects of His Most Catholic Majesty were a pious people, and, whatever their faults may have been on the dry land of Porto Bello, aboard ship they were assiduous in their devotions. Every ship had its chaplains, of course, and these led everyone — seaman and soldier, officer and passenger — in the chanting of Matins. Later, the chaplain general of the fleet celebrated Mass on the deck of the flagship. Preparations for weighing anchor, therefore, were made by the seamen as they sang hymns.

Their preparations were not easy. A galleon's masts, or "trees," were hung with great square sails, emblazoned with the Cross of Jerusalem, for no one had yet discovered the secret of using several small sails. To hoist these stretches of canvas by hand required great effort; and, to make matters worse, the fleet was short-handed, for, now as always, a considerable fraction of the crew had been lost by disease and desertion. Even in the best of circumstances, the seamen of the fleet were not of the highest caliber, most of them being ignorant and untrained, or beggars and criminals hurriedly assembled in all the ports of Spain and the New World. Even so, their movements were co-ordinated as they seized the halyard of the enormous mainsail and, to the rhythm of a hymn, hoisted it aloft. (The area of the mainsail could later be increased by the use of two additional strips of sail. Two series of initials — an acronym — were embroidered along the lower edge of the mainsail and each of the strips, A.V.M.G.P.: *Ave Maria gratia plena*. This invocation served a double purpose; it assured that the strips would be hoisted in the proper position relative to the mainsail, and it placed the ship under the protection of the Virgin.) As the mainsail was being hoisted, other seamen were cranking the windlass to raise the last of the anchors — an iron anchor more than twenty-five feet high and weighing a ton.

Finally, the weak breeze filled the sails, and the great galleons began to move, slowly, as the pilots struggled to keep the prow turned toward the neck of the cove. It was a difficult and frustrating job. The action of the rudder had very little effect upon so heavy a ship moving at so slow a pace. The galleons, like all the vessels of the fleet, responded only to movements of its sails; and their four masts generally allowed it to move only when the wind blew from behind or from the side. Even so, the square bowsprit sail (at the prow) and a triangular sail at the poop, made it possible for a dexterous captain or the pilot to have some control over the movement of the ship.

The clumsiness and lack of maneuverability of the galleons made them virtually defenseless against the forces of nature, and hampered them considerably in engagements with hostile vessels. To the disadvantages thus presented, there was another which was ever present in the minds of every man aboard, and that was the danger of fire aboard these wooden ships. There was a large iron lantern, decorated with fine scrollwork, on the poop of the *Santa Ana*. This was the sole permanent source of light — that is, the only fire — allowed on the deck of any ship in the fleet. It was the insignia of authority, and only the captain general had the right to display it. And below deck, no lamp and no candle was allowed even during the night, except one which served to illuminate the compass in the *bitacora* — which later generations of mariners would know as the binnacle.

The King's Quintal

Everyone aboard the ships of the Fleet rejoiced in the calm of the sea and the gentleness of the wind. In a heavy sea, the *Santa Ana*, the *Margarita*, and the *Nuestra Señora del Rosario,* would have been in considerable danger, for they were so heavily loaded with cargo that the lowest part of their decks, in the center of the ship, were barely six feet above the waterline. The fore and aft sections of the ship — the two "castles" — were much higher, but their height entailed another disadvantage: in heavy weather, they had an adverse effect upon the stability of the ships; and this was particularly true in the storms of the Caribbean and in the great Atlantic swell.

In theory, the function of the galleons of the fleet was to transport the goods of the king of Spain — the king's quintal; for the Spanish kings received one-fifth of all the wealth that came from the New World. The remaining four-fifths of the gold, silver and jewels remained in the possession of the king's subjects who had mined it, or taken it from the Incas. The theoretical arrangement was that the colonization and exploitation of the New World was an area of private enterprise, and that the king received a percentage of the profits of that enterprise as a sort of precursive "income tax."

Such was the theory. The reality, however, was something else. The opening of the world of the Indies had engendered a frenzy of disorganized commercial activity. In order to impose some control, the Catholic Kings, Fer-

A Spanish ship as seen by the Indians. (From a Mexican ms. in the Bibliothèque Nationale, Department of Oriental Manuscripts, Paris.)

dinand and Isabella, in 1503, had established an agency called *La Casa de Contratación*. The Casa was at the same time a commercial clearing house and a maritime bureau controlling naval traffic and security. It was also an information agency and a meeting place for speculators and sea captains eager to do business with one another.

Since the offices of the Casa were at Seville, every ship leaving for or returning from the Indies was required to call at that inland port, which was reached by sailing up the Guadalquivir River. After several decades, however, the presence of shifting sand bars in the Guadalquivir made its navigation dangerous for galleons, especially since larger and larger ships were being built which required deeper and deeper water. Another port of call had to be chosen, and, in 1680, Cádiz, at the mouth of the Guadalquivir, was designated. The headquarters of the Casa de Contratación, however, was not moved there until 1717.

It was the duty of the Casa's officials to decide on every detail of a galle-

The *Calypso* heading toward the Silver Bank.

on's voyage. They determined the itinerary, the route, matters of discipline aboard ship, and the strategy to be followed in battle. Since there was no means of long-distance communication, everything had to be foreseen and provided for. (Light, fast vessels were used for communication between different parts of the fleet; but it would have been almost impossible for even these cutters to catch up with it en route to deliver instructions from Spain.) As so often happens, however, these careful instructions and orders, which had been worked out to the smallest detail, had been formulated by men who knew little about the Indies, and less about the sea; and so the regulations had little application in practice.

The gigantic and complex bureaucracy of the Casa was designed to assure the safe transport of the cargoes on which Spain depended for its economic survival. The task, however, was beyond the technical abilities of the age. And it was beyond the competence of the Spaniards assigned to the Casa, who were often poorly fitted for their work because of personal dishonesty, and poorly equipped for it by lack of training. And so, of course, it grew, as bureaucracies do, into an administrative octopus with a tentacle in every phase of Spain's maritime life. It had agents in every port at which galleons called, to see that the Casa's rules were obeyed. At Porto Bello, officials of the Casa de Contratación — had counted the ingots of gold and the bars of silver, and had inspected the galleons down to the bottom of their holds before the fleet weighed anchor. And they had pretended not to notice that these holds were filled to overflowing with merchandise that had nothing to do with the king's quintal. There was the personal property of Captain General Don Francisco Rodriguez, and that of Admiral Gaspar de Vargas. And there was hardly a seaman aboard who had not managed to load his own personal "treasure" onto the king's galleons: logwood, spices, rare fruits such as bananas and pineapples, and animals — parrots, monkeys, and turkeys. Sometimes, there was even a precious emerald, or some other stone.

The officials of the Casa were hardly in a position to protest these abuses; for, in with the possessions of the officers and men of the galleons, was their own personal loot — which they knew their colleagues at Seville or Cádiz would ignore, so long as they received a share of it.

In short, everyone was in business for himself. The Casa de Contratación from top to bottom was a vast system of double-dealing and pay-offs, and complicity and intrigues, all designed to drain the New World of the whole of its wealth. In this system, the king had a share; but it was far from being a controlling interest.

In addition to the clandestine merchandise aboard the three galleons of the fleet, there were also several hundred passengers who had been permitted to book transport for themselves and their goods because the admirals of the Casa received a share of the passage money.

The presence of all these passengers was particularly dangerous during storms, when they milled about the decks and made it even more difficult than usual for the seamen to maneuver the galleons, and in the event of an attack by pirates, when they often made it impossible to defend the ship. In addition, the passengers, not being seamen, frequently panicked in times of danger, and more than once were responsible for revolts aboard ship.

Shipboard Mass

For the moment, however, all was peaceful aboard the three galleons of the fleet. As they made their way into the open sea, Mass was being celebrated on the poop deck; for there were always several priests aboard each galleon. Some of them were *conquistadores a lo divino* — "God's conquerors," or missionaries — who were returning to Spain after working among the Indians. Others, however, were the chaplains who always accompanied the soldiers and seamen in order to hear confessions, administer the sacraments, and generally to supervise the moral and religious behavior of the seamen.

Everyone recommended themselves to God's care with great devotion. For everyone knew that they were at the beginning of a long and perilous voyage. With luck, the fleet might reach Cádiz in two and a half to three months. Before that, however, there would be storms to be ridden out, perhaps pirate ships to be escaped, and certainly misery to be endured in conditions of the most horrendous discomfort. For no food had been provided for the illegal passengers aboard. Those who had experience with galleons had brought their own supplies — even their own water; and they spent their time aboard in guarding these supplies as carefully as they guarded their treasures stored below. It was axiomatic in the fleet that the two principal diversions aboard ship were gambling and stealing. And, in addition to human thieves, one had to be ever on the alert against the depredations of the innumerable colony of rats that infested every ship, as well as against other vermin: lice, fleas, worms, roaches, and weevils.

The immediate destination of the *Santa Ana* and her sister ships was not Spain, but Cuba. At Havana, they would be joined by the Fleet of New Spain, and together they would make their way eastward across the Atlantic. As a matter of principle, the fleets of Spain comprised the maximum number of ships available. There seemed a certain comfort in numbers in so venturesome an undertaking as the voyage to Spain; and, more important, a large convoy of ships might discourage pirate attacks. Even so, on the way to Havana, the *Santa Ana* and the ships that followed her were required to pass through the area that comprised the richest hunting ground of the pirates and privateers — the English, at Jamaica, and the French on the isle of Tortuga, who frequently joined forces on the Island of the Cow, south of Hispaniola, in order to attack Spanish convoys.

Cuba remained the hub and center of trade and conquest during the Spanish domination of Latin America. Its port, Havana, was heavily fortified and well defended, as befitted its role in the Spanish scheme of things. The city was built of stone; and, in the sixteenth century, it could have passed as a city in Spain. It combined the advantages of European civilization and comfort with the delights of tropical life. Its reputation, and its importance, had made of Havana the gathering place of adventurers determined to amass a fortune by any means.

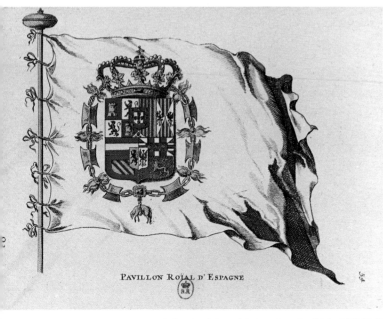

PAVILLON ROÏAL D'ESPAGNE

PAVILLON DES GALIONS D'ESPAGNE

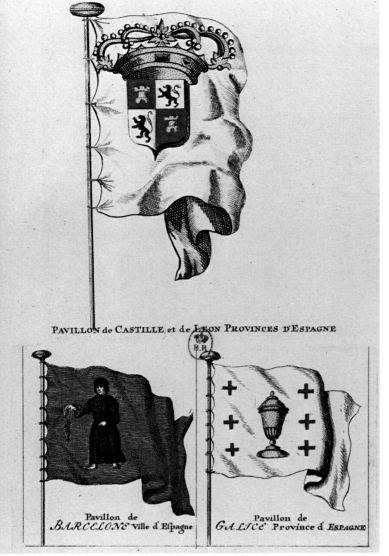

PAVILLON de CASTILLE et de LEON PROVINCES D'ESPAGNE

Pavillon de
BARCELONE Ville d'Espagne

Pavillon de
GALICE Province d'ESPAGNE

3

Standards shown by Spanish ships:
1. The royal Spanish standard, showing the arms of Castille and Leon,
   Aragon, Sicily, Granada and Portugal. The shield is decorated with
   the Order of the Golden Fleece
   and surmounted by a royal crown.
2. The standard of Spanish galleons,
   showing a crowned black eagle
   and encircled by the collar of the
   Order of the Golden Fleece.
3. The standard of Castille and
   Leon; the standard of Barcelona,
   showing a monk holding a rosary;
   and the standard of Galicia, showing a chalice.

(From the Bibliothèque Nationale,
Cabinet des Estampes, Paris.)

Right: The Spaniards in the tropics
fought in their heavy armor, and it is
thus that they are depicted by Indian
artists. (Codex d'Histoire Chi-
chiméque, Bibliothèque Nationale,
Department of Oriental Manuscripts,
Paris.)

quex
yao
cazu

The Veracruz Convoy

It was to this hub of the Caribbean that another fleet, the Fleet of New Spain, comprising several galleons — the *Almirante de Honduras*, the *Nuestra Señora de Atocha*, and the *San Josefe* — and numerous merchant ships, were also sailing, from Veracruz. This city, on the Gulf of Mexico, was, like Porto Bello, a port of call for the ships of Spain. And, like its Panamanian counterpart, it was a relatively inhospitable place. It was situated on low-lying, sandy land; and from May to September it was relentlessly baked by the tropical sun. The only water in the vicinity was a muddy stream, the Tenoya, to the southeast of the town. The surrounding countryside was sinister in appearance, and bare of vegetation. And the settlement itself was little more than a country road, with no protection from the summer hurricanes and the winter winds. For the galleons that called there, the only shelter was a small island that lay at water level. On this island was the Fort of San Juan d'Ulloa, which dominated the town and served to protect the port. The port itself, which was bad enough, was made even worse by the presence of reefs along the coast. And, of course, the entire area abounded in malaria-bearing mosquitoes, and in cases of *vomito prieto* — yellow fever — as well as other diseases.

The voyage from this miserable spot to the comparative paradise that was Havana took several weeks. It was impossible to sail directly to Cuba across the Gulf of Mexico, for one had to follow the winds. One had to sail northward, skirt the coasts of present-day Louisiana, and then turn southward along the entire coast of Florida. The Fleet of New Spain, its heavily armed galleons and the merchant ships, on this occasion took four weeks for the trip — which was considered a fairly rapid crossing; for it often required five weeks to sail the semicircular route between Veracruz and Havana. In addition to contrary winds, one had also to take into account the possibility of heavy weather; for more than a few galleons had been blown aground in the course of a sudden gale.

The ships from Veracruz, having survived the perils of nature as well as the danger of pirate attack, approached Havana from the north, and their arrival was the signal for great rejoicing. The city, supplied with the luxuries of civilization, and characterized by the prodigality of the great lords who lived there, and by an atmosphere of moral laxity, offered numerous distractions to men who, for months, had been leading a life of privation and danger. And the city was determined to show its gratitude to such men.

The fleets now in the port of Havana were already behind schedule, and the festivities and pastimes of Havana delayed them even more. And yet, it was necessary for the galleons and merchantmen to call there, for only at Havana could they obtain the food and water that they would need for the long crossing of the Atlantic. Even so, the ships were already so loaded with goods and passengers that it was only with difficulty that room could be found for these provisions.

Another delay was caused by the necessity of making repairs on some of the ships; for many of the vessels of Spain were old, or hastily built, or both. Overloaded as they were, they leaked outrageously, and the pumps available at that time, which were made of wood and leather, were unable to handle such large amounts of water. Also, the hulls of the ships were regarded as a delicacy by *teredos*, or ship's worms; and they were burdened by the growth of barnacles and algae on their exteriors. It was therefore necessary to make at least a minimum of repairs, even if these meant delaying the departure of the fleet. And Havana was the only place in which this could be done. Moreover, the shipyards of Havana were the best in the New World. The Spaniards may not have always been good seamen, nor were they particularly competent as naval architects, but one must admit that they were active and accomplished maintenance men. Their ship's carpenters, whether aboard the vessels themselves or on the beach at the various ports of call — Havana, San Juan d'Ulloa, Cartagena, or San Juan de Puerto Rico — accomplished marvels in keeping afloat ships that had been poorly designed, badly built, and constantly abused by overloading.

The combined fleet now numbered some eighty vessels: the six galleons mentioned above, and dozens of merchant ships belonging to various shipping firms, Spanish noblemen, and private enterprises. These latter, however, although their journeys were strictly commercial in nature, were required to carry armament in keeping with their size. Generally speaking, no less than a dozen cannon were stipulated by the rules of the Casa de Contratación. Here again, however, the rules were applied in an arbitrary manner, and the merchant ships actually depended for their defense on the cannon of the galleons. The space that they should have devoted to weapons, they preferred to fill with more profitable merchandise. The general assumption seems to have been that the merchant ships were assured of protection because of the *averia*, or fee, they paid in order to join the convoy. The rules of the Casa concerning the personal weapons to be carried aboard ship — each male passenger was supposed to have either an arquebus or an arbalest (a mechanized version of the crossbow) and ammunition for his weapon: but this rule was no more enforced than that which applied to the armament of ships.

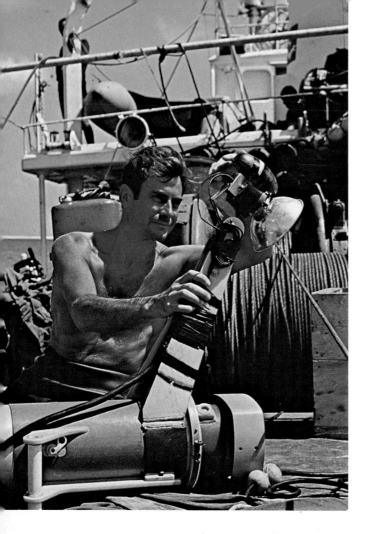

To the left: Michel Deloire, our cameraman, readies his equipment for a dive.

Above right: From the *Calypso*'s observation deck, where our radar is mounted, we try to pick out a clear path through the coral.

Below right: Everywhere in our work area there are coral massifs, and any one of them may conceal something of importance. We must therefore examine them one by one and take soundings.

Toward Europe

The route to be followed by Spanish ships upon the return journey to Europe was as well defined as that followed by the ships on their way to America. And both were based upon years of experience and observation, and upon rules and regulations. During the voyage from Spain to America, ships sailed southward to the Canary Islands, where they picked up the trade winds and, turning westward, crossed the Atlantic to arrive at the Gulf of Mexico. The itinerary for the return trip required the galleons to sail northward through the Bahamian canal after leaving Havana — a route in which they were constantly in danger of running aground on the reefs which abounded there. Then they continued upward along the Atlantic coast of North America as far north as the present-day Carolinas — at the approximate level of Bermuda — until they caught the west winds and entered the Gulf Stream. (The latter was an important factor in the speed of the ships on the return trip, for it flows at a speed of three knots.) The next stage of the crossing took them to the Azores, from which the fleet sailed in a straight line

to Spain. The usual time of arrival there was toward the end of the year, usually in December.

If all went well, the round trip usually required eight months. But it sometimes happened that all did not go well. In 1565, for instance, the Fleet of New Spain was sunk, en masse, by a storm. In 1572, five galleons sank, another burned to the waterline, and two others were abandoned. In 1581, eight galleons disappeared without a trace, including the vessel of the admiral commanding the Fleet.

The dangers and uncertainties of the Atlantic crossing were surely never far from the minds of the men of the combined Fleet as it finally sailed out of Havana harbor. At the head of the convoy was the flagship of the captain general of the fleet, who had been personally appointed by His Most Catholic Majesty of Spain. This vessel was instantly recognizable, for from it fluttered a standard of red damask, on one side of which was embroidered a crucifix, and on the other, the arms of Spain and those of Captain General Don Francisco Rodriguez himself. This official insignia had cost one thousand escudos; and it had been presented to the Don Francisco by the king. It was hoisted only on three occasions: when the fleet was getting under sail; during battle; and on the Feast of St. James, who was the patron of Spain. The rest of the time, the standard was entrusted to the care of a high official, the *alférez major*, who undertook his duties with the full understanding that a moment of carelessness might cost him his head. The banners of the other galleons were less grand, and consisted of three horizontal bands, one red, one white, and one yellow. On the middle, or white band, was superimposed a black eagle, surmounted by a crown and encircled with the collar of the Order of the Golden Fleece.

For all his splendid insignia, Don Francisco did not receive any remuneration from his rank of captain general as such. To the contrary, the ships' cannon, provisions, and instruments of navigation were all his personal responsibility. Moreover, upon his nomination by the king, he had been expected to donate a large sum to the royal treasury — and to make smaller contributions, all the way down the line, to the royal officials who had been helpful to him in obtaining his office. In spite of all this, however, it was well known that the captain general of a fleet could count upon amassing a fortune after a single voyage to the West Indies.

The Perils of Navigation

Behind the captain general's ship sailed, in an orderly formation, the eight other galleons which carried (theoretically) authorized passengers, mer-

No coral formation can be dismissed as unimportant. We have to examine every one of them for evidence.

chandise from the colonies, and the king's quintal. Last came the ship of Admiral Don Gaspar de Vargas, which guarded the rear of the convoy. Around the galleons sailed smaller, lighter, and faster cutters, whose job it was to encircle and maintain order among the sixty-or-so merchant ships of the convoy. These latter were of various sizes and tonnages; and one could be sure that, without the cutters to ride herd on them, most of them would have been dispersed and lost in the first strong wind. Despite the vigilance of the cutters, such accidents did occur occasionally during storms or as the result of a battle with pirates; and, in such cases, the Casa de Contratación had specified certain places where the fleet was to regroup.

In principle, this was a wise precaution. In practice, however, it was virtually useless because of the primitive navigational skills of the age. In order for a scattered fleet to be able to find one of the Casa's gathering points, it was necessary for every ship's captain or pilot to know the precise location of his vessel at any given time; and this necessity far exceeded the navigational science of the time. Experienced seamen, combining guesswork with the use of the compass, could discover their latitudinal position; but they were often unsuccessful in discovering their longitude. There was no instrument — and there would not be one for another century or so — capable of determining exactly the difference between an hour of the terrestrial meridian and that of the local meridian. The essential apparatus in establishing one's position was a simple hourglass, which served as the ship's clock. Every half hour, the sand ran out, and the hourglass had to be reversed — a task that was the responsibility of the seamen- apprentices.

The problems of navigation were further complicated by the fact that the Casa de Contratación had yet to establish a hydrographic service, a map bureau, or even a naval academy. The result was that Spain never once had a sufficient number of competent captains, or, above all, of trained pilots. The lack of pilots was particularly serious, for the responsibility for the ship's course rested entirely in the hands of these specialists. Today, navigation and command are both functions of the ship's captain; in the days of the galleons, however, they were separate and distinct responsibilities, and navigating was the exclusive domain of the pilot. He set the course; and he held it. And, in both, the pilot was dependent upon a combination of data with intuition that had very little of theoretical knowledge in it. It could hardly have been otherwise, for man had only recently begun to turn his ships away from the comfortably familiar coastlines of the Old World and into the great unknown Atlantic, and his science had not yet caught up with his love of adventure. The pilot therefore relied more upon personal experience, upon the accuracy of his memory, and upon a complex of mysterious "signs" and "feelings," than upon charts — as well he might, for the latter were notoriously vague and incomplete. Moreover, each pilot guarded his secrets as his greatest treasure, and no pilot would have thought of sharing his own store of knowledge concerning winds, currents, and reefs.

The fact that the ships of Spain always traveled in convoy was not only because of the danger of pirate attack, but also because the navigational skills of the time were so primitive, and so monopolized, that not every ship was able to have an experienced pilot. But even this arrangement led to other problems, for the pilots of the fleet often did not agree among themselves.

Captain General Rodriguez could hardly have been surprised to discover that, even before leaving the American coastline to sail toward the Azores, several of the merchantmen of his convoy had wandered away and been lost. And Admiral de Vargas, whose galleon was sailing in the rear of the convoy, and whose responsibility it was to keep an eye on the smaller vessels of the fleet, was unwilling to spend too much time waiting for them to find their way back to the main body of the convoy. He was eager to be well on his way across the Atlantic before the bad weather set in.

The whole procession of ships moved slowly in the wind, at a speed of no more than four knots, for a galleon's rounded shape (even at that time French sailors called galleons *barriques* or *bailles* — tubs) made it slow-moving as well as unwieldy. By now, the galleons' square sails had been supplemented by two triangular ones; for square sails made it difficult to maintain a direct course on the open sea. One of the triangles hung from the mizzenmast, and the other from the quartermast. Smaller sails, such as a square sail rigged underneath the bowsprit, were used as a mean of maneuvering rather than of increasing speed. Even with these precautions, however, a crosswind arose and, despite the best efforts of the pilots, the fleet was soon hopelessly off course. The ships could do no more than let themselves be carried, day after day, in the general direction of Europe. As disagreeable as the situation was, however, it would have been worse for the fleet to have been becalmed. Mariners feared these calms as much, or more, than they did rough seas; for they prolonged voyages indefinitely, and the ships were perennially short on water even in the best of circumstances.

Shipboard Life

It was a nightmarish voyage, and an interminable one, in conditions of extreme discomfort. The ship's personnel was a motley collection of nationalities and classes. All of the ship's officers were Spaniards, with the exception of the pilots, who were often Portuguese or Italians. Only a small part of the crew, however, was Spanish, and the rest — sometimes as much as four-fifths of the crew — were drawn from every country in Europe. There were ships manned by natives of no fewer than twelve countries. And the result was a veritable Tower of Babel, with no one understanding anyone else, and fights breaking out on every occasion. The situation was not helped by the fact that many of the sailors, whether volunteers or conscripted by force, were not of the best sort. (Columbus himself, for example, had two convicts aboard the *Santa Maria*: an Englishman and an Irishman.)

One can imagine the conditions aboard a ship only 125 feet long and 45 feet wide with between six and seven hundred passengers. Everyone, from the most refined grandee to the lowest seaman, whether he were lodged on the forecastle or on the poop, was exposed to the same lack of privacy, the same diseases, the same filth and vermin. And there was one toilet, a seat with a hole in it, which had been attached to the forward deck, for everyone aboard.

The sailors, soldiers, and passengers all slept on the open deck, exposed to the elements. Most of them never had occasion to remove their clothing from the beginning of the voyage to the end — a period of perhaps three months. (Uniforms, of course, were unheard of, for both soldiers and sailors. The latter wore red conical hats — a product of Toledo — and, when they could afford it, gray capes with hoods to protect them from the rain and waves.) Passengers and crew took shelter below deck only in case of rough seas; and there their plight was even worse, for they were packed like sardines in a can. It happened occasionally that passengers made the entire crossing below deck, crammed into the holds and surrounded by the stench of human waste; for there were no portholes, and no other means of ventilation.

The ships were naturally made of wood; and, overloaded and overtraveled as they were, they leaked at every seam. On many ships, the pumps were manned twenty-four hours a day. They were located in a special compartment, so constructed that all the water in the bilge collected there. The air was so bad that before entering the pump room, it was necessary to let a candle down into the compartment. If the flame went out, then it was concluded that the air could not be breathed until the compartment had been "purified." This operation was simplicity itself: fresh water, mixed with vinegar or urine, was poured into the pump room before the seamen climbed down.

Pastimes

One of the greatest enemies of shipboard life was boredom, and in the course of the fleet's haphazard trek across the Atlantic everyone aboard vied in organizing feasts and entertainments. Into this category fell religious celebrations. Mass was said every morning on the bridge, High Mass was sung on Sundays, and the feast days of the various saints were celebrated with unalloyed enthusiasm by everyone.

Considerable time was also devoted to entertainments of a less wholesome nature. There were cockfights, pig races (the pigs were destined for the dinner tables of wealthy passengers), and bull races — the bulls being soldiers and sailors who raced about in the limited space available on deck. And, of course, huge sums were bet on champion cocks, pigs, and "bulls."

On some of the ships — particularly the merchant ships — there were women. The regulations formulated by the Casa clearly required that they be segregated from male passengers, but the nobles and the ship's officers were the first to ignore this rule. In fact, there was a regular exchange of ladies

Right: A sixteenth-century vessel as depicted by Pieter Brueghel (1525-69): The Fall of Icarus. (Musée des Beaux-Arts, Brussels.)

A view of the Port of Havana, with the Fortress of El Moro.

among ships; and it happened occasionally that this traffic led to nocturnal orgies on the poop decks.

On the whole, the fleet lacked food more than entertainment. What was available was hardly suited to maintain the health of men exhausted by a sojourn in the tropics and unprotected by any notion of personal hygiene. The food aboard was, for the most part, discovered to be rotten and inedible. The passengers suffered continually from hunger and thirst; and a good number of them died of privation. Even more, however, died of disease, for there were no sanitary or medical facilities aboard, and scurvy was endemic. To make matters worse, many of the passengers had brought aboard with them the diseases of the colonies, and yellow fever and dysentery were everyday occurrences. It was only by chance that not everyone aboard was infected. In these conditions, death became a commonplace, and no sooner had a passenger or sailor breathed his last than the last rites were hurriedly administered and the body dropped overboard. Then, everyone smiled at the thought that there would now be a bit more room . . .

Of the original eighty ships in the convoy, almost two-thirds finally dropped anchor at the Azores. No one had dared hope that so many would make it. The remaining third, barring a catastrophe, would eventually reach

Europe; but at what point, exactly, only God knew. For the ships that had succeeded in reaching the Azores, the worst of the voyage now seemed over. The only danger that remained to be faced was that of strong westerly winds and storms near the coast of Spain. And certainly that was not to be discounted.

But the thought of past disasters did not cloud the celebrations or the optimism of the fleet now at the Azores. Admiral de Vargas promptly dispatched a fast cutter to the port of Cádiz, with the tidings of the safe arrival of His Majesty's Fleet in European waters.

The King's Debts

Everyone from the king to the smallest clerk in the offices of the Casa had been waiting for this news. And now that it had come, steps were promptly initiated for celebrations to mark the impending arrival of the fleet. Everything was in readiness for an explosion of official welcome. But, before the first wine bottle could be opened, there were certain formalities to be observed; formalities imposed by the regulations of the Casa de Contratación.

No one could disembark from the ships of the fleet, and not one item of merchandise could be removed, until the inspectors of the Casa had completed their official inventory of each vessel's contents. This inventory, however, was not as formidable as it might sound. The inspectors were willing to ignore the supernumerary passengers, to close their eyes to the vast piles of merchandise, belonging to great nobles and rich merchants, that had been transported illegally on His Majesty's galleons — so long as they were assured that their lack of attention to such details would not go unrewarded. Such matters were settled amicably in the quarters of Captain General Don Francisco Rodriguez, where, with many smiles and bows, everyone stated the price of his complicity.

Despite the peculations of the ship's officers and crew and of the merchants and the officials of the Casa, the flood of wealth discharged from the holds of the galleons seemed inexhaustible: gold, silver, gems, pearls, spices, tobacco, sugar, cacao, indigo. And yet, this vast treasure was not destined for the coffers, strongboxes, and kitchens of Spain. No sooner had the cargo been unloaded, registered and stored in warehouses, than it began to be redistributed throughout Europe to pay for goods needed by Spain: linen from Flanders, to make into galleon sails; iron from the north, to forge into anchors, swords, and picks. For Spain herself produced almost nothing.

Three masterpieces of Incan art: two vases of wrought gold, and a small female idol, also of gold. (The vases are in the National Museum of Anthropology in Lima, and the idol is part of a private collection in the same city.) Among the treasures found by Phips in the wreck of *Nuestra Señora de la Concepción* were idols and golden vessels of Peruvian origin.

Thus, although wealth poured into Seville, via Cádiz, the other cities of Europe were the ones who controlled European trade. In the sixteenth century, it was Antwerp; in the seventeenth, Amsterdam. There was a well-known saying: "Spain eats the New World, and the Low Countries are getting fat." But it was not only the Low Countries who profited. The king of Spain had so many debts that, in order to pay off some of them, he had to allow a German banking family, the Welsers, to operate, for their own profit, his mines in Venezuela. And cities other than Antwerp and Amsterdam also profited from the golden cornucopia of the New World: Genoa, Bourges, Ostend, Rouen, Nuremberg, Augsbourg, London . . .

Not only did the treasure of the New World never enrich Spain herself,

but, worse, it contributed, each year, to increase the cost of living in that nation. From the beginning of the sixteenth century, Spain's prices were the highest in the whole of Europe. Moreover, Spain's overseas adventures were depriving the nation of its vital resources and wasting its young men on military adventures and overseas conquests. Christopher Columbus' discovery, which had seemed capable of conferring infinite wealth upon Spain and power beyond anything of which European countries had ever dreamed, was in the final analysis, causing Spain to become stagnant. It was slowing her evolution, preventing the development of her own resources, discouraging industrial progress, and leading her into a state of social and economic stasis which was to endure for three centuries. Such was the curse of Spanish gold.

THREE

The Sunken Ship

Monday, July 15. This morning two completely equipped groups are going to visit the Bank. We can see it from the *Calypso*, mauve and bluish green, its masses of coral alternating with the colors of open water in the distance. One of the groups, headed by Remy de Haenen, is going northward in the launch. This team will try to find out whether or not there is a reef projecting above the surface on which the Spanish seamen might have camped while waiting to be rescued. The area that these men will investigate is at the position indicated by Phips; that is, 20 degrees 43 minutes north.

At 11:30 A.M., Remy's team returns to the *Calypso* and reports that they have found nothing. No projecting reefs and no artifacts of any kind, even though they searched carefully among the coral.

Thereupon, the second team — consisting of myself, Bernard Delemotte, Michel Deloire, Serge Foulon, and Riant — sets out in the launch. We head for the semicircular coral table that was discovered yesterday, intending to examine it again. Delemotte dives first, and attaches himself to a weight that is being towed by the launch. This enables him to be towed alone slowly beneath the surface. Our reconnaissance is initially concentrated on the sheltered and barren side of the reef. On this side, coral does not grow unless it can find something on which to grow — something like a sunken ship.

The bottom of the leeward (southern) side is very different from that of the windward (eastern) side. In the former case, the water is deeper, and the wall of the level reef goes straight down for 80 to 100 feet. Here, we find large golden Acroporians growing everywhere, and it is impossible to make out the contours of a sunken ship — especially one that may have been here for over three hundred years. On the windward side of the reef, coral growth is much denser. The water is more shallow, and the bottom more regular. There are patches of bottom covered with sand and bits of dead coral. And here we find all the forms of marine life that are usual in coral waters: large sea fans, giant clams, spirographs, etc. No single coral area, however, is exactly like another; and this one is subtly different from those that we have seen in the Red Sea and in the Indian Ocean. These differences are immediately perceptible to the trained eye — differences in the distribution of species of coral, in the size and shape of certain corals, in the various colors, and in the limestone algae and the sponges. In the sea, one never has the feeling that he has seen something before. The flora and fauna may be the same; but each place is somehow different.

Delemotte finally surfaces to tell us that he has indeed found a sunken ship — but it is made of iron, and therefore of comparatively recent date.

A Cannon

It is now Michel Deloire's turn to go down. Only a few minutes later, he is back on the surface, waving his arms and obviously excited about something. "There, on the left. There's a sort of hill, and on top of it is some very strange-looking coral form. I'm almost sure it's a cannon."

He climbs into the launch, finds a pick, and immediately dives back into the water, to reappear a short time later. "It's a cannon, all right. And there are two more just like it a short distance away."

Three cannon, I think. Is it possible that there is a treasure ship after all? Delemotte and I dive with Michel and begin looking around the area. We see three large mounds of coral and debris, each one a good distance from the other. The base circumference of the first one is 130 feet; of the second, 175 feet; and of the third, 250 feet. The lowest point of these mounds is about 50 feet below the surface of the water. There is a fourth mound, much smaller than the others, a short distance away. On top of the northernmost mound I find a piece of iron — a crank handle. On top of the largest one, I find bits of rigging, several large nails, and a few objects that could be tools. I cannot see them very well, since they are all partially sunk into the coral.

There seems to be no doubt about it. There is a sunken ship at this spot, a very old ship. I feel a shiver of excitement. Michel and Bernard signal their impatience to continue our reconnaissance.

The ocean floor of the Caribbean presents an extraordinary diversity of life forms. Shown here are sponges and sea fans, and, swimming among them, a *Thalassoma* and a *Scarus taeniopterus*.

I see, to the south, Deloire's cannon. One of them has a small chain lying over it; the chain was probably used to secure a lifeboat, but broke and sank to the bottom when disaster overtook the ship.

Two more cannon are resting on the flank of the third mound; one small and one larger. At the foot of the mound, I see two cannon breeches, perfectly parallel to one another, sticking up out of the bottom. Farther on, there is a heap of broken pottery. To the east, there are two craters, apparently recent ones, in the bottom. In one of them, I find several clay bricks — no doubt from the oven of the ship's galley. I surmise that we are probably standing near the site of the forward mast. In one of the other holes, Michel finds some planks lying on the bottom. Then, we see something else; something in the shape of a section of column, about twenty inches long and fifteen inches in diameter. By signs, Michel says that it may be a strongbox of some kind. He strikes it with his pick, and a small cloud of rust rises. He strikes it again, harder. A piece falls off: a nail. The mysterious object consists of a number of rectangular nails rusted together; probably, they were in a bag that dissolved in the seawater. Apparently, we are in the workshop of the ship's carpenter.

Near this same crater we see two large anchors, each about fourteen feet long. Each one has a broken hook. Under them, another cannon is lying.

Another anchor, this one about twelve feet long, lies a short distance to the north.

Then we notice something strange. The whole area around these anchors, for a distance of about fifty feet, is surrounded by a cord of some kind, as though to mark out a work area. The cord seems of fairly recent manufacture, and is of cotton or nylon; no more than five or six years old, surely. On the bottom, we see bits of electric wire — an indication that someone has used dynamite here recently.

A little farther out, the bottom seems untouched and is covered with small coral formations as far as the eye can see. But there Bernard and Riant make some surprising discoveries: a refrigerator part; a carburetor; a centrifugal pump; and the dashboard from a motorboat.

The Explanation

At first, it is difficult to make sense out of what we are seeing. After climbing back into the launch, however, and sorting out the information that we have picked up, things begin to fall into place. The only possible explanation is that a very large and very old ship, probably from the seventeenth century, is lying on the bottom below us, buried under tons of coral. The ship has obviously been found and worked on, and perhaps damaged, by someone before us. Moreover, the depth at which the wreck is lying, its location close to the reef, and its latitude, all correspond closely to those of the galleon that William Phips described. One might therefore say that, very likely, this is the same galleon.

The three large mounds and the single smaller one seem to be heaps of rubble resulting from earlier attempts to uncover the ship. They may even date back to the time of Phips's own expeditions. On the other hand, there are indisputable traces of a much more recent expedition, one which proceded more roughly and more hurriedly, and which seems to have been superficial and suddenly halted. It is not impossible that the divers were too ambitious in their use of dynamite and blew up their own boat.

At this point, Remy and his team join us, and Remy immediately begins inspecting the top of the reef, which lies at water level. He calls us to point out two caldrons. One of them is very large and is partially buried in coral on the slope of the reef, under about seven feet of water. We can only guess that the shipwrecked sailors attempted to survive on the reef, and that the large caldrons were perhaps intended to hold their drinking water. It may be that they even constructed some kind of platform on the Bank, and that in the course of time the platform was swept into the sea along with the caldrons. The presence of the caldrons, in any case, is an indication that the survivors were able to exist on the reef for some time. And, all at once, I find myself believing that we are on the right road. I make up my mind to do everything that I can to make sure that our quest will have a happy ending.

The whole of the afternoon is devoted to preliminary work. A team headed by Bernard and Michel begins marking the location of everything that is found and making a sketch of the site, with the aid of a compass and a tape measure. Yves Agostini and Riant are busy taking vertical color photographs. We hope that, by the time we return to the *Calypso*, we will have gathered enough information to make up a map of our work area.

Before we know it, however, the sun is setting, and the water is becoming dark. We can do no more today.

According to what we already know, the situation is good, though not perfect. The water here is not more than thirty-five to forty feet deep, which means that there will be no problem in diving. There are tide currents, however, and these can sometimes be troublesome. And, of course, there is the coral; but we expected that.

On the whole, it has been a good day, almost a day of triumph, or at least a day that seems to promise success. Everyone aboard is happy, including myself. I think it is not so much the anticipation of the "treasure" that pleases me, but rather the enthusiasm of my friends on the *Calypso* — and the prospect of the fascinating and unusual job that seems to await us. To do battle with the coral, to rip from its grasp the secrets of a ship three centuries old — this is the real excitement of our treasure hunt.

Aboard the *Calypso*, nothing is talked about but the discoveries of the day. Remy's two caldrons seem particularly exciting. Everyone, including myself, is certain that we have found the site of a large sunken ship. Why not that of *Nuestra Señora de la Concepción*? Skepticism has its uses, but there are times when it is wise to ignore one's doubts. It seems that Remy's experience and information, and Deloire's air reconnaissance and the films he took, have paid off handsomely. And, of course, we have had our share of luck.

Everyone is impatient to get to work and dig out the "treasure." No one seems to have the slightest doubt that the ship down there is *Nuestra Señora*. I am not nearly so sure as everyone else that we will find a pot of gold at the end of our rainbow; but I am convinced that we will find another kind of gold, an archaeological treasure. Still, I cannot bring myself to disappoint the other members of the team by showing less enthusiasm than they; or rather, less certainty that we will all end up rich beyond our wildest dreams.

While everyone is discussing and celebrating, however, I am thinking about what we have already done, and what we should do next. Given the fact that we have found the remains of a large ship — the size of the anchors alone indicate its dimensions — it is very possible to conjecture that the ship may indeed be a galleon. A galleon, with its armament scattered around it on the ocean floor.

What I would like to do would be to get to the wooden hull as quickly as possible. This would tell us a good deal, both about the direction in which we should begin digging and about the amount of work that will be entailed. Moreover, the details of the ship's construction should furnish information about the time in which it was built and used.

Gold Fever

Our first task will be to find a way to get the *Calypso* from its present position to the site of the wreck — across 2900 yards of coral. I send out a team of divers with Paul Zuéna in the launch to try to find a passage. According to their radio report, it will be possible to maneuver the *Calypso* onto the site, but it will be a long and difficult operation. No one, however, is discouraged. Moving our ship seems a minor detail after our good luck in finding the wreck so quickly. I, however, am not quite so optimistic. I would feel better if I could be sure that my friends will not be disappointed at what we will find eventually. And I would be less uneasy if it were not so obvious that the *Calypso* — has suddenly been overcome with an epidemic of gold fever.

Actually, I hardly expected it to be otherwise. It is easy enough for someone of my age and experience to be detached, and to be preoccupied with archaeological treasures rather than with Spanish gold. It is different, however, for these men — our divers, camera crews, and mechanics. They are all young, excited, enthusiastic; and they are fascinated by the idea of "sunken treasure." I had told them, with a smile, that we were going to go on a treasure hunt. They remember the word "treasure," but they seem to have forgotten the smile. Perhaps I had better remind them.

I should mention that my wife, Simone, from the very first has been unrelentingly opposed to this treasure hunt. She is afraid that, if we are successful, we will have sacrificed our team's solidarity for nothing more than a bit of gold. And, since she lives aboard the *Calypso* and takes part in all our expeditions, and since she considers herself responsible for the health and well-being of everyone aboard, she is opposed to anything that might affect adversely the human quality of the *Calypso*'s team.

After the second service of dinner, I ask everyone to assemble in the wardroom. There, I explain our situation in detail. Then, I suggest that, if everyone is willing, we will spend one month, and no more, digging out the wreck. I am careful to point out that we may well spend the entire time working like demons and still not find the treasure that almost everyone seems so sure is there.

Everyone listens, their glasses of rum on the table before them, their eyes bright. My speech has not diminished their optimism one bit. On the contrary, they are more enthusiastic than before. The whole atmosphere of the wardroom is that of a seventeenth-century privateer. What is foremost in the minds of these young men, certainly, is the attraction of Spanish gold; but it is also a burning curiosity about what they will find down there, buried among the coral, in that phantom ship from a fabled age.

The Fantastic World of Coral

Remy de Haenen is certain that the sunken ship is indeed *Nuestra Señora de la Concepción*, and his optimism has infected the rest of the people aboard. For my part, I will wait until we find proof one way or the other before making up my mind. Moreover, I hardly expect to find such proof immediately. In shallow water, on a windward wall, coral can grow at a rate of about a half inch per year. If this is indeed *Nuestra Señora*, it has been lying on the bottom for 329 years — which means that the hull is encased in a shell of coral that may be anywhere from ten to fifteen feet thick. This is the first time that anyone has attempted a "dig" on a site in which coral is so abundant. I have a feeling that we will soon discover the problems implicit in archaeological work in tropical waters.

It seems to me that our basic work must proceed at two levels. First, we must film every phase of yesterday's discoveries before we do anything to change the appearance of the worksite. Then, we must organize our future work area very methodically and very carefully, and we must decide on the

Above right: Parrotfish, unintimidated by the presence of human beings, are on familiar terms with divers from the *Calypso*.

Below right: Michel Deloire hits a coral formation with an iron bar to make sure that there is a cannon underneath the limestone.

Calypso's anchorage both above the sunken ship itself and among the reefs.

I was thinking last night about the danger of the *Calypso* — being trapped among the reefs in the event of a sudden gale or hurricane. As we try the passage into the Bank that Zuéna and his divers found yesterday, we will have to mark it with buoys so that we can get through it quickly if we have to do so, without having to spend hours picking our way through the reefs. Right now, Zuéna and Remy de Haenen are working with a team of men to set up radar poles and buoy anchors in the channel. A metal sighting board about five feet wide (fifteen times the width of the radar wing) is attached to the main reef at the end of a vertical galvanized pipe about six feet long. Then, five colored inflatable buoys are anchored to the most dangerous of the reefs, and their positions are established by radar and radio in relation to the position of the *Calypso*. We are beginning to put together a workable chart of the area. The Fantastic World of Coral

The underwater plateau at the edge of which the *Calypso* is anchored is, at its deepest point, less than a hundred feet from the surface. It abounds in coral life, and especially in branched coral. The "branches," like towers or cathedral spires, often rise almost to the surface.

There is no reef barrier here. One can sail over this plateau without seeing it; and it is as though one were going through a forest that is sometimes very dense, and sometimes dotted with clearings. It is a world of fantasy, like a series of buildings set down without any preconceived plan. There seems to be no rule governing the growth patterns of these living organisms of coral. At one point there may be five hundred yards of clear space with hardly any coral in it at all; and then, just a short distance away, the growth will be so thick that our divers can hardly find their way through it.

It is obvious that this bank is virtually impassable, even if one knows it well and has more than one's share of a navigator's intuition. It is impossible to keep one's bearings among these haphazard coral towers.

The Silver Bank is a far cry from the Far San and Suakin archipelagoes of the Red Sea that we know so well. In the Far San, for example, there are coral towers that rise 750 feet from the bottom. With our sonar and our mini-subs, we have studied the configuration of these banks. At a distance of no more than 150 yards from the reef, the water is already 800 feet deep, and we know that these towers rise from the depths. Here on the Silver Bank, however, the forest of coral spires rises from a plateau. And this enormous accumulation of limestone will have to be broken away, and the rubble will have to be removed; an overwhelming amount of work, and perhaps all for nothing.

A Secret Ballot

The rear deck of the *Calypso* sounds like a discussion club. Since our meeting of last night, everyone is in a state of great excitement. And the most excited of them all, certainly, is Remy de Haenen, closely followed by Michel Deloire and Bernard Delemotte.

Remy takes me aside for a word in private. He reminds me that he has been looking for this wreck for two years; that he has spent a lot of money and a lot of time on it. He would like to stay with us, he says, and to put his airplane and his boat at our disposal. In return, he asks to be reimbursed for half his expenses, and to receive 20 per cent of anything that we may eventually find. I tell him that I am willing, but only if the team as a whole gives its consent.

That night, everyone is once more called to the wardroom. I begin by trying once more to abate their gold fever; this time by talking about the amount of work involved in our project:

"You all know by now that this is going to be a great deal more work than we imagined. To remove the tons and tons of coral that are down there will require an enormous effort, and it may take a long time. I know that you have courage. But I know too how tired you will become; and fatigue may bring on discouragement. Before we do anything else, therefore, I want to know how you feel about it. We are going to take a vote. And I want to remind you, before we do, that it is by no means certain that this sunken ship contains a treasure, or, if it does, that we will be able to dig it out. We do not even know for sure that it is *Nuestra Señora de la Concepción.* You all know what my feelings are about this. The important thing is that there is a ship, and an old ship, down there; whether or not it is full of gold is beside the point. I hope that no one will let himself be carried away by visions of a fortune, buried or not, in the Silver Bank.

"I want you to vote Yes or No on the question of whether or not we should continue with this expedition. If you vote Yes, we will have to get some more equipment sent out from Puerto Rico. And I will also cable Frédéric Dumas and ask him to join us. His experience in marine archaeology and as a diver will be valuable to us. It is Dumas, remember, who dived down to the hull of the *Andrea Doria*, in almost three hundred feet of water.

"And now, let's vote."

It is a secret ballot, of course, and the atmosphere of the wardroom had a certain solemnity about it which befits the occasion. I imagine that pretty

The first cannon has been marked with a red buoy. The diver is now swimming toward another cannon to mark it in the same way.

much the same sort of thing went on three hundred years ago aboard the pirate ships of the Caribbean. The pirate captain was not an autocrat, and direct democracy was a way of life aboard pirate ships, the most liberal way of life possible.

Everyone in the wardroom has now placed his vote in a hat. While waiting for the votes to be counted, everyone reacts according to his temperament; some joke; others sit quietly, their faces serious. Then the voting results are announced, and it is a unanimous Yes. Everyone has voted to become a ditchdigger.

Later that night, I make a list of the new equipment that we will need. Some of it can be brought from Puerto Rico, but a few items will have to come from France. We will also need specialists in this kind of work, and that is why I mentioned Frédéric Dumas in the wardroom meeting. "Didi," as we

Captain Cousteau giving instructions to the divers prior to an inspection dive among the coral.

call him, is an expert in marine archaeology, and his works on ancient sunken ships are considered authoritative. During the night, I contact a friend in France, Commandant Brenot, by radiotelephone, and ask him to get in touch with Dumas for me — and also with two other specialists: Alan Landsburg, the co-producer of our films, who has much documentation at his disposal, and John Soh, our chief film editor. Then, Caillart and I sit down and write telegrams to Brenot and to Fred Imbert (our agent in Puerto Rico), giving a long list of the material that we will need.

Dynamite

Wednesday, July 17. Another splendid day, with small, fluffy clouds on the horizon, floating over the blues and greens of the Silver Bank.

Everyone has been hard at work since dawn, and there has been no diminishing of interest or enthusiasm.

Already we are referring to the sunken ship as the "work area." Two teams are there now. One, Deloire and Delemotte, are recording the site as it is now, with Delemotte photographing the sunken ship and Deloire making moves of Delemotte at work. The second team is doing more exploring in order for us to be able to make a more detailed map of the area.

A third team, which includes myself, now sets to work to clear away the recent or "modern" debris to the south of the work area: the pieces of motor, the pumps, compressors, etc., that we found the first day.

The riddle of these items remains unsolved. Obviously, the men who left them here were at this spot rather recently. A part of a pump, for instance, is hardly rusted at all. Why on earth did they leave so much material behind? Did they have an accident? Did their boat sink? If so, where is it? Did they find "the treasure"? Perhaps we will never know.

Caillart went out early this morning with the buoys to select anchorage sites for the *Calypso*. He returns satisfied: six buoys have been put down, and there is sufficient clearance for the *Calypso* — to be able to get through the channel. Moreover, the chart of the channel, as marked by the buoys, is almost finished. But — there is always a but — it will be necessary to dynamite a coral head that is dangerously situated (or rather, to use TNT on it). De Haenen says that he will take care of it. We prepare six charges of TNT and bring out the detonators. At three o'clock, the charges are exploded — neat, limited explosions, without unnecessary destruction. The coral head has been shortened, and partially dislocated. Even so, we will have to have another go at it tomorrow, for we have to be certain that there will be no less than six feet of water under the *Calypso*'s keel.

De Haenen and Serge Foulon now take the *Zodiac* to explore the area to the southeast of us. There, about ten miles away, they find a sunken two-master, about a hundred years old. They bring back several objects, none of them of great interest: a bronze thimble, a brass lamp, assorted plates and jars.

In the meantime, the men in our two launches are working to secure steel lines to blocks of coral on the bottom, in order to prepare anchorage sites for the *Calypso*. Caillart, as captain of the *Calypso*, is in charge of this operation. With him are Paul Zuéna, Delemotte, Raymond Coll, Riant, and Marcel. By late afternoon, this onerous job is done. Marius is making several anti-swell Alinat buoys out of Afcodur tubing. Tomorrow, I will go down for a look at the anchorage sites. Perhaps we will be able to test them during the day.

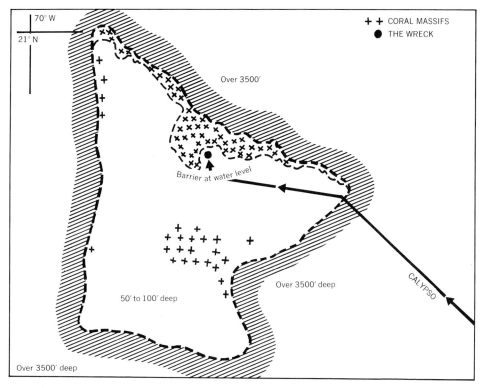

A detailed map of the Silver Bank, showing the location of the wreck.

There is a telegram from Commandant Brenot announcing that Didi Dumas will arrive, with the requested supplies, on July 24, at 4 A.M., at San Juan, Puerto Rico. There will be a problem finding quarters for Didi and John Soh on the already crowded *Calypso*, but we will work something out.

In the Heart of the Silver Bank

Thursday, July 18. At 7:30 A.M., Remy and Serge Foulon get to work, this time with a block of ten TNT charges, to finish the demolition of the coral head. By nine o'clock they are back, their mission accomplished. Meanwhile, Deloire, Delemotte, and I have gone over the photographs that Agostini took yesterday, but without turning up any new information. The photographs only confirm what we already knew.

By ten o'clock we — Delemotte, Deloire, Jean-Clair Riant and I — are on our way toward the Bank in a launch. Foulon, Remy, and Agostini are accompanying us, in the Zodiac. Agostini, of course, has his camera on hand.

Once there, we dive to inspect the work area, and I point out to Bernard

Following page: Sea fans and giant sponges on the fringes of the Silver Bank.

Delemotte a spot on the bottom beyond the area marked off by our predecessors here, to what I assume was the starboard side of the ship's forward anchors. There, Bernard uses his "sounder," a metal rod, to discover that the mud on the bottom is only about eight inches deep. Below that, however, the bottom seems relatively soft; it is not coral, certainly. Bernard and I set to work with our hands, digging in the mud, and uncover several planks. We note carefully the direction in which they are lying, and determine that they are parallel to the planks we found yesterday. The axis of the ship, it seems, runs east-west.

Next, I must check out the *Calypso*'s projected anchorage. I inspect the steel slings installed by Caillart and his men yesterday. The one to the east is secure; but the one on the west has come loose and will have to be changed. We will have to postpone moving to our new anchorage until tomorrow.

During the afternoon, a team goes out to install a new sling on the bottom, to the south of the reef, and establishes, by means of radio and radar, a deep-water anchorage point to the southeast.

In the meantime, Bernard Delemotte and Michel Deloire, along with several other divers, set out in the launch for a detailed survey of what we think is the forward section of the galleon. Michel discovers more planks — probably inner siding or planking — and these too are lying east-west.

Later that evening, a map of the work area is put together in my cabin, and then posted in the wardroom. The ship — the Treasure Ship — is instantly christened by the *Calypso*'s wits: *Nuestra Señora de la Sanctissima Recuperación.*

The Treasure Committee

The most important event of the day takes place that night. After dinner, the entire crew meets over a few bottles of rum. This meeting (which is on film, with sound) is certainly the most colorful of any I have ever attended in my checkered career as a sailor, diver, or treasure hunter.

My purpose in calling the meeting is to eliminate the possibility of discord aboard the *Calypso*. I want nothing to compromise our friendly relations with one another. If we should indeed discover pieces of eight, or ingots, or any object of value, it is essential for us to have agreed beforehand on the division of spoils. This is in the best tradition of treasure hunting in its classic form.

I therefore call for another vote, this one to determine the share of each one, including that of the shipowner. Once again, the ballot is secret. And the results are as follows:

It is unanimously decided that 20 per cent of anything we find will go to

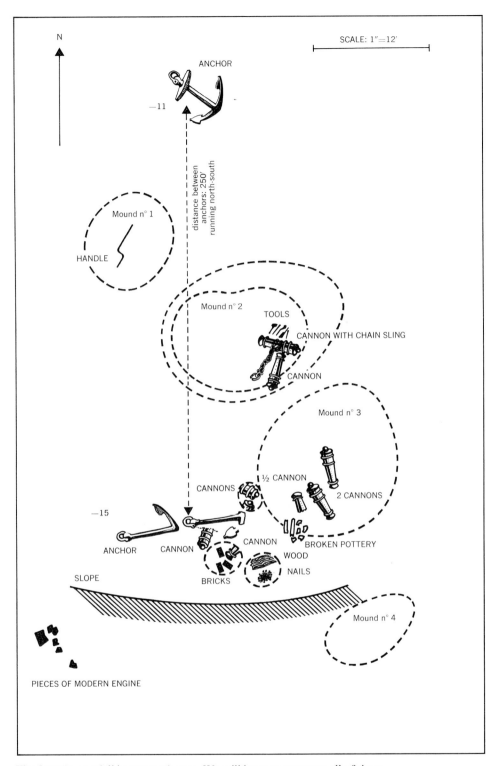

The four "mounds" in our work area. We will have to excavate all of them.

Coral fish, having recovered from their initial fright, are now back in our work area. They become readily accustomed to our presence.

Remy de Haenen, 40 per cent to the shipowner (Les Campagnes Océanographiques Françaises), and the remaining 40 per cent to be distributed in equal shares among all members of the crew. It is agreed that Frédéric Dumas, who is supposed to arrive next Wednesday, will also have an equal share.

Next, we proceed to the election of three delegates to preside over the

The colorful fish of coral waters are everywhere around us. Here are some specimens of *Myripristis* (red), a *Fissilabrus* (vertical white and blue stripes); and, in the middle, a small *Chromis*. The yellow fish in the foreground is probably a surgeonfish.

inventory of our treasure, and to take care of the disposition of what we find. Paul Zuéna, René Robino, and Raymond Coll are elected. They are the oldest and most experienced of our team — which shows the wisdom of the electorate. Remy de Haenen and I are to be *ex officio* members of the newly elected "Treasure Committee." There is a round of heartfelt applause, and everyone seems confident and enthusiastic.

Bad Weather

Friday, July 19. Since our arrival at the Silver Bank, the weather has been variable. On July 14 and 15, the trade winds were from the east at about 20 knots. There was a light swell at our anchorage, and the water was a bit choppy. At the site of the sunken ship, however, the swell was almost broken, and the water was relatively calm.

On July 16 and 17, the trade winds slackened to 15 knots; and, on July 18, to 10 knots. The weather was clear and calm. During the night, however, the wind rose to 30 knots and shifted to the southeast. The swell increased also, and the *Calypso* rolled as a result. This morning, the sky was completely overcast and gray, and the weather remains unpleasant. The wind is blowing at 25 knots.

An Accident

Yesterday, Dr. Tassy, our ship's doctor, ruptured an eardrum while diving. It seems that he dived with a spool of steel line, intending to attach a sling to a coral head. The spool was too heavy, however, and he sank like a rock. He also grazed his right leg against coral, and has developed a violent allergenic reaction, aggravated by infection. He is very upset at the thought that he will not be able to dive for a month. To console him, and with only a little malice, we suggest various activities to keep him busy: he can become the postal clerk, and sell tobacco. He can also keep the maps of the work area up to date. He can take charge of whatever we find on the bottom. And when we will have installed lighted buoys along the *Calypso*'s channel into the Silver Bank, he can be in charge of lighting them every night and putting them out every morning. (Actually, for the rest of our stay on the Bank, Dr. Tassy was to perform the latter duty with great diligence.)

This morning, despite the threatening weather, we are continuing to work. Three teams are in action. Deloire and Delemotte are trying to fill in details on the map of the work area. Coll and Riant are using the small suction device (which we call the "Bic") to locate pieces of wood forward of the anchors, on the ship's axis. They find neither the bowsprit nor the stem; but they do find various pieces of wood, partially splintered, beyond the work area laid out by our mysterious predecessors. These pieces, too, lie east-west.

A Predicament

After lunch, and despite the poor visibility, we weigh anchor and turn the *Calypso* into the channel — not quite two miles long — that we hope will lead safely to the work area. The big red buoys on either side of the channel are a comforting sight. The passage is managed without incident, and, as soon as we have reached our destination, Caillart sets to work, in liaison with the launches, to anchor us down at six points. Soon, the *Calypso* is at the center of a six-pointed star of steel lines: three forward, and three aft. Forward, the *Calypso* is floating above several coral formations that were partially destroyed by TNT. We are now secure in the heart of the Silver Bank — a situation that, only a short time ago, it had seemed impossible to realize.

Even before the anchorage was complete, Raymond Coll went down with the miniature suction, which he hooked up to reserve air tanks by means of a narghile pipe. He is supposed to begin digging in the crater where I found the clay bricks, and try to find either the keel or the timbers. Serge Foulon, who went down with Raymond to photograph the operation, brings back miscellaneous objects that the suction has turned up: fragments of pottery, a pig's tooth, a coffeepot — and two belt buckles, the smaller one of which still has its tongue. I scrape the larger buckle a bit. It is made of silver! It is a modest treasure, but the first silver object that we have found on the Bank of the same name. Everywhere on the *Calypso*, faces light up.

Raymond remains for an hour and three-quarters on the bottom, working the suction. He is relieved by Delemotte, who must work by artificial light, since it is getting dark. Everyone would be disappointed, however, if I called a halt to the work.

Delemotte finally reappears when the second service of dinner is almost over. He brings two sheaves, which he believes — wrongly, in my opinion — are the wheels of a cannon. He also has a pulley with its sheave, smaller than the other two. He says that he has uncovered a framework of ironwood, which could be a cannon truck. And he found and demolished the oven made of clay bricks.

That night, we sit around talking about ways to speed up the excavation. Basically, of course, the two essential operations will have to remain the same: we will have to dig by means of suction, and we will have to clean off and identify whatever we find. But, above all, we will have to *understand* what we are doing — something that we have not yet succeeded in doing. We know that we are working somewhere on the forward section of the ship; but we do not know exactly where, and therefore we do not know in what direction to work in order to find the rest of the ship.

A more immediate problem is that of the weather, which remains threatening. The knowledge that the *Calypso* runs the risk of being trapped in this maze of reefs is not comforting. If the weather should worsen, we will have to get out in a hurry, through the lighted buoys, and ride it out in the open sea.

Where is the Rest of the Ship?

Saturday, July 20. Everyone is awake early. Deloire, Delemotte, Coll, De Haenen and I discuss the problem of finding the rest of the ship. Then, I dive with Delemotte and Coll, taking the microsuction with me. The water is clear, and I have no trouble finding the site of yesterday's excavation. From that point, I go far forward, to where the stem of the ship should be, and I try to visualize the lines of the buried ship. The only possibility, it seems to me, is that the hull lies between two of the mounds of debris and coral, the third and fourth ones. I work my way aft in that direction until I reach a sort of em-

Bernard Delemotte thought at first that this was an interesting archaeological vestige. It turned out to be a huge sponge.

bankment about twenty inches high — which could mark the stern of the ship. About a hundred and fifty feet aft of the putative stem of the ship — that is, where the poop should be — the only thing to be seen is an immense field of staghorn coral. I am willing to admit that staghorn coral can grow on the timbers of a sunken ship. But between them? The microsuction is brought and applied: nothing.

The suction is then moved forward, about twelve feet from the anchor farthest to the east. We immediately find a large piece of wood. In my mind, I draw a line from it to the foot of the third mound of debris, and the microsuction goes to work there. We dig three feet down, but without finding any more wood.

Next, Deloire films the securing of a line to the block of rusted nails that we found the first day, and the process of hoisting it onto the deck of the *Calypso*. Remy and I noticed earlier that these nails had been tied around the middle with an electric wire; and then we found the case of an unexploded dynamite charge. Apparently the people who were here before us tried, for some unimaginable reason, to blow the nails apart with dynamite. As soon as the nails are aboard, we can see that they were originally contained in a cask.

According to the state of the weather, we have to hoist our small craft aboard the *Calypso* or lower them back into the water.

The lower part of the block of nails, in fact, is still covered with part of the cask. Everyone gathers around to have a look, and Gaston notices that, on the upper part, which is exposed, there is a series of regular ridges — suggesting that the nails were stored in separate bags within the cask.

A Preliminary Balance Sheet

Within two days, the *Calypso* is covered from stem to stern with bits of broken coral. Everything is filthy, and the ship is almost uninhabitable. I have organized a sort of revolving work schedule for the divers. No one works for more than two hours at a stretch on the sunken ship, cutting away blocks of coral which are then hoisted onto the rear deck of the *Calypso*. There, everyone who is not on the bottom sets to work breaking open the blocks with hammers. The debris must then be hauled away to a safe distance, so as not to bury our work area under a layer of coral fragments.

The results of all this work have been meager. Here is the total of our discoveries to date: the galley oven; the ship's carpenter's store of nails; and a few jars. Several pieces of wood have been uncovered, but not enough for us to be able to identify them as being part of this or that section of the ship.

Every night there are marathon discussions on the day's activities, and everyone pores over the chart of the area and the map of the ship while the cameras grind away to record these immortal moments. And we are beginning a series of marathon discussions on history, sailing ships, and the relations between Europe and the New World which, in spite of our fatigue from the day's work, will occupy all our evenings in the wardroom. To these conversations, everyone contributes something — either from his knowledge of the subject, or from his imagination.

Everyone is still full of courage and optimism, but, to my mind, the work is discouragingly slow. The amount of work to be done seems incredible, and the *Calypso*'s equipment is inadequate. For one thing, the suction that we have been using is too weak; it is unable to "swallow" anything but sand, and a fragment of any size at all causes it to jam. The holes that it digs are negligible in comparison to the area that must be excavated. Moreover, we on the *Calypso* are not able to break open the coral fast enough, even though everyone is working at it — even the cook. (Even so, there seems to be no place aboard that does not have its share of coral fragments.) We do not have enough hammers; and the number of those we have is steadily diminishing, because the handles break. We also need sledgehammers, drills, wheelbarrows, and protective glasses for those breaking open the coral.

Despite all these problems, everyone aboard is exuberant. It seems that, for these young men fired by the spirit of adventure, there is no such thing as an obstacle, and they are confident of being able to overcome any difficulty. And, somehow, they never seem to tire.

They would never admit it — either out of superstition or out of prudence — but they *believe*. They really believe that there is a treasure. What gives them so much energy, however, is a love of the game; a love of battling against odds; a desire to prove that, with their limited means, and with their experience, they are invincible, and neither the sea nor the coral will win out over them.

It is left to me to be reasonable, to see the situation clearly, and to make them aware of it. I must do two things. First, I will have to try to convince them that we do not have the equipment that is necessary to do a complete job of excavation; that we must either have professional equipment, or give up the job. The second thing is more complex. If ever we do find gold, what will it do to the spirit of friendship that binds together the men of the *Calypso*? I have tried to answer that question before it was asked, by calling for a vote on the sharing of anything we find. But who can tell what will happen the first time that the glitter of gold is seen on the deck of the *Calypso*?

Reinforcements Arrive

Saturday, July 20. Today we must leave the Silver Bank for Puerto Rico, where we are to pick up Frédéric Dumas and our supplies. Our six anchorage points are loosened, and we get underway, maneuvering carefully among the reefs, through the channel bordered by red buoys and radar poles.

Sunday, July 21. We are en route, making good time against a fairly strong headwind and sea. I use the time to rest and to think. The problem remains the same. Was it a mistake for us to get involved in this project? It remains to be seen if we are capable of doing the job; or if we have gotten ourselves involved in an endless and impossible task — as we did at the Grand Congloué in 1953.

I am also concerned about the possibility of hurricanes, for the season is well upon us. I have my doubts about whether we will have time to get the equipment we need, organize our work area, and do a great deal of excavation, before a storm catches us in the middle of the Silver Bank. On that score, however, I console myself with the thought that I can depend on the intuition and knowledge of Caillart, the *Calypso*'s captain, who pays close attention to the American weather bulletins.

A breastplate of gold, of Colombian origin. It is an example of the accomplishments of the Chibcha civilization. Such artifacts were among the "idols" that Spaniards melted down into ingots. (Musée d l'Homme, Paris.)

FOUR

Blood and Gold

There was mild excitement aboard the two Spanish galleons cruising at the mouth of the great river Orinoco. In the surrounding marshes which bordered the green walls of the jungle, a canoe, apparently adrift, had just been sighted. Even so routine an event was sufficient to shatter, at least momentarily, the boredom of shipboard life; for although Spain now regarded herself as the conqueror of the Americas, there was still much that Spaniards found strange in the vast New World.

In a few moments, a launch, under the command of an officer, was sent out from one of the galleons. As it drew near the canoe, the officer saw, stretched out in the bottom of that Indian craft, a human shape. It was not, however, an Indian, but a white man. A Spaniard; for, when he spoke, it was in the purest Castilian. Yet, he refused to explain where he was from, or how he had gotten to the mouth of the Orinoco. Even more mysterious than his reticence was his baggage, which consisted of two hollowed gourds — filled with gold nuggets the size of rosary beads.

The galleons took the man aboard and, at his request, put him ashore at their next port of call, San Juan de Puerto Rico, where he would be able to find transportation to Spain. On land, he was as silent as he had been on the sea, and he never allowed his precious gourds to leave his side. In a short time, he fell seriously ill. And, sensing that the end was near, and being a good Catholic, he relented, and told his story to the priest who came to hear his confession.

The man's name, it seemed, was Martinez, and he had been an officer in an expedition organized by Don Diego Ordaz for the exploration of Guiana. Don Diego's troop, comprising some six hundred men, had disappeared in the vastness of that land and had never been heard of again. The only trace ever found, other than Martinez himself, was a rusted anchor from one of the expedition's ships, which had been found at the mouth of the Orinoco.

Martinez confessed that he had been guilty of a grave sin, for which he had been justly punished. He had been made responsible for the expedition's store of gunpowder, and, one night, he had been foolish enough to light a small fire nearby. There had been an explosion. For this crime, Don Diego Ordaz had condemned Martinez to death; but, rather than execute the sentence in the customary way, he had decided to set the culprit adrift in a canoe on the Orinoco, without supplies.

Martinez was soon found by a band of Indians who had never before seen a white man. Their curiosity aroused, they decided to take him home with them, so that their friends might see this marvel for themselves. For fifteen days they cut their way through the jungle. On the fifteenth day, they had blindfolded Martinez. When the blindfold was removed a short time later, Martinez had thought that he was dreaming. Spread out before him in the distance he saw an immense city, sparkling like gold in the sun. The palaces, the roofs of the buildings, even the streets themselves, seemed covered with the precious metal. The name of this great city, the natives told him, was Manoa; and it was the capital of a great chief, a mighty prince who was called the Inca.

Another two days were required to reach the city. And, once there, Martinea realized that he had not been the victim of a mirage, but that the reality he saw before him was more fantastic than any dream. There were great palaces and towers, all wrought of gold, of an alien design, and yet more beautiful than anything he had seen even in his native Castille.

Martinez was the first European to see the palace of the Inca. It was a place of incredible wealth, he said, filled with statues of gold in the shape of animals, birds, trees, plants, and even fish. Every piece of furniture, every chest, every fountain was made of gold or silver; and all the plate of the household was of massive gold.

There were feasts being celebrated in the city, Martinez recounted, and, on these occasions, the Inca, and the lords of his house, appeared nude, but with their bodies covered by a golden powder or dust, so that they resembled statues of gold rather than ordinary men. Then, Martinez said, the Inca seemed to be truly the Golden King — *El Dorado*. And this was the name that the dying man gave to the City of the Inca: El Dorado. It was a name that was to haunt the dreams of Spaniards for the next two centuries.

In Search of El Dorado

Europe in the sixteenth century was desperately hungry for gold; and Spain, it was believed, held the key to a world of it. The first hidalgos to set foot on the shores of Hispaniola were certain that they would have only to bend down and scoop up a handful of nuggets from among the pebbles of the beach. (Actually, they were not far wrong. The beds of the streams glittered with the metal, which was too common even to be of interest to the natives.) Many Spaniards, more daring than their fellows, were determined to find the City of Gold described by Martinez; and they all perished in the attempt, from disease, hunger, and exposure, or at the hands of the natives.

Martinez' El Dorado, was not wholly fantastic. There was, in fact, such a city, in a land rich with gold. It lay, however, on the other side of the continent. And it was Francisco Pizarro, the bastard offspring of a captain general, a daring but brutal adventurer, who found it in 1531. Pizarro's first act was to arrest the great Inca himself; and his second was to execute him for "rebellion against His Catholic Majesty, the Emperor Charles V." Then, he did what he had come to do, and seized the treasure of the Inca.

From that time, the Spanish conquest of the New World was no longer confined to the lands surrounding the Caribbean, it spread to the shores of the Pacific. America now had two faces, one toward the east, and the other toward the west.

Beginning in 1540, there were Spanish galleons permanently assigned to the Pacific; a fleet whose duty it was to transport the wealth of Chile and Peru to Panama, from where it would be carried across the Caribbean to Havana, and from there across the Atlantic to Spain.

The gold and silver of the Incas, however, was not the only wealth that Spain sought. There was something else, something just as precious, in which the New World was disappointingly poor; and that was spices. The true land of spices was not in the New World, the Spaniards discovered, but in Cipango, in the East Indies, the fief of the Arabs and the Portugese.

The Spaniards were disappointed, but not deterred. Hernando Cortez, the conqueror of Mexico, ordered four caravelles to be built at Zacatula, and these set sail across the Pacific and reached the Philippine Islands. By 1565, the Spanish were solidly entrenched there, and were active in trade in the Far East. Every year thereafter, a galleon called the *Nao de China* sailed westward from the Philippines, loaded down with a cargo which, while not the richest in gold, was the most astonishing of any carried by the ships of Spain, for it abounded in works of art, fabulous jewels, and exotic objects. By means of Chinese junks, Manila maintained commercial relations with Japan, China, and the Indies; and from these places came silks and ivory, plumes, brocades, spices, perfumes, and porcelain, all of which were eagerly sought by the Spanish merchants of the Philippines. The voyage of the *Nao de China* from Manila to its port of Acapulco was relatively fast: ten weeks. When it arrived, its cargo was loaded onto the backs of mules and carried across Mexico to Veracruz, the port of call of the Fleet of New Spain.

There was only one voyage each year across the Pacific, and only one galleon made that voyage. This was the command of the king. For Spain was perennially short of ships and of men, and she did not wish to dissipate her strength on two oceans. The bulk of her forces, therefore, was reserved for traffic between the Old World and the New World. The "galleon of the Philippines," however, was always the largest one of its time. In the sixteenth century, it was 700 tons; in the seventeenth, 1500; the eighteenth, 2000.

The Conquistadors

The most famous of Spain's conquests, whether in the Americas or in the Far East, were not those of official expeditions financed and patronized by the king. They were the result of private enterprise and were organized by a captain — always of gentle birth — in collaboration with merchants, bankers, and shipowners. The captain recruited his men and was in command of the expedition. His collaborators furnished the ships, supplies, and arms. The booty was carefully portioned out, according to the terms of a contract.

The soldiers who were recruited for one of these commando operations, the sole purpose of which was profit, belonged to one of two classes: there were *caballeros* and there were *peones*; that is, horse soldiers, and foot soldiers. Horses, unknown in America, were regarded as a precious possession; and firearms, which were still rare at this time, were also a distinct advantage to their owners in finding a place in a captain's troop.

The demand for men devoted to their swords and their horses explains both the epic achievements of a Cortez and a Pizzaro, and the inefficiency of

Two merchantmen of the sixteenth century with very high rear decks. (Painting by Lemoyne de Morgues, 1564, in the Service Hydrographique de la Marine, Paris.)

Spain's maritime activity. It seems that Spain never considered her ships to be anything more than a means of transport for her soldiers and her loot. And this accounts for the constant opposition to any initiative on the part of her ships' captains and pilots. Never did Spain understand, as England did, that the solution to her problems lay in maritime techniques, in the improvement of ship construction, the advancement of navigational skills, and the experience and initiative of her seafaring men.

The dangers that threatened the transport of Spain's wealth from the New World to Europe arose not only from the condition of Spanish ships and the fact that Spanish ships habitually chose to sail during the hurricane season, but also from the greed aroused in the whole of Europe by the sight of this river of Spanish gold flowing across the Atlantic every year.

The Ancestor of the Dollar

This greed was all the greater because most of the gold and silver had already been transformed into coins by the mints of the New World. The first of these coins, which went into circulation in 1537, were called reales, and were in denominations of 1, 2, 3, and 4. They were also known as escudos (shields) because they were stamped with a shield bearing the royal arms of Spain: the castles of Castille, and the lions of Leon; or doblones (doubloons) because they were worth double the value of the pistole.

In the former Empire of the Incas, the Potosí mines (in present-day Bolivia) had been opened in 1545, and a mint had been established there. Others followed, at Santa Fe in New Grenada (Colombia), at Lima, and at Cartagena. And, as befitted these houses of gold, the mints were constructed on a scale only slightly less sumptuous than that of the churches. The one at Potosi, for example, had cost two million piastres to build.

These mints, or *monedas*, produced an enormous number of coins. The most common one was worth eight reales, for this was the most convenient and sought-after denomination. For three centuries, these coins — the "pieces of eight" of pirate lore — were regarded as the most prestigious medium of exchange both in Europe and in America. They were, moreover, the ancestor of the modern American dollar. The great trading houses of that time used to designate these pieces of eight on their books by a peculiar sign composed by the letter *P* and the number *8* intertwined. After a while, for the sake of speed in bookkeeping, the *8* was written as *S*, and the *P* was reduced to a straight vertical line. The result was a symbol which has become instantly recognizable: $.*

These pieces of eight were stamped with the sign of Spain's pride in her colonies: two columns, the bases of which were bathed by the waves of the sea. The columns were the famed Columns of Hercules; that is, Gibraltar. And they gave notice to the world that the Mediterranean alone was no longer sufficient for the mistress of the seas, but that Spain was pushing beyond, into the unknown. This symbol stood for the whole of Spain's enterprise in the Americas. And for that reason, the coins of Philip II (reigned

*The word *dollar*, however, is of German rather than Spanish origin. Beginning in the sixteenth century, the Joachimsthal silver mines of Bohemia began minting a coin which became common in Europe and was known as a *Joachimsthaler*. The name was abbreviated as *thaler*; and then transcribed as *dollar*.

1556-98), son and heir of the Emperor Charles V, were stamped with the motto, *Plus ultra* — — "Farther still." On the reverse were these words: *Philippus II Hispaniarum et Indiarum Rex*, "Philip II, King of Spain and of the Indies." The word *Indiarum* always appeared on coins minted in the New World.

Pirates of the Caribbean

The subjects of the king of Spain were by no means the only ones whose greed was stirred by the sight of so much gold. The French, the English, and the Dutch — all of whom, as seafaring peoples, were noticeably superior to the Spaniards in maritime skills — were determined to have a share in it. The means by which they proposed to do this were in the use of light, fast, maneuverable ships. For the pirates, privateers, and corsairs of the Caribbean — which was called "the Spanish sea" — realized that such craft could easily master the cumbersome and slow galleons of Spain. Galleons normally carried sixty to seventy cannon, while the pirate ships generally had no more than five or six. Therefore, speed and mobility were the essential elements of a successful pirate attack.

Even the crushing superiority in armaments of galleons, however, was often nothing more than an illusion; for the cannon required by the rules of the Casa de Contratación were often removed to make place for merchandise. At Cartagena, Havana, and Veracruz, there were businessmen who made a living by renting cannon, on a short-term basis, to ship captains. Thus, the captains were able to have the required number of cannon on board during the inspection by officials of the Casa, before sailing. Then, as soon as the inspectors had left the ship, the cannon were returned to their owners ashore, and the space was filled with a more lucrative cargo.

The pirate ships carried only seventy to eighty men, as opposed to around eight hundred on the galleons. But this also was an advantage, for when the pirates boarded a galleon, the Spanish officers and men were almost always unable to put up a fight because of the large number of civilians on board who, along with the illegal merchandise, filled the ship.

The ships of Spain, however, were not totally defenseless. A boarding net was installed on the galleons, which represented one more obstacle to be overcome by a boarding party before they could reach the ship's cargo. At the extremities of the yards of the mainmast and foremast there were hooks, designed to tear the rigging of any ship moving in for close-quarter combat. And, finally, at the end of the long bowsprit, a grapnel, or grappling iron, was permanently installed.

Elizabeth I, Queen of England. (Engraving of 1596.)

Right: Titian's portrait of Philip II, King of Spain. (Palazzo Pitti, Florence.) Philip was characterized by, among other things, his lack of understanding of anything having to do with the sea.

Elizabeth I and Philip II

By the sixteenth century, the English had made giant strides in naval science and left the Spanish far behind. Their ships, with low forward sections, were light and mobile, and fast. Spain was hopelessly outclassed on the sea; and, since her overseas empire could be reached only by sea, by the middle of the sixteenth century she could no longer govern that empire. Everywhere, Spain's situation was deteriorating, and the threat to the royal galleons was increasing, as English sea power in the New World increased.

The fault, in large measure, was that of the king of Spain, Philip II. Philip was an austere man, devoted to his work; but he had never been interested in maritime affairs, and he had never understood the problems of navigation. On two separate occasions, he refused to accept the services of the famed English mariner, Sir John Hawkins — a cousin of Sir Francis Drake — who offered (for a price, of course) to protect the Spanish fleet from pirates and privateers. Sir John then took to attacking the king's galleons instead of protecting them; and so successful was he at his trade that his ventures led to an open break between Spain and England.

The resources of the English sovereign, Queen Elizabeth I, were much more limited than those of her contemporary, Philip of Spain. Her kingdom, however, was rich in courageous seafaring men of great ability, who asked for nothing more than the opportunity to fleece Philip of his American gold. It

was not Elizabeth, however, who gave them this opportunity; for Spain and England were not at war, and Elizabeth did not wish to provoke such a war if it could be avoided. The English privateers therefore operated as private enterprises. They were financed by wealthy noblemen and businessmen, who provided the ships and arms in exchange for a share in the profits.

Ambush at Panama

On May 24, 1572, a young man of no more than thirty years, small, energetic, and wearing a short red beard, sailed from Plymouth with two ridiculously small ships. There was the *Pasha* (70 tons), and the *Swan* (25 tons), the combined contingents of which numbered seventy-three men, all of whom were even younger than their commander. The name of the latter was Francis Drake. Drake was born of a family of stanch Protestants; and, with his seaman's daring and his pirate's courage, there was combined a streak of religious fanaticism. Europe, in the sixteenth century, was a place of fierce and implacable religious hatreds, and Catholics and Protestants were constantly at each others' throats. In Drake's case, this hatred found a logical target: Catholic Spain, the greatest power on the face of the earth.

Thus, while Philip II was busy suppressing heresy and intriguing against the Protestant powers in Europe, a religious war of a different sort was being waged in the Caribbean. It was a bloody war, with the Protestant English and Dutch, along with a number of French Huguenots, against the Spanish Catholics. Piratry and pillage were supported and justified by theological hatred. And of all those who fought against Spain in the cause of the reformed religion, Francis Drake himself was the most ardent champion.

Drake's men were divided into three groups, according to the kind of weapons they carried. Some were armed with pikes, for close combat; others had muskets; and a third of this small band consisted of archers. Most of the nations of Europe had long since abandoned the longbow, but the English had remained faithful to the weapon that, in 1415, had won the Battle of Agincourt for them, and had made them the best foot soldiers in the world. Drake's plan, however, justified the presence of these anachronistic weapons; for his project was one for foot soldiers. It was his intention to ambush, in Panama, the mule train carrying the gold of Peru and Chile to Porto Bello.

Drake's transatlantic dash set a world's record for his time: twenty-five days, from Plymouth to Nombre de Dios — which he took, but could not hold. Then, he learned that twenty-eight official mule trains, as well as several private ones, were already cutting their way through the Panamanian jungles.

A *real*, one of the celebrated pieces of eight. This one dates from the reign of Philip III, and was coined at Potosi. On one side is the Cross, the castles of Castille, and the lions of Leon. On the other, the columns of Hercules, waves symbolizing the Atlantic, and the word "Potosi."

Between the two columns is the figure 8, and the motto *Plus Ultra* — "Farther Yet." (Bibliothéque Nationale, Cabinet des Médailles, Paris.)

Each train comprised about fifty mules, and was protected by an advance guard and a rear guard. He decided that the moment was opportune.

Drake's situation did not seem encouraging. Of his original force of seventy-three men, twenty-eight had died, and many of those still alive were ill — probably of yellow fever. Besides himself, only eighteen men were in condition for combat. But Drake set out with this small troop, in the company of a Frenchman he had found at Nombre de Dios, named Guillaume Le Testu, a Huguenot from Le Havre, who was one of the best hydrographers of his time. Guided by cimarrones — escaped slaves — he began hacking through the tropical vegetation, carving each step of the way by machete, oblivious to hummingbirds, orchids, and snakes, until he came within sight of the Pacific coast. Then gazing down on the city of Panama and on the unknown ocean, he swore to be the first Englishman to set sail on the Pacific.

It was well known that the Spanish preferred to travel by night, in order to avoid the heat of the day. Drake therefore gave his orders: they would attack that very night.

At sundown, the cimarrones reported that the convoy was drawing near; and soon the Englishmen could hear the faint tinkling of the mule train's bells. By some extraordinary coincidence, the muleteers gave the signal to halt at the top of the very slope on which Drake and his men were hidden. Almost immediately, Drake gave the signal, and a volley of arrows and musket shot rained down on the soldiers of the escort. Then the assault began. The Spanish guard had been taken completely by surprise; and, having no idea of the size of the attacking force, they fled into the jungle as Drake and his men set to work hamstringing the mules.

Then, heavily loaded down with Castilian ducats and pistoles, with ingots and sacks of coin, the adventurers began the return journey through the jungle. The fifteen tons of silver ingots taken from the caravan, they buried. On the way, they were attacked by a troop of fifty Spanish soldiers fast approaching from the rear. Le Testu, with eight men armed with muskets, mounted a rearguard action to stop the Spanish. He succeeded, but was killed in the operation. He was the only fatality.

The Englishmen continued their trek through the jungle, a handful of exhausted men, many of them feverish, struggling under the weight of as much gold as they could carry. For two days and two nights they struggled, alternately baked by the sun and drenched by the tropical rain, until they reached the Rio Magdalena. There, they found that the dugouts, which they had used on their way to the ambush, had been taken by the Spaniards. Drake ordered his men to build a raft. He himself, with three men, set out to find help. Eventually, the troop was sighted by an English frigate and taken aboard. The most intrepid of the Englishmen, however, insisted on returning to dig up the silver ingots that lay buried in the Panamanian jungle. They were lucky enough to avoid any contact with the Spanish, and they returned to the frigate laden with an enormous amount of booty. Drake returned to England with all his treasure, but with only thirty of his men still alive.

Up till then, English privateers had confined themselves to attacks on Spanish ships in the Antilles. Drake had gone further. He had attacked the forces of Spain on dry land, at Nombre de Dios and at Panama. And now, he wished to go further yet, and attack where Spain had always thought herself to be invulnerable: in the Pacific.

Thus it was that, in 1577, he sailed from Plymouth again, this time with four vessels. One of the ships was lost in a storm — a storm which carried Drake southward and made him the discoverer of Cape Horn. Another of his ships returned home, and a third was lost in the River Plate while attempting to do the same. Drake, in his own vessel, the *Golden Hind*, proceeded to the Peruvian coasts, where he cruised until he had taken and plundered a score of Spanish ships. Loaded down with rich booty, he thought it unsafe to return to England via Cape Horn, and struck out across the Pacific. He reached England, having circled the globe, on September 26, 1580, after an absence of three years.

At first, Queen Elizabeth hesitated to recognize and reward the exploits

Left: Our Lady of Potosi, from a sixteenth-century Spanish engraving. The Virgin's mantle evokes the shape of the Mountain of Silver, and one can make out the forms of llamas, Incas, and prospectors. At the bottom are the Pope and the Emperor.

Jules the Barracuda. Apparently, he cannot bear to be separated from our teams.

Right: Our work in the Silver Bank was made considerably more difficult by the abundance of coral, sea fans and fixed animals that thrive in that spot.

of this great captain, for fear of provoking a war with Spain. Drake, however, had powerful friends at court; friends who had derived enormous profit from his ventures, and who were in a position to plead his case before the queen. In the following year, therefore, at Deptford, Elizabeth arrived with great ceremony for a banquet aboard the *Golden Hind*, in the course of which, having ordered Drake to kneel, she took a golden sword and tapped him lightly on both shoulders. When he rose, the great mariner had been converted into Sir Francis Drake.

Our divers discover more cannons. By the end of our dig, we had uncovered thirteen of them, all from the same ship.

The capture of the entire Spanish fleet in 1628, in the waters off Havana, by a Dutch fleet commanded by Peit Heyne. (Musée de la Marine, Paris.)

Drake had shown that, with a few ships and a small number of men, the whole edifice of Spanish power in the New World might be shaken to its foundations. And, indeed, in the latter part of the reign of Philip II, Spanish sea power had entered on a dangerous decline. The shipyards of Spain found fewer and fewer experts and specialists, and fewer and fewer ships were built. Finally, almost everything, including ships, had to be purchased abroad.

The deathblow to Spanish power on the seas came in 1588, by the destruction of the Invincible Armada, when 132 vessels had been lost. At the end of the sixteenth century, the golden century, England's star was in the ascendancy, and that of Spain was declining rapidly. By 1597, the year before Philip's death, it became necessary, in order to organize a fleet for the transatlantic crossing, to buy over twenty galleons from Holland. Spain had not discovered that prosperity is not measured by the amount of gold that a nation absorbs, but by the production of its people. And this failure was her nemesis.

The *conquistadores*, in their greed, had virtually enslaved the natives of the New World and forced them to work against their will; and the Indians, unaccustomed to servitude and to labor, had died in great numbers, or run away. By the close of the golden century, the populations of Cuba, Hispaniola, and Puerto Rico were greatly reduced, and it became necessary to import slaves from Africa. This was a traffic at which the English and the French excelled, and, through it, they established new commercial ties to the West Indies. Spain, for her part, had no moral scruples as far as slave trading was

A panel of the sixteenth century, probably depicting Cortez. (From *L'art des Conquistadors*, by
C. Arthaud and François Hebert-Stevens. Arthaud, Paris.)

concerned. Her problem was economic. She could barely afford to provide her colonies with shoes, let alone with slaves.

Because of the weakness of the maritime forces of Spain, and because of the venality of the officials of the Casa de Contractación, relations between the Spanish colonies in America and the mother country became increasingly difficult. Even within the New World, the exchanges between Peru and Mexico became less frequent. At the same time, the smuggling of merchandise by the English, Dutch, and French developed proportionately.

In the meantime, the privateers were making Spain's position in America almost untenable, and the Spanish king rapidly lost control of all his Caribbean islands except Cuba and Puerto Rico. Spain was virtually cut off from the source of her wealth.

The Dutch were as effective as the English in bringing this about. On September 8, 1628, for the first and only time, the whole of the Fleet of New Spain was captured. It happened in the Bay of Matanzas, on the north coast of Cuba; and the captors were Dutch privateers under the command of Peit Heyne. Twenty-four vessels — under the command of Captain General Juan de Benavides y Bazan — were taken, along with a booty of some twelve million guilders or fourteen million pesos.

The palmy days of the pirates and privateers, however, were almost over, at least so far as Spanish loot was concerned; for after the death of Philip II (1598), the production of silver in Mexico and Peru decreased, and, by 1630, it had slowed to a trickle. By the middle of the seventeenth century, more than half the mines of the New World were closed for various reasons: the lack of laborers, or technical problems.

The rivalry between Elizabeth I and Philip II, between the two great maritime powers and the two great religious powers, had extended over the whole of the sixteenth century. If it ended, finally, in victory for England, it was because Elizabeth had been astute enough to foresee that ships were the key to victory, and energetic enough to have ships designed and built. To accomplish this, however, she needed more than foresight and energy. She needed men; seafaring men, and especially naval architects. And she had them. The best ships of the English fleet responsible for the destruction of the Armada in 1588 had been designed by a master carpenter, Matthew Baker. Baker grasped at once what the Spanish had never been able to recognize: that warships had to be light and fast. He therefore designed his ships without the exaggeratedly high poop that characterized Spanish ships, and had them built with long, elegant lines, close to the water. Another master designer was Phineas Pett, the scion of a long line of naval architects. Pett was

Galleons in port. (Painting by Lemoyne de Morgues, 1564. Service Hydrographique de la Marine, Paris.)

responsible for at least two masterpieces: the *Prince Royal* and the *Sovereign of the Seas*; the latter carried one hundred cannon, and was a full century and a half ahead of its time.

The difference in shipboard personnel between the vessels of England and Spain was as great as the differences in the ships themselves. While the galleons were loaded with soldiers who were only effective (if at all) during a boarding action, the English ships were manned only by sailors. They did not depend upon the risky process of boarding an enemy ship, but placed their trust in their naval artillery — a decisive factor in the defeat of the Armada.

FIVE

The Treasure-Hunter's Panoply

Monday, July 22, 1968. The heat here in the port of San Juan is almost unbearable. What a contrast to the fresh breezes of the Silver Bank.

At eight o'clock in the morning, after instructing our agent to accept delivery of the material arriving from France — lighted buoys and a suction nozzle — Remy and I go into town by taxi to buy the rest of the equipment we need.

We visit two construction-material yards to buy the pipe we need for the airlift, or suction apparatus, but we have trouble deciding on the size of pipe we want. Six-inch pipe, or eight-inch pipe? We are told that six-inch pipe is as much as a man can handle under water, and so we have to take the smaller of the two, almost against our wishes. We also buy some unusually good, flexible suction pipe; it is also six inches in diameter, and comes in fifty-foot lengths.

Remy and I part at eleven o'clock. He has several errands to do — to buy marine plywood, lumber, nails, bolts, glue, mastic, and various tools. He intends to leave, later in the afternoon, for a visit to his family on St. Barthélemy, and promises to return tomorrow evening — with a case of rum for the *Calypso*.

Philippe Sirot, our chief mechanic, and Zuéna, Bassaget, and Delemotte, are also in town with lists of items to be bought. We have rented two cars, and that is none too many. Everyone is courageously whittling away at their shopping lists, but the noonday heat makes us think longingly of our beautiful, cool, coral waters. And we are struck by the hustle and bustle everywhere and the harried looks on the faces of the people. This is a phenomenon of which we are aware whenever we come ashore after a stretch at sea. It may be that all this hurrying about is symptomatic of another kind of gold fever.

Our Noisy Monster

By a stroke of luck, I have been able to rent a large (200-horsepower) Worthington air compressor. It is almost new, and the negotiations were interminable because the owner had to be assured that his machine would be transported below decks on the *Calypso* — rather than remain in the dampness of the open air. Finally, a bargain was struck, and the compressor was delivered to our pier (number five) at three o'clock in the afternoon, as promised.

I have no doubt that this beautiful piece of machinery will make our lives miserable. It seems that, so far as air compressors are concerned, there is a direct connection between noise and efficiency; and I can see that this one will be very efficient indeed. I know that there will be no escape from its pounding when it is in operation, and that the entire *Calypso* will vibrate to its rhythm. And we will have to learn to live with its pounding in our ears for twelve hours a day, not only aboard the *Calypso* itself, but also everywhere on the surface of the water for a good distance around, and even below the surface. But it will be well worth the trouble. This noisy monster will make it possible for us to dispose of tons and tons of coral.

Wednesday, July 24. Didi Dumas arrived at San Juan on schedule, at four o'clock this morning. And there was no one to meet him. He was furious; and he was perfectly justified. Our agent, who was supposed to meet him and bring him to the *Calypso*, did not show up, for some reason.

Now that he is aboard the *Calypso*, Didi has calmed down. He is too eager to get to work to remember that we left him stranded at the San Juan airport; and he is already throwing out ideas on how to go about excavating our sunken ship.

In his book *Epaves Antiques (Sunken Ships of Antiquity)*, he formulated the theory of the use of the airlift in marine excavations. And he suggested a method of using suction, in certain cases, that has not yet been verified in practice, but which he is certain will work. Hence his excitement; for he says that our treasure ship will be ideal for testing his theory. He shows me a sketch of what he has in mind, and I am immediately infected by his enthusiasm. The device consists of a large, heavy vertical tube, heavy enough to allow us to make it stationary by anchoring it to the bottom. From the lower end of this tube, runs a flexible and movable pipe, from thirty-five to fifty feet long, which will always be filled with water. The necessary supply of air will enter from the lower end of the fixed tube. The problem with airlifts has always been that the exhaust jams with material and becomes blocked at its extremity, because that extremity is always in a more or less horizontal position. The ingenuity of Didi's theory is that it enables us to eliminate that problem of blockage (we hope).

Didi's Shopping List

The *Calypso* has become an oven under the tropical sun. It is almost a relief to get back into the blazing streets of San Juan. We must do so, in any case, for there are still things on our shopping list that we have not bought — hammers, sledgehammers, nylon line to divide our work area into sections, and cable buoys to bring up anything that we may find on the bottom. The items are divided up, and everyone scatters into the city.

Dumas, with a quiet smile, announces that he has a list of his own. With his long experience in marine excavation and archaeology, he has thought of dozens of things that escaped me completely. He and I begin a tour of stores of every kind, from street bazaars to drugstores, for what he needs: plastic shovels, which Didi says will be useful in trimming coral fragments; an assortment of brooms — big, small, and medium-sized brooms, commercial brooms and household brooms, straw brooms and nylon brooms — which, I am given to understand, are indispensable tools for a marine archaeologist in coral waters; and a collection of garbage cans, to be used for soaking our finds in fresh water.

Then, since we are afraid that these precious items will not be delivered to the *Calypso* in time, we carry them ourselves back to the ship, down the narrow sidewalks of old San Juan, through the crowds of gaping tourists and amused Puerto Ricans in flowered shirts. Dripping with sweat, clutching garbage cans, and with broom handles sticking out in every direction, we finally stagger aboard the *Calypso*, where we are greeted with mild surprise and many unkind remarks.

"Let them joke," mutters Didi. "They'll thank me later on."

Bernard Delemotte at work with the auxiliary airlift that we call the "pointe Bic."

Final Preparations

Remy de Haenen, who returned last night in his Cessna, went out this morning with Caillart, Deloire, and Agostini for another reconnaissance flight over the Silver Bank. They intend to film the area around the sunken ship.

Meanwhile, no one is idle aboard the *Calypso*. We have begun building the large metallic baskets into which the airlift will dump what it brings up from the bottom. We continue working all day, and then, at night, we move onto the pier in order to take advantage of the lights there. Everyone works away enthusiastically, soldering, cutting and nailing, until 1 A.M. — to the astonishment and amusement of an audience of nocturnal Puerto Ricans.

Thursday, July 25. We have been loading since early this morning. The compressor, in accordance with the wishes of its owner, is lowered into the hole and bolted down. The pipes, tubes, baskets, lumber, nails, screws, straps, gutters, T pieces and coupling pieces, the food and water, the rum brought from St. Barthélemy, and even the brooms, are finally stowed in their proper places. In order to make room, I decided to store the two minisubs, the "sea fleas," and their material, ashore. They are now safely locked in a San Juan warehouse. The process of unloading them from the *Calypso* created a mild sensation among the spectators on the dock.

Finally, at twelve-thirty, we get underway. I am very pleased. The loading of our equipment, considering the amount of material involved, was accomplished in a surprisingly short time.

The silhouette of the island of Puerto Rico, its old fort, its mountain covered with forests and crowned with clouds, have not yet disappeared from sight, and already I hear the sound of saws and hammers from the rear deck. Remy, along with Foulon, Coll, and Gaston, is building what he describes as a "launch-catamaran-basket carrier." There is widespread skepticism concerning this monstrous craft's ability to float.

The sea is rough, and navigation is hit-or-miss. During the night, the *Calypso* passes the Bank of the Nativity without sighting it on the radar screen.

Late at night, Remy announces that his creation is nearing completion. The critics are silenced, and then converted into admirers. Remy, everyone agrees, knows exactly what he is doing. And, in fact, his contraption will no doubt prove to be one of the essential tools in the next stage of our work. We will have to find a proper name for it. In the meantime, everyone is trying to come up with suggestions for its improvement.

Work Begins Again

Friday, July 26. Early in the morning, the *Calypso* passes over the shallows that we missed the last time. The charts of this area are very inexact. Moreover, at this time of the year the currents are unusual and variable. We turn toward the north, but seem to have missed the line of reefs that we are looking for. We are too far to the west. We turn back toward the southeast. Eventually, we get a blip on our radar — from a distance of five miles. An exceptional stroke of luck. Soon, we are in the buoyed channel which leads to our anchorage in the middle of the Silver Bank. It is quite late, however, before we are ready to drop anchor. It was more difficult than we expected to navigate along the channel, despite all the precautions we have taken to mark it out. I feel a twinge of apprehension at our situation if a hurricane should come — one of those spiraling storms that springs up four or five times a year, between July and October, in the Caribbean. I wonder whether our luck will hold.

Saturday, July 27. This morning, Didi, impatient to get to work, dives down to examine the wreck. When he reappears, everyone crowds around to hear his comments. But Didi only shrugs. Like a cabinet member burdened with secrets of state, he refuses to make any comment at all. He feels it is too soon to judge. Like us, he wants to become thoroughly familiar with the site.

It is obvious that everyone aboard is waiting eagerly for some word from him. Our personnel are all young men, for whom Didi, with his vast experience and his formidable reputation, is an authority and an oracle. Even when they speak of him among themselves, they refer to Didi as *Monsieur* Dumas.

It is hard for them to bear the suspense that Didi's silence has created. They are certain that they will find a treasure; or at least some gold and objects of value, if not an actual Hollywood-style treasure chest. They have even decided what they will do with their shares of the booty. Morgan, the cook, plans to buy a race horse and bet the races. He cannot place bets while on the *Calypso*, of course; and he misses this very much.

During the day, we put out three Norwegian buoys — buoys with blinking lights — that I had sent from Marseilles.

Remy's basket-carrying raft is now complete. We have found a name for it: the *James and Mary*. We hope that it is a lucky name. The original *James and Mary* was the ship that William Phips used to carry away enormous wealth from *Nuestra Señora de la Concepción*, and Phips named it after the English sovereigns of his time. Philippe Sirot and Dr. Tassy (who is still not allowed to dive), eager as always to be helpful, have painted the name, in many colors, on several places on the raft. With this done, we proceed to the launching of the *James and Mary*,, which is accomplished by hoisting it over the side and lowering it into the water. Despite its strange appearance, and earlier opinions to the contrary notwithstanding, it floats.

The metal baskets begun in San Juan have been finished and installed in their proper place, to catch whatever treasure the airlift may choose to spit out. The bottoms of the baskets are made of a fine mesh so that no pieces of eight may slip through.

Didi, still thoughtful, still preoccupied by the archaeological problems posed by the wreck, goes down for a second visit to the site. Bernard Delemotte and Michel Deloire, following his instructions, measure the dimensions

Leaving Puerto Rico, the *Calypso* makes for the Silver Bank.

Below: Aboard the *Calypso*, we work frantically to put together the *James and Mary*.

of the work area once more, and also the distances between various points marked by Didi. It is his opinion that these points may correspond to certain parts of the galleon. I have not said a word to him on this subject, for I do not want to influence his judgment one way or the other. There will be plenty of time to compare conclusions later.

The Pieces Begin to Fall into Place

Sunday, July 28. Dumas spends most of the morning in the water. In order to establish a perimeter of research, he takes soundings all around the site with the microsuction device. He is particularly interested in the south-eastern edge, where he finds several pieces of wood and some dishes. He

The Silver Bank is home to a large number and variety of animal colonies.

brings up an especially fine dinner plate, blackened by its three centuries in the water. We will try to clean it off with acid.

Later, during lunch, Philippe Sirot tells us a frightening story. It seems that last night, while he was on watch, he saw "a large ship passing quietly through the reefs of the Silver Bank." Caillart and I exchange shocked glances. From what we know of these reefs, I would say that a ship has only one chance in ten of getting through. What probably happened was that the ship's captain was not very sure of his position (we know from experience how difficult it is to ascertain one's position in this area), but, seeing the *Calypso* riding serenely at anchor, he concluded that he was in safe waters, and blithely took his ship right through the most treacherous complex of reefs in the Caribbean. What a terrible feeling of guilt we would have experienced if the ship had not succeeded in getting through.

During the afternoon, I send Bernard and Michel below again to take a few more measurements. When Bernard returns with them, I record them on my map, using a scale of two centimeters per meter (approximately ¾ inch to every 40 inches). And then suddenly, it all falls into place.

With Bernard watching, I write down the measurements of a typical galleon of the time: 150 feet long, including the bowsprit; 35 feet wide; 75 feet of rectilinear keel, etc. And then I draw the galleon, in red ink, on the map. And there it is, if one takes into account that there is a list — to starboard, probably. The forward section of the galleon lies near the two anchors, which are both to starboard; and there are the cannon of the lower battery, of the upper battery, of the prow, of the poop. And the latter is undoubtedly the cannon that is sticking out of mound number three.

There are still several questions, however. Why are there two cannon on mound number two? And, above all, where is the poop? Regarding that latter question, I have three hypotheses. First, it may be buried under mound number three, which seems unlikely. Second, it may be the mound itself. And third, which seems the most likely explanation, the aft section of the galleon may have settled on top of the coral and was not buried like the rest of the ship. Phips would then have taken his treasure from that part of the ship, which was relatively accessible at the time, but which was subsequently destroyed by storms and has now entirely disappeared. I discuss this explanation with everyone on board, and arguments pro and con rage for the rest of the day. Only Didi says nothing.

This afternoon we must complete the difficult job of clearing our anchorage. There is still a reef lying at water level to the west, which for the protection of the *Calypso* must be removed. The surface explosion is spectacular, but when divers go down to examine the results, it becomes obvious that we will have to blast again. The broken coral has settled in a large (and dangerous) pile in the same place as the original reef. By the time the job is finally done to our satisfaction, we have used thirty charges of TNT.

I am very unhappy about these underwater explosions. I have refused, perhaps a bit childishly, to have anything to do with them; and, in fact, I was inclined not to allow them. It took all the persuasiveness of Captain Caillart, who is responsible for the safety of the *Calypso,* to make me give my reluctant consent to this sad, but apparently necessary, step. Any destruction of marine life, even when in the interests of minimum security, seems outrageous, even sacrilegious.

A team of divers takes down the port anchor and line. We should be perfectly stable from now on. I must admit that, despite my harsh words to Caillart on the use of explosives, I will now be less worried about the *Calypso.*

All the new buoys have been put in place and lighted by Dr. Tassy. His job has not turned out to be a sinecure after all.

And finally, the large suction apparatus, making use of the six-inch tubing we bought in San Juan, has been completely assembled.

The Bearskin

Tonight, there are movies on the rear deck: our film on sharks, and a reel of rushes brought by John Soh. Afterward, we have another meeting, this time to confirm what was agreed to in principle at the last one: that Frédéric Dumas would have a share in the treasure. This meeting has since become known as "the sharing of the bearskin." A resolution is proposed: "That, because of the importance of Mr. Dumas' technical contribution, he receive a share in the treasure equal to that of other members of the crew." The ballots are cast, and it is announced that Dumas has been admitted to the company of those entitled to a share in Spanish gold. I am appointed a committee of one to bring him the glad tidings.

Of course, all this was done half in jest (but only half). No one can bring himself to believe completely that there is really a pot of gold at the end of the rainbow. Since Didi's arrival, I have sensed that he, for one, is skeptical about the whole thing.

The weather is not especially good. There is a sharp wind from the southeast, a swell, and the water is choppy.

Monday, July 29. It seems that we will never be done with our prepara-

The elaboration of an excavation plan in the *Calypso*'s chartroom. To the left is Frédéric Dumas.

Right: Bernard Delemotte discovers another cannon.

tions. They are necessary, of course; but I am impatient to begin the real work of excavation. And my impatience is aggravated by the suspicion that we will very likely see a storm before long. Even if I am wrong, there is still some doubt in my mind that we will be able to do much excavating before the hurricanes really do begin in this area.

Unfortunately, we cannot begin excavations today. We must still put down three solid anchor lines to hold in place the float of four cans that we are using to support the airlift. Then, we will need three more lines, equally strong, to anchor the *James and Mary*. The placement of this equipment, of course, must be calculated carefully in relation to our work area. Moreover, the *Calypso* must be close enough to the *James and Mary* to be able to hoist aboard the heavy load-baskets with a minimum of risk.

The two pipes, totaling twenty feet in length, which comprise the airlift proper, are installed beneath the float. Then, a sturdy elbow of cast-iron pipe (angled at 90°) is bolted to its lower extremity. By means of this elbow, the vertical pipe, which is rigid and heavy, is attached to the flexible pipe which will be used in the work area. The swell makes this whole apparatus rise and fall about a yard, and sometimes it smashes violently against the surrounding

coral heads. Divers go down with pickaxes to chip away these formations — a hard job, which goes on until late in the night.

The rest of us struggle with the Worthington compressor, which must now be brought up on deck for use tomorrow. It is staggeringly heavy and seems to grow even heavier with every move. Finally, the job is done, and we go on to take care of a hundred other details.

Tonight, another showing of rushes on the forward deck. (I am astonished that we are not too exhausted even for this.) There are two reels this time, both showing shots of the wreck. These films were made by Deloire and Omer, using my new four-lamp lighting system, each lamp being 750 watts. I think that this system has opened the door to a new age of marine cinematography.

The Loch Ness Monster

Tuesday, July 30. I have decided that the honor of being the first man to begin excavation should go to Raymond Coll. Raymond has been with us a long time; and, more significant, he is of Spanish origin, a Catalan. It seems to be fitting, somehow, that he strike the first blow in the liberation of *Nuestra Señora* from her coral tomb.

The morning is spent making a final inspection of the various anchorage lines, and then of the airlift apparatus. First, I examine the whole thing, inch by inch; and then Bernard Delemotte comes behind me, doing exactly the same thing. Since yesterday, the suction platform has been covered with large plywood panels, painted bright yellow, so that it can be located instantly. It is now securely anchored in fifty feet of water, with the flexible pipe extending for twenty feet along the ocean floor to the first point of excavation.

We are now ready to test the compressor, and I give the signal for it to be turned on. We have calculated that the airlift is able to bring up, every hour, fifty tons of water, sand, mud, and coral debris from the bottom. It is a rather fearsome apparatus, and one which will require the greatest care on the part of the divers. Its power is so great that it could rip off a man's arm. And, at the pressure of one atmosphere, at which we will be working, it is capable literally of drawing out a man's blood through his skin. For those reasons, the apparatus is known among the divers as the Loch Ness Monster.

As an added precaution, I have distributed red diving gloves to the divers — gloves which, by some chance, we had aboard. Hopefully, these gloves will make it possible for whoever is working airlift to see the hands of his shipmates below, and avoid them.

Frédéric Dumas has also suggested a gadget to facilitate the divers' work: large lead weights, weighing about ten pounds each and ending in a ring. When a diver is working on the bottom, it is difficult for him to stay in one spot because he has no traction. It is for that reason that helmet divers weigh themselves down — so that they may work more comfortably. Dumas' gadget applies the same principle. The purpose of the ring, however, is to enable the diver to attach the weights to his belt. Then, when his shift is over, he will pass the weights to the man who goes down to relieve him. It has also been decided that, in order to gain more stability, the divers will wear boots instead of their fins.

Frédéric Dumas was hesitant in suggesting that we make these weights. He was afraid of asking us to do something that we might not be equipped to do. Actually, he should have known that the *Calypso* — is capable of doing a number of unexpected things. At the end of the morning, there were a dozen lead cylinders, shimmering like silver, lined up on the rear deck. They end, however, not in a hook or even a simple ring, but in a safety clasp — which will greatly facilitate their use on the bottom.

Roger Dufrêche made the weights without telling Dumas what he was doing. It was intended as a surprise. And Didi was indeed surprised; so much so that he could not help muttering "*Very* good!" Which is reward enough for Roger.

One thing I always insist upon, when we are working at a project the conditions and problems of which we do not know thoroughly, is that we take as much time as we need to continue until we have investigated all aspects of the project. This was the system we followed during our archaeological expedition to Grand Congloué; and it is the one that we will follow here. It is the only way to avoid having to say, later on, "We should have done this, or that." That is the reason why the *Calypso* always carries a maximum supply of water and food.

Now, finally, it is time to get down to the real work.

Raymond Coll dives. The compressor is turned on. And Coll begins using the airlift on mound number three. It works beautifully.

Three teams of divers have been organized, headed by Dumas, Coll, and Delemotte. One team — Coll's, in this case — handles the airlift, and the other two break open and sift what the lift brings to the surface and dumps into the

Following page: We have had to clear a work area on the ocean floor, but all around it, coral life continues unabated.

metal baskets. Each team will spend two ninety-minute shifts on the bottom, interspersed with six hours of breaking and sorting. A workday of nine continuous, grueling hours.

Using the map of the worksite, I have explained to the divers how we will approach the wreck. We will dig a trench across the ship, even with the two parallel cannon on the starboard side.

Didi, however, believes that the bottom is too hard around mound number three for the airlift to be used to maximum advantage, and he decides instead to begin in the crater in which we found the barrel of nails. And there, in fact, the lift works away with a vengeance.

It is now time for Delemotte's team to go down, and I accompany them. I am eager to try the airlift for myself. Once on the bottom, I decide to start by digging a trench toward the north, beginning at Didi's crater. The trench will run around the three cannon that are amidship-starboard, and then, turning southward along the mound, will run into the trench originally planned.

An Accident

It was inevitable that, in breaking in the airlift and learning how to use it, there would be problems. One such problem has arisen almost immediately: the lift's airline has ruptured.

My only previous experience with a lift of this kind has been at Grand Congloué. There, we were working at about 140 feet, and using pipe 120 millimeters (four inches) in diameter. Here, it is essential that we work more rapidly; and, for that reason, I chose 150 millimeter (six- inch) pipe, basing my decision on such common-sense factors as the return per section of pipe at a given pressure, etc. The novelty of the system suggested by Didi consists in putting as much distance as possible between the work area and the area in which the mud is ejected; and this is done not by using a horizontal exhaust on the surface, to which the mud is drawn through the vertical suction pipe, but by using a horizontal pipe *on the bottom*, before the vertical pipe is reached. Obviously, this arrangement presupposes the use of a superior quality of flexible air hose; one that will not collapse if there is any blockage.

There is an art in the use of the airlift. Thanks to Didi's innovation, that art is now reduced to its simplest form, and the flexible hose of the lift can be used like a vacuum cleaner. Didi prefers to compare the airlift to an animal, which must be fed intelligently. It must be given as much sand and rock as it can handle, but without giving it indigestion. In order to avoid a malfunction, the airlift must have water. Water allows it to rid itself of what it swallows. The problem, now that we are just beginning, is that the divers are neglecting to see that the airlift gets the proper amount of water; and blockages have resulted. But they are beginning to get the knack of it.

Everyone is delighted with Didi's lead weights, and the divers are now wearing two of them on their belts: twenty pounds of supplementary ballast. And they report excellent results.

Didi, however, refuses to use the weights, and he is teased about it by the divers, who point out that he makes them wear these outlandish contraptions but refuses to use them himself. Finally, he explains why: "I prefer to hold on to the lift, or to the coral. I don't like to load myself down. I prefer to be able to move about easily in the water, so that I can keep an eye on everything and get to any spot where I am needed."

Didi's explanation, as usual, makes sense, particularly in view of the nature of the bottom where we are working. There are often rocks or coral fragments that are too big to be drawn into the suction pipe, and these have to be removed, quickly, before they reach the pipe. Two men are required for this, while the third member of the team handles the Monster.

The divers' red gloves are working out well; that is, they are easily visible, even in the cloud of mud that hovers over the work area. I am hoping that we will be lucky enough, and careful enough, to avoid any kind of accident. Dr. Tassy is even more concerned than I, and, since work began, he has been standing by for the first sign of trouble. In the meantime, in addition to his duty as chief buoy lighter, he is spending his days breaking coral on the deck of the *Calypso*, like an ordinary deck hand.

The debris on the bottom is beginning to be a problem. It must all be removed from the work area, but carefully. The larger pieces may contain something valuable. The divers therefore pick these out by hand and place them in a net basket. When the basket is full, a buoy is inflated (by compressed air) and the net rises to the surface to be taken aboard the *Calypso*.

The work area is constantly under a cloud of mud and coral dust. Sometimes visibility is so bad that the divers have to stop working until it disperses.

On the surface, the situation is hardly better. The rear deck of the *Calypso* is already buried under coral fragments of various sizes.

One of the teams, by using the *Calypso*'s hoist at maximum power, has managed to haul aboard some strange blocks of coral weighing several tons. Michel Deloire refers to them as "coral cannon." We strike one of them with a sledgehammer, and it reverberates. We chip away some of the coral and see the glint of metal. Michel was right; they are cannon.

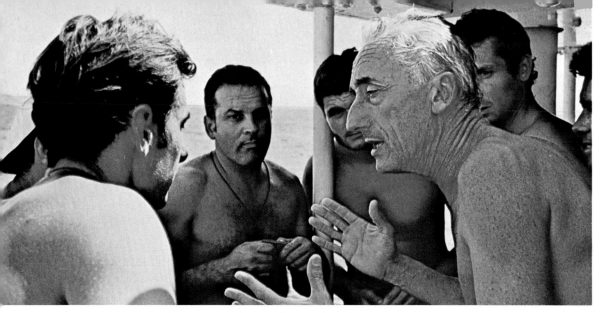

Captain Cousteau, Deloire and Canoë, discussing the direction of the next dig.

A low-flying American plane has carefully inspected us several times. He no doubt thinks that we are a group of lunatics to have chosen this particular spot in which to drop anchor. He must be puzzled, though, by the airlift apparatus and our radar equipment.

Today, we have our first personnel problem, but it is a very understandable and human problem. One of our companions, Raymond Amaddio, has reached the point of exhaustion, and he can no longer sleep. He feels that it

Everyone on board has a hand in hauling aboard the debris brought up from the bottom.

On the bottom, Captain Cousteau supervises the excavation of one of the mounds.

In the work area, surrounded by a cloud of mud, the divers inflate a floater. The floater will be used to raise to the surface a basket of fragments of archaeological interest.

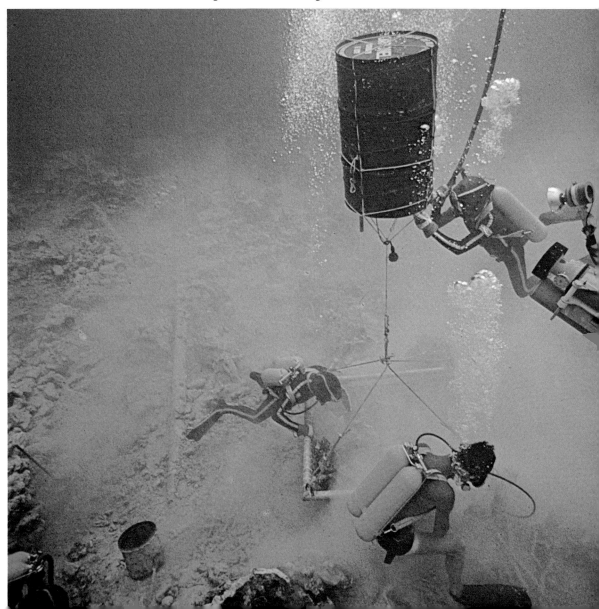

may be necessary for him to return to France, and he feels very bad about it. It is not the possible loss of the "treasure" that bothers him, for Raymond is one of the few people aboard who has never believed that there is a treasure. I have done my best to make him feel better; and, in any case, I would like him to relax and rest for a while before making up his mind about what to do.

SIX

Galleons in Peril

Aboard the galleon of His Most Catholic Majesty, the *Almirante de Honduras*, everything was as ready as it would ever be. The soldiers' muskets were at the ready, and the wick for their powder had been lighted. The cannoneers were at their posts. Sand had been scattered over the deck to enable the combatants to maintain their footing in the blood that seemed certain to be spilled. Buckets of sand and of water had been spotted about the ship for use against fires. The boarding net was spread out at the foot of the mainmast and covered the entrance to the hold. Beneath the feeble protection afforded by the net, a terrified mob of women, children, colonists, and merchants, moaned, trembled, cried, and prayed, each according to his own temperament. Two friars and a priest were leading the people in a hymn; and, in a corner, a Capuchin monk was hearing confessions and giving absolution with unaccustomed liberality.

The *Almirante*, a vessel of 600 tons and carrying sixty-eight cannon, had only recently sailed from Cartagena, bound for Cuba, from which, along with the other ships of the Fleet of Tierra Ferma, it was to return to Spain. Along the way, however, the galleon had sprung a serious leak, and had been forced to fall behind the two vessels accompanying it. Finally, it had lost sight of its convoy altogether. The captain and officers of the *Almirante de Honduras* had not been particularly worried. The wind was steady, and the hurricane season had only just begun. With a little luck, all would be well.

But the *Almirante*'s luck had run out. The optimistic calculations of the officers had been interrupted by a shout from the seaman on watch. A ship had been sighted, coming up fast in the wind. There could be no doubt that it was a pirate ship. Its rigging, the design of its stem, and the fact that it was showing no colors,* proclaimed its identity even to the most inexperienced sailor aboard.

A council of war was called immediately, and word of the pirates spread like lightning throughout the crowded ship, striking panic into the hearts of the hundreds of passengers. Even the officers who assembled on the poop for the council seemed solemn and preoccupied.

David and Goliath

The little pirate ship was hopelessly outclassed by the galleon. It was a two-master, its unusually tall masts rigged with triangular sails and topsails. It rode low in the water and was of modest size: about a hundred feet long, and twenty feet in the beam. Compared to the imposing mass of the galleon, it seemed little more than a toy. Despite its size, however, it had a large crew — almost a hundred men — all of whom were now assembled on deck. But, so far as armament was concerned, its cannon were so few that they could barely be seen from the galleon's deck.

The less than formidable appearance of the pirate ship served to allay the panic of some of the passengers and crew of the *Almirante*; at least among those who had had no previous experience with pirates. It seemed a foregone conclusion that the great Spanish ship, with its preponderance of cannon and its great size, would make short work of this presumptuous enemy.

The pirate ship was now only a short distance behind the galleon which, although it was under full sail, was unable to broaden the gap between them. Still, speed was not everything. The Spanish vessel had other defenses. For instance, the *Almirante* incorporated the latest innovation from Spain: the helmsman now controlled the ship from a cabin facing the mizzenmast, from which point he could observe the sails while steering the galleon. Previously, he had been unable to see the sails — a decided disadvantage on a ship where the rudder exercised a minimum of control, and maneuvers were generally effected by the position of the sails. Also, the rudder was now controlled di-

*The famous "Jolly Roger," or skull and crossbones on a field of black, did not come into use until much later, when the age of pirates was almost at its end.

A brigantine, the vessel favored by pirates in the middle of the seventeenth century, depicted by Gustave Alaux. (Musée de la Marine, Paris.)

rectly, by means of a long tiller (known as the manual), rather than, as before, by a block-pulley apparatus.*

As the pirate vessel continued gaining, the officers of the galleon buckled on their swords, donned their helmets, and began loading their pistols. Orders were shouted; and the mizzen sails on the poop, and the bowsprit sail, were angled accordingly. Slowly, the great ship began to turn to port. The purpose

*Two celebrated sailing vessels furnish detailed information on seventeenth-century ships: the *Mayflower*, which dates from 1620; and the *Vasa* (1628), which was raised from the bottom off Stockholm in 1960-61.

A galleon gives battle. From a drawing by Leon Haffner.

of the maneuver was clear: the galleon was preparing to fire a broadside. But the maneuver itself was so painfully slow as to defeat its purpose, for the pirate vessel, being much lighter and more mobile than its prey, had more than sufficient time to move in such a way as to remain to the rear of the galleon. And the galleon's cannon were mounted so that only two of them, mounted below the poop, could then fire upon the pirates. Even these two did not present a real threat, for, like the other cannon aboard, they were stationary and could not be aimed individually. In order for a galleon's cannon to point in the direction of an enemy, therefore, the galleon itself had to be aimed, rather than its weapons. In such a situation, one wave was sufficient to send the cannon balls zooming into the sky, or down into the water a few feet from the galleon. Then, the time-consuming loading process had to be begun again, since these were barrel-loading cannon. The cannoneers ran back and forth among the cannon, on the exterior walks which ran around the ship, stuffing powder and cannon balls down the muzzles. And, of course, they were at the mercy of the waves — and of the pirates' firearms — as they did so. The master-cannoneer, exasperated, ordered another round of ten-pound cannon balls; and these also fell far short of their target.

By now, the two ships were close enough for the Spaniards, from their high poop, to see their attackers far below them on the deck of their little ship. They knew that they would soon have the opportunity to inspect them at closer range; for, with the pirate ship sailing to the rear of the galleon and out of range of its cannon, it was inevitable that the Spaniards would be subjected to a boarding assault. Ordinarily, a boarding took place aft, to either the starboard or port. The pirate vessel would close with its victim, and the pirates would climb from the deck of their own ship to that of the galleon. They were all seamen, agile as cats, and experts in their profession; while the soldiers of Spain, inexperienced in this sort of attack, could think of nothing to do but stand on deck waiting for the assault.

Knives and Halberds

The pirates were armed with short sabers and cutlasses. They also had pistols, but these were not very effective in a boarding operation. They could be fired only once, for they were too long to be able to be reloaded in hand-to-hand combat. For this reason, pirates sometimes carried as many as eight pistols stuck into their belts, or hanging from bandoliers.

Now the pirate ship was upon the galleon, and its grappling irons found

The anchor we discovered was a very large one. In the foreground is the anchor ring.

a hold on its starboard. Shouting pirates leaped from their own deck onto the hull of the other ship, and then scrambled up onto its decks. They were well organized. One group attacked the officers. Another was responsible for the soldiers. And a third, after cutting the boarding net, went below deck to find the powder magazine; for it was a pirate custom to threaten to blow up the ship, and everyone on it, unless the officers surrendered immediately.

Meanwhile, on deck, the Spanish soldiers and their officers were trying desperately to organize some semblance of resistance against the boarding party which, suddenly, seemed to be everywhere. But the decks were stacked with merchandise, and terrified civilians were running about, crying and shouting, some of them trying to find a way to protect their treasures. In this situation, it was impossible for the soldiers even to reach the pirates, let alone launch an effective counterattack. The pirates, however, were under no such handicap. When they wished to reach a particular spot on the deck, they simply cut their way through the panic-stricken mob.

Moreover, the Spaniards were not armed for combat at close quarters. They were somewhat protected by their breastplates and helmets, but their principal weapon — halberds — were difficult, if not impossible, to wield in the middle of a mob. The cutlasses and sabers of the pirates were much more effective. The Spaniards also had arquebuses, a weapon which they had used since the beginning of their conquest of the New World. They had discovered that its loud noise terrorized the natives; and its large ball — of which several could be loaded at once — assured effective results. Even if a man was only slightly wounded, he was almost always knocked to the ground by it. The disadvantage of the arquebus, however, was that it was necessary to hold a lighted wick to its powder for it to fire. It was a dangerous procedure, and one which became impossible when there was rain or wind. Another weapon, the musket, was less expensive and easier to handle than the arquebus, but it had not yet replaced the latter as the standard weapon of the Spanish Army. It was a Spanish invention, even though the Italians had given it its name. Even the musket, however, was so heavy that it could not be fired unless it was supported by a fork, or unless it rested on a deck railing.

The third group of pirates by now had found the powder magazine and made their usual threat, with the usual results. Rather than see their galleon destroyed, the captain and the admiral preferred to surrender it.

Actually, they had no other choice. The pirates, being seamen, had already taken over the ship by seizing control of the manual, the mainsail, and the mizzen sail. Their officers who had chosen to fight, sword in hand, were now dead or wounded. The few soldiers still struggling with the pirates were begged by the terrified civilians to lay down their arms.

After the captain and the admiral had been bound and the last sign of resistance had disappeared, the pirates, who now seemed perfectly at home on the galleon, went below to the treasure room. They threw open the wooden hatch and thrust a torch into the enclosure — the same torch with which they had threatened to blow up the ship. There were eight or ten soldiers guarding the treasure, and ready to fight; but the struggle was brief, and soon the Spaniards lay dying on the deck. Then, the treasure chests were opened with axes, and the pirates' eyes saw the reward for their daring: stacks of leather bags, filled with coins and gems. Most of the men chose those containing coins; others took the sacks of pearls; and still others were perceptive enough to choose a few handful of emeralds from New Granada—present-day Colombia.

Those who seized the coin sacks were doomed to disappointment when they opened them later, aboard their own vessel. They would be astonished to discover that these sacks contained more silver than gold. For pirates of this period, like historians of a later age, had come to believe too easily the tales of unlimited gold in the New World. There was gold, it is true, and a great deal of it. And the Tower of Seville, to which the wealth of the Americas eventually found its way, was indeed called the "Tower of Gold."* But much of the treasure that found its way aboard the galleons, and then into the Tower of Gold, was silver, from the mines of Mexico and Peru, rather than gold.

A man lighting the powder of his arquebus. (Taken from a work by Jacques de Gheyn, entitled, *Maniement d'armes, d'arquebuses, de mousquets et piques réprésenté par figures*, Amsterdam, 1608. Bibliothèque du Fort de Montrouge, Arcueil.)

The pirates who seized the *Almirante de Honduras* were less bloodthirsty than one might think. Which is to say that almost every woman aboard was almost immediately gang-raped, but that the lives of the soldiers, sailors, and civilian passengers were spared. As for the captain, the admiral, and the nobles, they were worth far more alive than dead, and they would be kept in chains until ransom could be arranged.

Next to the women, the group that fared least well was probably the clergy, for most of the pirates were Protestants. The pirate captain, who maintained strict control over his men and did not allow them to drink aboard the galleon, was a Frenchman, and a Huguenot. His men, however, were as motley an assortment as the crew of the *Almirante*. There were Hollanders, Englishmen, Danes, and even Indians among them.

After a conference with his lieutenants, the new master of the *Almirante* announced his decision: the galleon would be taken to the island of Tortuga,

*The Tower was built in 1220, by Cid Abu el Ola, the Moorish governor of Seville. Its name originally was taken from the *azulejos*, or ceramic tiles, with which its walls were covered, though it was amply justified later by the use to which the Spanish put the building.

and its merchandise sold there to the highest bidder. He then assigned half his men to duty on the *Almirante* and, after a threatening speech to the assembled Spanish crew of the galleon, he returned to his own ship. A short time later, sails were hoisted, and the ships, one following the other, were on their way to the most notorious island of the Caribbean.

The Pirates' Den

The island of Tortuga was, at that time, a safe haven for the pirates of the Caribbean; or at least for the French pirates, for their English counterparts preferred the island of Jamaica.

The first pirate settlement in the Caribbean, however, was neither Tortuga nor Jamaica, but the island of St. Christopher, which would be known in the twentieth century as St. Kitts. St. Christopher belonged partly to the French and partly to the English, and was governed at this time, in 1623, by a French adventurer named Belain d'Esnambuc.

The proximity of pirates to the traditional return route of Spain's galleons, however, was disturbing to the Spanish. And, in 1630, Admiral Fadrique de Toledo attacked St. Christopher and expelled the pirates, both English and French. His attack force consisted of forty-nine ships, of which thirty-five were galleons — an overwhelming force, for at that time Spain's power in the New World, both in ships and men, was still considerable.

Eighty of the now homeless pirates, under Belain d'Esnambuc's command, then moved to Tortuga. The island had been named by Columbus. Tortuga means "turtle"; and the island has, in fact, the shape of a turtle, being round, with its "head" to the west and its "tail" to the east. The choice of Tortuga as the pirate's new home proved to be a fortunate one, for the island was pleasant, fertile, covered with shrubs and tall trees, and had a plentiful supply of fresh water. Moreover, it was skirted by steep cliffs, and there was only one spot where it was possible for ships to land; and therefore it was easily defensible. Tortuga's most important advantage, however, was its location. It was separated from the island of Hispaniola by a strait only six or seven miles wide. The Silver Bank, therefore, was very near; and the Bank, of course, was the nemesis of Spanish galleons that were blown off course on the return trip to Spain.

The Spaniards were no more pleased with the presence of the pirates on Tortuga than they had been with it on St. Christopher, and they attempted to expel them. In 1638, they succeeded in landing a group of soldiers there; but

A team of cameramen films the work site.

the following year this garrison was attacked by a group of English pirates and ejected. The island was now dominated by the English.

The English, in turn, were expelled by a Frenchman named Le Vasseur. Le Vasseur had been a follower of Belain d'Esnambuc, a former resident of St. Christopher, a former officer of the French Navy, and a Huguenot. He received a commission from the new governor of St. Christopher, Philippe de Longvilliers de Poincy, to take Tortuga from the English; for the pirates of

Tortuga, under D'Esnambuc, had recognized the sovereignty of the French king over their island, and, English or no English, France still claimed the island as hers. Le Vasseur's reward was to be the governorship of Tortuga. He succeeded in his project by hiding out on a neighboring island (Margot) for three months, and then launching a surprise attack against the English. The assault was so unexpected that Tortuga fell to Le Vasseur's invading force — which consisted of forty-nine French Protestants — almost instantly.

Under Le Vasseur's rule, forts were constructed, and cannon were brought in to protect the island against future invasion. Then, under the stout walls of those defenses, he established a thriving market place. For Tortuga was inhabited by French colonists who cultivated the land, and it was to the pirates' advantage to have a refuge to which they could safely come for provisions and relaxation. Many of the colonists, however, became pirates, or rather privateers, themselves; and the authorization to do this, in the form of royal commissions issued in the name of King Louis XIV of France, was readily available from the hands of Governor Le Vasseur. Thus, Tortuga became the home as well as the haven of pirates, who came there periodically to drink, gamble, and dispose of their booty. Soon, Tortuga was one of the most prosperous markets in the Caribbean, where one could buy anything from the simplest items to gold or silver plate. And, naturally, payment was made in pesos or pieces of eight. At this time, the population of Tortuga was about ten thousand, of which some three thousand were pirates.

The Spanish, of course, were outraged, and more than once they attempted to take Tortuga. But now they were facing a leader who was as foresighted as he was well informed. On one occasion, Le Vasseur repulsed, with heavy losses, an invasion force consisting of five ships and six hundred Spanish soldiers. Never before had Spain's commerce with the New World been in such danger. Never before had the Spanish king had so many enemies in the Caribbean, or such well-organized enemies.

The English were hardly less active than the French in their opposition to His Most Catholic Majesty, or in their fondness for his gold. From their own stronghold on Jamaica, these buccaneers, as they called themselves, preyed relentlessly and daringly on any ship showing the royal standard of Spain.

These two colonies of pirates, at the very heart of Spain's lines of communication with her colonies in the New World, represented a mortal danger. But the French and the English were not the only dangers in the Caribbean. There was also hurricanes, and coral. And the galleons were as helpless against these as they were against the pirates and buccaneers of Tortuga and Jamaica. The convoys that were indispensable to communications and trade between Spain and America, the ships that were supposed to protect Spain's ports and colonies, because of their poor design and equipment, were little more than playthings of the wind. They were driven into reefs and blown aground in the shallows of the tropical sea; and the hidalgos, whose bravery on land was unsurpassed, were helpless in the face of these dangers. They could not even swim.

The Mastery of the Seas

The taking of the *Almirante de Honduras* was but one instance of many such pirate victories.

Spain, for three centuries, had pillaged the works of art of the ancient American civilizations, melted them down into coins and ingots, and carried them — along with the natural riches of the tropics, and even with treasures from China — in an unending stream across the Atlantic. It was too much to expect that the other nations of Europe would control their envy and greed for so long a time. And the fact that they could not control it is the central fact of the history, not only of Spain, but of Europe itself during this period. The period is characterized by Europe's determination to exploit the New World and to develop a maritime capability proportionate to that determination.*

This vast process of exploitation occurred, for the most part, in a very limited geographical area: the Caribbean — the "Spanish sea," that New World equivalent of the Mediterranean, enclosed by a double crown of islands. The Caribbean was the unavoidable antechamber of the New World, the vestibule opening onto the Americas. Spain's position in the New World required that she dominate and control the Caribbean basin by means of her maritime power and by naval bases on the islands of this sea. And she succeeded in doing this — but only for a short time; and thereafter, the maritime history of Spain is a repetition of the same mistakes and the same abuses. The galleons were always too heavily loaded; too encumbered with illegal mer-

*According to a report submitted to Colbert in 1670, trade with the West Indies in the preceding year amounted to 38 million *livres*. Of this total, France's share was 6 million; England's, 5 million; Holland, Hamburg and Danzig together had 10 million; Flanders, Sweden, and Denmark had 4 million; Genoa, Naples, and Leghorn 7 million; Portugal, Galicia, and Biscaye 2 million; and the Barbary states, 1 million. Spain's share was only 3 million. (Cited by A. Thomazi, in *Les Flottes d'Or*).

The Tower of Gold at Seville, in which the treasures of the New World were stored temporarily. (Office National du Tourisme Espagnol, Paris.)

chandise; too crowded with passengers who had no business on the king's ships; too poorly designed and haphazardly constructed. Their crews were always poorly trained, and their officers could never be persuaded that the tactics that had worked so well on land would not work equally well on the sea.

The pirates of the Caribbean, who plundered this inadequate, undisciplined, untrained, badly equipped and poorly commanded fleet, could hardly have failed to show themselves more competent and more daring than their prey. The Dutch, especially, had already given evidence of a true vocation for the sea, and were particularly effective in the Caribbean. (The word "free-booter" is the corruption of a Dutch word meaning the same thing: *vrijbuiter*. The linguistic cross-pollination among pirate bands is itself indicative of the multinational origins of the Caribbean pirates.) So efficient were they as naval architects that, in 1603, Sir Walter Raleigh had occasion to complain that an English ship of 100 tons required a crew of thirty men, while a Dutch ship of the same tonnage required only ten. They put this talent to use in the Caribbean by engaging in smuggling and privateering; and their specialty was providing the Spanish colonies with the necessities which the fleets of Spain could not supply. Every year, from sixty to eighty Dutch ships arrived in the Caribbean with cargoes of high-quality manufactured goods — such as cloth, tools, and construction material — which they traded for colonial products. So profitable was this traffic in contraband that one-fifth the cargo of a Dutch convoy, seized near Martinique by a French pirate named Grammont, was worth 80,000 livres. The value of these Dutch cargoes became a byword even among pirates, and their ships became known collectively as "the Amsterdam stock exchange." And Spain was as inefficient at putting a stop to this activity as she had been in suppressing the pirates.

The Agony of the King

It is difficult to understand why Spain, given her lack of ships and technical proficiency, did not attempt to solve her problems by organizing a naval headquarters in the Caribbean. If such a command had been established, and if the administration of the West Indies had been organized along more flexible lines, it might have been possible for Spain to find in the New World the means to combat piracy and smuggling that she lacked in the mother country. This is particularly true in view of the fact that the men of the colonies were perceptibly more vigorous and enterprising than their contemporaries in the Old World, and understood the problems better than the bureaucrats of Seville or the members of the Council of the Indies.

As it was, Spain came to depend for all her resources on a handful of adventurers beyond the sea, who were robbing her mercilessly, and on a fleet under the command of men who were a far cry from the conquistadores who had audaciously seized a continent. The result was that the kings of Spain, who owned the galleons that transported those resources, spent their lives waiting in an agony of suspense for the arrival of their ships from the New World.* There were many years in which no ships came at all, because of storms, pirates, lack of ships, lack of personnel, or because of several of these causes combined. And in those years a painful contrast was evident between the financial condition of the king, the court, and the nation as a whole, and the apparently inexhaustible wealth of Spain's American possessions.

While the king waited in anguish and while the bureaucrats compiled regulations, the great lords and captains were lining their own pockets. The colonies were left to develop as best they could on their own. There is a direct connection between these two latter phenomena. If the Spanish colonies were never allowed to organize at the economic level, it is because the Spanish commanders in America were not administrators or governors, but profiteering nobles whose only concern was the filling of their family exchequers. They gave little thought to the good of the colonies, or even to that of Spain herself. And, under their domination, the decline of Spanish maritime power was accelerated. Between 1570 and 1599, Spain had 110 ships in the Caribbean. By 1610, there were only 55. And by the middle of the seventeenth century, only 25 were left. In 1661, Spain had to hire the Dutch ships, under Admiral de Ruyter, to carry her goods back and forth across the Atlantic.

Nuestra Señora de la Concepción

There were, of course, some officials who were the exception to the rule. In 1640, Diego Pacheco, Duke of Escalona, was appointed viceroy of Mexico by King Philip IV. The duke recognized immediately the causes and implications of Spain's worsening situation in the Caribbean, and ordered the shipyards at Veracruz to set to work building the ships that the mother country needed so badly. In less than a year, eight galleons and a frigate had been completed. The largest, strongest, and most imposing of these galleons was the flagship of the new fleet, and the Duke of Escalona himself christened it: *Nuestra Señora de la Concepción.*

---

*Despite the steady flow of treasure not only to Spain but also to other countries, the "golden century" marked a low point in the finances of the European powers. The monarchs who profited most (in one way or another) from the wealth of America — Charles V, Philip II, Elizabeth of England — were perennially short of money, and were head over heels in debt to the merchants and bankers of Europe. Indeed, Spain, even at the apex of her glory, was literally bankrupt on several occasions — in 1557, 1575, and 1596, for example.

As befitted a flagship, *Nuestra Señora*'s poop was adorned with carved figures, crowns, and garlands. (This ornamentation added useless weight to the galleon; but it was considered *de riqueur* if a galleon was to be imposing, and therefore forbidding, in the eyes of an enemy.) A carved frieze ran the length of the ship above the upper deck; but there was not sufficient time for it to be gilded, and it had simply been painted yellow.

The intentions of the Duke of Escalona were certainly above reproach. He was not, however, a man of the sea, and he had had no idea of the experience, the number of specialists, and even of the time that was required to build a fleet of nine ships. This lack of knowledge, combined with the makeshift techniques, lack of planning, and hit-or-miss workmanship of the shipyard employees, was to have its effect.

The fleet, with *Nuestra Señora de la Concepción* at its head, sailed on its maiden voyage from San Jose d'Ulloa (the port of Veracruz) on July 23, 1641. Its first port of call was to be Cuba, where it would join forces with the Fleet de Terra Firma under the command of Captain General Juan de Campos and Admiral de Villavicencio. Thence, across the Atlantic to Spain. On this first stage of its journey, the new fleet could count on the protection and support of the Armada de Barlouento.

The Mexican fleet reached Havana without incident. There, she dropped anchor and settled down to wait for the galleons of her sister fleet, while the nobles and officers amused themselves in the city — which, now more than ever, was a tropical paradise of magnificent palaces, ostentatious wealth, and handsome slave women of many hues. The Fleet of Terra Firma finally arrived, and after more delays, the combined fleet — now numbering thirty-one ships; and including a number of merchantmen — weighed anchor on September 13, 1641, in the middle of the hurricane season.

On the second day out from Havana, it was noticed that *Nuestra Señora de la Concepción* was taking on water at a dangerous rate, and its hold was filling rapidly. The pumps were unable to handle this volume of water. There was nothing to do but for the entire fleet to return to Havana. The shipyard carpenters of the port worked night and day with extraordinary diligence, but it was September 28 before the repairs had been completed. The use of the dry dock was not among the skills of the time, and the customary technique was to heel over a ship, first on one side and then on the other, for the carpenters to make their repairs. For this to be done, the entire cargo had to be unloaded, along with the cannon. Given all these factors, it is certain that ten days were sufficient to do only cursory repairs. Even so, two more weeks of precious time had been lost.

Above: Searching among the coral on the floor of the Caribbean.

Below: Bernard Delemotte, on the rear deck of the *Calypso*, breaking down the larger blocks of coral with a sledgehammer.

Right: A block of coral is being hoisted by sling from the bottom, as a group of divers and cameramen watch from beneath the *Calypso*'s hull.

Starting out again from Havana, the fleet followed the Bahamas canal along the northern coast of Cuba to Matanzas, and then turned northward toward the Florida straits. Before the fleet was the Bahamas Bank, the island of Andros and its innumerable reefs. It was the most dangerous area in the waters of the Antilles. From that point, the fleet had to sail through a narrow corridor between the Keys and the Cay Salt Bank. The water was dotted with what are known in the Antilles as *cayes* (stones).

The Hurricane

It was at this point, when the fleet was surrounded by rocks and coral reefs, that the storm struck. Seamen had often noted that September was the worst possible month to set sail for Spain; and the fleet was now to verify that observation. Under the impact of a violent wind, the ships, poorly constructed as most of them were, could not hold their places in the convoy and were scattered in all directions. Three of them sank in full sight of the others. Others were smashed against the rocks. Four ran aground on the Florida coast. And there were no survivors from any of these ships. A cutter, which had been used for liaison among the galleons of the fleet, was washed up on a reef, and a few men who had clung to it were saved by a ship sent out from Havana. The rest of the passengers, soldiers, and sailors were either drowned when their ships sank, or were devoured by sharks when they tried to swim to land.

The death agony of *Nuestra Señora de la Concepción* was more prolonged than that of the other ships. Driven before the wind, she had her rigging completely destroyed by the storm. Then, buffeted by enormous waves and tossed about among the reefs, she drifted out of control for several weeks along the Bahamas canal, driven sometimes to the east and sometimes to the west, at the mercy of every wind.

Aboard *Nuestra Señora*, the situation was beyond description. The forecastle and the bowsprit had been demolished, and the waves had ripped away both the *batel* (a large canoe) from the starboard, and the *chalupa* (a smaller boat) from the port. The passengers were huddled below deck, in darkness, filth, and despair. The ship, as everyone knew, could not stay afloat much longer.

The crew jettisoned the expendable excess weight: some of the cannon, the cannon balls, and everything that had no commercial value. It occurred to no one, however, to throw overboard the heaviest cargo of all: the gold and silver.

When the storm abated somewhat, the crew managed to fashion a mast of sorts out of the main yard, and a sail was hoisted. Hope was renewed, but not for long. *Nuestra Señora* had been built with too much haste and too little skill, and the repairs effected at Havana had been poorly done. The seams of the hull began to split, and the hold to fill with water. Everyone — soldiers, sailors, passengers — took turns at the pumps, but it was all in vain. *Nuestra Señora de la Concepción* was already nothing more than a hull driven by the wind. And it was being pushed steadily toward the most deadly of the Caribbean coral reefs, those that mariners called *abreojos* and feared above all others.

A sailor was constantly on duty, in a barrel at the prow, taking soundings. Depth soundings were virtually the only safeguard in navigation at this time, for charts were primitive and undependable, and position was a matter of guesswork. Soundings at least were an indication of the depth of the water, and warned of shallows and reefs. These warnings, however, often came too late. In the Caribbean, coral reefs often rise almost vertically from the bottom.

On November 1, at nine o'clock in the evening, the watch announced that the dreaded reefs were in sight. The thunder of the waves breaking against the coral almost drowned out the shrieking of the wind, and everyone began to prepare themselves for death. As a last resort, the anchors were dropped: the davit anchors — a sailor released the davit with a blow of his ax — and the two auxiliary anchors, each weighing more than a thousand pounds; and, finally, the *misericordia*, the largest and heaviest anchor of all. For a moment, it seemed too late; the galleon's hull was already scraping the bottom. But then, by some miracle, *Nuestra Señora* was free again, and in open water. Again, the violence of the storm abated, and the men of *Nuestra Señora* looked up in renewed hope.

At dawn, on November 2, the crew succeeded in launching the few small boats that remained aboard the ship. All day, they worked at towing *Nuestra Señora* as far away as possible from the reefs. Then, that night, after the exhausted crewmen had returned to the ship, the anchors were dropped once again. The few cannon left aboard were used as auxiliary anchors.

Toward midnight, the wind rose with renewed fury. At two o'clock in the morning, the anchor lines gave way, and the galleon was hurled toward the reefs. Her prow scraped the coral — and then the wind and the waves pushed her headlong into the bank. The agony of *Nuestra Señora de la Concepción* was not yet over. For one entire day she was thrown about in the midst of the bank and ripped open by rocks and coral until most of her passengers and cargo had been lost. And then, finally, she turned over, and sank, stern first. Striking a coral slope beneath the surface, the galleon broke in two. The broken prow disappeared into the water, taking with it the galley with its brick oven, and most of the food and water. Her stern rested on the bottom, while the rear section of the ship still projected above the surface. Then the rear section disintegrated under the hammerblows of the storm.

Not all of the people, however, were drowned. Many of them were struggling among the breakers on the reef, and succeeded in gaining a foothold on the rear section of the ship. Then, when this refuge was destroyed, they moved onto the reef itself. But the reef was barely at water level, and the waves began dragging the men, one by one, into the sea. By now, sharks had gathered and were waiting for their prey.

The most courageous among the survivors made an attempt to escape by lashing together rafts from drifting lumber and planks. But then, they could not agree upon the direction to be taken. The pilots believed that they were near the Puerto Rican coast, and, with several of their fellow survivors, they set out on one of the rafts in what they believed was the proper direction. They were never seen again. Admiral de Villavicencio concluded that the *Nuestra Señora* had gone down to the north of Hispaniola, and took a raft, with a number of the other survivors, in that direction. All of these eventually reached safety.

About thirty of the survivors refused to join either the pilots or the admiral, but chose to remain behind on the reef and wait to be rescued. And, since the reef remained covered with water even at low tide, and the men were in water to midcalf, they built a platform for themselves out of lumber ripped from the hull of their sunken ship. On it they placed their caldrons and their meager provisions, and all the gold and silver that could be removed from the ship.

After waiting for several weeks on their precarious platform, these survivors — burning with thirst, ill nourished, sunburned, and dehydrated — concluded that no rescue party would be sent for them. They therefore built a crude boat and, taking what remained of their supplies, they set out toward the south. Their craft sank just north of Hispaniola, and one man was saved.

Out of the five hundred and twenty-five people aboard *Nuestra Señora de la Concepción*, over three hundred perished in either the storm or its aftermath.

Such is the story of the galleon to which Remy de Haenen believed he had guided the *Calypso*.

SEVEN

The Excavation

Wednesday, July 31. This will be the first full day of digging with our new equipment. This time, I think we have what we need, and a new phase of our treasure hunt is beginning. I give the starting signal by ringing the ship's bell. Immediately, the compressor's roar begins, and the divers, already in their equipment, slip into the water.

As before, we will work in relays of three teams for ninety-minute intervals, beginning at 6:30 A.M. and continuing until 7 P.M.

Work on the trench seems to be progressing. It has reached the cannon lying across one of the mounds. Yet, on the two occasions that I go down to watch the teams at work, I sense that something is wrong. We do not seem to be going as fast as we could, at any stage of the operation. This certainly is not because of lack of energy or enthusiasm on our part. The divers are working relentlessly; and Remy de Haenen sits all day on the *James and Mary*, scraping away at the fragments that are sent up to him in the basket. He does not even look up.

After dinner, I ask Dumas, Paul Zuéna, Caillart, and the diving teams, to come to the wardroom for a meeting, and I state the problem without preliminaries:

"We will have to find a way to double our output."

I suggest having four diving teams of two men each, rather than three of three men each. In this way, the airlift will be in action three additional hours every day.

Another problem: the work area is now encumbered by the presence of large blocks of coral, which makes it difficult for the divers to excavate at maximum speed. After discussing various solutions, we decide to try what seems to be the most effective suggestion: we will move the *Calypso* so that her stern is directly over the work area. Her hoist will then be able to haul up the larger coral pieces and the baskets of fragments.

St. Francis

Thursday, August 1. At six o'clock in the morning the divers go down to begin work. Then, without interrupting the actual work of excavation, the *Calypso* is moved in accordance with last night's decision. Then, a partially full basket from the *James and Mary* is hauled aboard. We set to work immediately, sifting the fragments through a fine screen. It is discouraging work. Once more, we find only broken pieces of pottery of no particular interest. Then, among the pieces of coral, we see two bright objects. Gold, at last. Not a great deal of it, but gold nonetheless: a medal, and a cross.

The small medal is attached to a chain by means of a ring. On it is the figure of a bearded saint, and an inscription: *S. FRAN. Ora P. NOS (S. Franciscus, ora pro nobis* — "St. Francis, pray for us"). On the reverse side is another image of the saint, this time in conversation with an angel who stands on a cloud. St. Francis, obviously; but which St. Francis? It could be St. Francis Xavier, the Spanish Jesuit who evangelized Japan and China. He was canonized in 1622, and it is certainly possible that a medal of his could have been aboard the *Nuestra Señora* when it sank in 1641. And it could also be St. Francis of Assisi, the *poverello*. What a bit of irony, and what a bad omen, if the very first piece of gold that turns up in our treasure hunt is an image of the patron saint of the poor.

We set to work breaking apart the blocks of coral that have begun to accumulate so rapidly that it is difficult to get around the deck of the *Calypso*. Everyone aboard is hard at it, breaking open coral, hoping that it contains some kind of treasure, while the compressor roars and the hammerblows resound. The pieces are taken forward, by means of a wheelbarrow and a dolly, and dumped into the sea at a safe distance from the work area. About six o'clock in the evening the wind rises and it begins raining. The divers are brought up, but everyone remains on deck, working in the warm rain. It brings welcome relief from the sting of salt and coral.

At the end of the day, the hoist takes the baskets from the *James and*

Debris of all kinds from the bottom is beginning to accumulate on the rear deck of the *Calypso*.

Mary and empties them onto the rear deck. We work far into the night, under the floodlights, while Didi examines each piece carefully with a magnifying glass that he wears around his neck on a piece of string. By using the accessories that Didi was foresighted enough to buy, we manage to go through between two and three tons of coral.

Morale is high, and everyone talks, laughs, and sings as the work goes on. The sight of gold, however slight, has been sufficient to put everyone in an excellent humor.

Late that night, we take inventory of the results of our labor. Besides the medal and the cross of gold, there are twenty cannon balls, weighing between six and nine pounds each; several culverin balls; a few lead balls for pistols and arquebuses; a well-preserved canvas bag of grapeshot; a piece of awning with a cord attached. In addition, the divers have finished digging out the three starboard cannon on the bottom.

John Soh, chief editor of our films, seems a bit puzzled by it all, but he expresses his admiration of the crew's high spirits, and his astonishment at the ingenuity and energy that they bring to their work. For my part, I am not surprised at the spirits or the ability of the men of the *Calypso*, for I expected nothing less. But I am astonished at the amount of backbreaking work that has been done.

Friday, August 2. Every time one team of divers relieves another team, nets filled with blocks of coral are dumped on our rear deck, and we set to work breaking them open. So far, we have found: a broken brass spoon, which was stuck to a cannon ball; a dagger hilt of bronze, the end of which is cast in the shape of a helmeted head.

After dinner, there is another squall, with a driving rain. We haul the *James and Mary* to the *Calypso* and empty two large baskets onto the deck. It is too late, however, for us to begin working on this enormous heap of coral.

In a sense, we are glad of the rain, for we are short of fresh water. Unfortunately, we will probably have to make a run to Puerto Rico in order to replenish our supply, even though everyone would prefer to continue excavating our galleon. We have taken steps to economize what little water we have left. The divers have agreed not to take showers, and the rest of us — the coral-breakers — whose skin is usually white with coral dust and salt, wash as sparingly as possible. Yesterday and today we have been lucky. The rain has washed us off better than we would have dared do it ourselves under the shower. We are hoping that our water will hold out at least until next Tuesday, but I have doubts on that score.

Despite our pleasure in the rain, these successive squalls are not very reassuring as to the future. If bad weather really sets in, it will become dangerous for us to remain at anchor in the middle of all these reefs.

Philippe Sirot has brought me a beautifully made sketch of a galleon, drawn to the customary topological scale: two centimeters to the meter.

Saturday, August 3. Shortly after dawn, we begin sifting through the fragments brought up from the *James and Mary* last night. One of the first things to catch our eye is a small leaden seal-clamp of the kind used to seal containers shut. It has an inscription: *ARO 100.* The consensus is that it may mean "100 pieces of gold." If that is so, then we can probably expect to find the coins themselves somewhere in this pile of fragments.

This morning's haul consists of the various pieces of a chair, a large jar which was sealed, but empty, and a broken plate which seems to be made of pewter. Didi believes that it is not pewter, but silver. He says that if it were pewter it would be less tarnished than it actually is.

Everyone's spirits fluctuate according to what we find. This time, our underwater booty has been a source of encouragement, particularly the plate. Galleons often had table settings of silver. We use acid to strip away the tarnish, expecting to see the soft gleam of silver. Instead, the platter turns out to be pewter, after all.

Next, the divers send up more plates, and then several bones. Dr. Tassy says, after a moment's hesitation, that they are the bones of animals. We conclude that the divers are working in the area in which the livestock was kept — which was always in the forwardmost section of the galleon.

We are now going through four or five tons of coral per day, and I have never seen such a dedication to work. Everyone is at it from morning to night. On the *Calypso* we must work at the same pace as the divers do on the bottom; otherwise, we will be buried under debris. But the job of breaking open the coral and chipping away at the fragments, all under the blazing tropical sun, is more exhausting than working on the bottom with the airlift. Even so, every man aboard devotes all his waking hours to the task: the cameramen, the chef, the electrician — everyone is on the rear deck, hammering away at blocks of coral that weigh one or two tons.

Meanwhile, the airlift has been continually regurgitating into the two enormous metal baskets of the *James and Mary,* Remy's raft, which has become both a good omen to us because of its name, and an indispensable tool. This river of mire from the bottom is capable of rousing strong emotions on

Following page: A school of *Lutjanus kasmiae* swims by as the divers watch.

the *Calypso*, and particularly in Frédéric Dumas, who spends a good deal of time examining it. Often, we catch a glimpse of a glittering object, which then is swallowed up in the avalanche of coral fragments, rotten wood, and sand. If the object seems yellowish, we are certain it is gold; if white, it is undoubtedly silver. Then, the airlift is shut off and we begin digging and sifting in search of the elusive bit of metal, with our arms in the muddy pile up to our elbows. Most often, what we find is only a bit of metal or copper that has been polished to the color of gold or silver by its passage through the airlift.

During the afternoon, Gegène goes down to install an underwater television camera, on a tripod, on the bottom. It is focused on the work area, and its images are picked up on a screen in the wardroom. Reception is excellent. Now we can follow the excavation step by step. And we can see that the excavation has turned into a battle between our divers and the dense forest of staghorn coral that lies, dead and broken, in the ooze of the bottom. The airlift handles these sticks of coral with difficulty; and sometimes it jams. In such cases, we try to dislodge the coral by the simplest possible means; that is, by opening and closing the air hose. The effect is the same as that obtained by the use of an ordinary bathroom plunger. If that does not work, we must then disassemble the pipe at the point where it is bolted to the elbow.

Gaston digs out another lead seal from the trench, on the side of the mound and toward the galleon's axis. On one side, there is an intricate and undecipherable escutcheon of some kind. On the other is a shield, emblazoned with three fleurs-de-lis and surmounted by a crown. There is an inscription, but we can make out only a few letters: QUO FERA . . . There are also more cannon balls. We have found many of these. When we first break open the coral around them, they appear to be intact; but after several days they begin to crumble, and end up turning into dust.

Despite our backbreaking labor during the day, our evenings are always devoted to discussions on history, to reading, or to the study of documents that could prove useful to us in our archaeological work.

Tonight, a fierce discussion is raging in the wardroom about the lead seals that we have found. The general feeling is that they are probably the seals from bags of gold; and the interpretation of the inscription ARO 100 seems to be the obvious one: *Real de oro ciento* — one hundred golden *reales*.

Sunday, August 4. A few drops of rain, accompanied by a sharp wind from the south and southeast. We must keep in mind that we are in the middle of a coral bank that has already claimed innumerable victims.

Remy de Haenen and I dive with the first team — Bernard and Gaston — at 6:30 A.M. Our purpose is to inspect the trench that has been dug at the foot of the mound. It begins at the two parallel starboard cannon, and follows the mound for five or six yards before turning outward toward the staghorn-coral embankment shown on the map. The divers are having a great deal of trouble at that spot.

The trench is about three feet deep, and, in its first section, it has been neatly cut. Above it rises the mound of coral fragments surmounted by a broken cannon and a culverin (or long cannon). On the northeastern wall of the trench, however, we find something unusual: an iron bar, and, farther on, a wooden billet. They are both projecting from the wall and are perfectly straight. This seems to support the hypothesis that the mound is actually the galleon. It is a wild guess, of course; but not too farfetched when one remembers the rapidity with which coral grows in these waters.

Dumas observes that this northeastern wall is of white coral. In it, there is an eight-inch layer in which vestiges of the ship are found — wood, pottery, broken glass, etc. Below that is more white coral. This is difficult to understand. How could the entire galleon have been compressed into a layer eight inches thick, even given the action of the sea, wind, and waves?

At noon, the airlift succeeds finally in penetrating the staghorn embankment over a small area. We find no port cannon, and no cannon balls, but a large quantity of broken pottery and — finally — some very large iron nails which could be planking nails. This is undoubtedly the portside of the galleon. But where are its cannon?

The divers are becoming more and more impatient to know whether or not this galleon is actually *Nuestra Señora de la Concepción*. Their opinions have changed somewhat since the first few days. Some of the divers who were the most enthusiastic believers in *Nuestra Señora* have gradually lost their confidence. And others, such as Bernard Delemotte, who were initially skeptical, have now come to believe that we will really end up by finding gold.

I ask Bernard what he will do with his share if we do find a treasure.

"I think I'll buy some land; a lot of land, with trees and hills and flatlands. And a river through it. Perhaps there will be an old house alongside the river . . . ."

A strange dream for a diver and a sailor. Or maybe not so strange.

Suddenly, there is a discovery in the work area that seems to substantiate Delemotte's dream. Serge Foulon, in using the airlift carefully, has uncovered four small, apparently fragile objects. Riant gathers them together, putting two of them in each glove, and brings them up to us. It is another group of lead seals. Perhaps these will give us information on the nature of the galleon's cargo, and perhaps even on its nationality and its proprietor. Is it possible

Some of this coral, unfortunately, will have to be destroyed.

Work with the airlift requires effort, and unwavering attention, on the part of our divers.

Captain Cousteau (center) supervises the operation of the airlift.

that it was owned by a king of Spain?

The first step is to clean the seals, so that we may see the inscriptions. I let them soak in vinegar for a while, then I brush them carefully. An inscription begins to emerge, the same one that we had been unable to decipher on the seal we found earlier: *Florebo quo ferar* — "I will prosper wherever I go." We can also make out three *fleurs-de-lis*. But it is too soon to draw any conclusions. The fleur-de-lis was popular among the Spanish as well as among the French. Even so, if our galleon is indeed a Spanish ship, it now seems possible that it dates back no farther than the time of the first Bourbon king of Spain, Philip V — the grandson of Louis XIV, who reigned from 1700 to 1746.

The other clues, it seems to me, are no more dependable. The use of Latin for the inscription tells us nothing about the nationality of the ship, for Latin was commonly used for such purposes by all European nations. And so far as the motto itself is concerned, it does no more than express a sentiment that characterized all exploiters of the New World, and all adventurers everywhere.

I will keep these thoughts to myself. We continue our work, and I sense that everyone is going about his job with renewed confidence.

Unfortunately, it is clear that there will be a mountain of staghorn coral to get through, which spells trouble for the airlift. Perhaps we could use another kind of suction pipe, a "stovepipe," which would have a larger diameter — say, eight inches — and be about ten feet long. It might be able to handle the staghorn coral and other debris more easily than the six-inch pipe that we are presently using. We get to work on it immediately. Robino, our chief mechanic, and Willy roll sheet metal into the proper size and weld it; and in a few hours we are ready to try it. Bernard and Gaston are the first to use it, and they report that it has sufficient strength for the job, but that there will have to be modifications made. It is not properly balanced, its handles are clumsy, and its anchorage is unsteady.

Caillart and Marius, during their customary swim late in the afternoon, use a string to measure the angle from the ring of the galleon's forward anchor to the culverin lying on top of the mound. It is an angle of 13 degrees.

Another round jar is discovered, this one containing grape seeds. These jars are another riddle. There must have been many of them aboard the galleon; we have found a number of them, and the fragments of many more. They are strikingly similar to the earthenware jars or pots that are made everywhere in Central America today. They seem to have been used to store food — preserved fish and salted meat, especially. It is doubtful that they were made in Europe, and it therefore seems that our galleon, at some point, took on supplies at a Caribbean port.

The work area that we first laid out on the bottom is now practically clear of coral. Below the *Calypso*'s stem, there is a mountain of debris that reaches almost to the surface; it is all that is left of the coral brought up by the airlift and subsequently broken apart by our sledgehammers.

The *Calypso* is filthy. The walks and the decks are covered with bits of rusted iron and pieces of coral. And the latter give off an unpleasant odor as they dry in the sun.

Water is still in short supply, and still rationed. The divers no longer wash off the salt that remains on their bodies after the seawater has evaporated, and it irritates their skin unmercifully. They accept this in good humor, just as they bear with the compressor's roar. And, after their shifts with the airlift, they continue to work on deck, breaking coral. Nonetheless, their enthusiasm seems to have lessened by a couple of degrees.

Dumas, de Haenen, and I have a long discussion about our situation. We agree that, up to now, we have uncovered only a relatively small part of the ship; perhaps not more than a third of it. In all probability, we have been working on the galleon's forward section. We have found the remains of a brick oven, and the food jars; and galleons usually had their galleys, and stored their food supplies, in their forward sections.

But where is the rest of the ship?

Down there, near our work area, is a mound of coral. Is it possible that the mound is the ship? We decide to find out. With some difficulty, we insert a metal rod into the mound. It passes through the mound and reaches the ocean floor without having run into a trace of the ship.

The galleon, except for its forward section, has apparently vanished. Certainly, the rest of it was shattered during the storm that caused it to sink.

Tonight, after dinner, we sit in the wardroom. At this time of the day we usually relax, talk, and joke. Now, however, there are long silences, and everyone is occupied in reading one or another of the *Calypso's* volumes on the history of the Caribbean. It seems that we are no longer able to unwind sufficiently to relax after a hard day's work.

By now, the men of the *Calypso* look like nothing so much as a pirate crew. We no longer shave, in order to save water. Everyone's face is covered with bristles, and our hair is uncut. Our bodies are black from the hours spent on deck, in the sun, breaking coral. We all carry the marks of that job; on our bodies and arms, on top of our suntans and salt burns, we have long white streaks from coral dust. We look like giant sergeant major fish, with our coral-dust stripes.

A Lover of Coral

If we have retained our confidence, it is because we have confidence in Frédéric Dumas's expertise, in our own strength, and in our equipment. The presence of this confidence is perceptible especially among the divers, even though they must spend several hours a day in the water, and the rest of their time smashing coral.

Gaston, one of our best friends, has taken part in our expedition in the Red Sea and the Indian Ocean, and he knows our equipment as well as anyone. On this trip, he is even more enthusiastic than usual about the means that we have on hand. "This is the first time," he tells me, "that we have had to actually dig into coral. Sometimes the airlift, powerful as it is, is simply not powerful enough. Perhaps what we need is a drill of some kind — though I'm not sure that we could use one in the water. Even so, with the equipment that we have, I don't see how we can possibly not find anything. I know that everyone on board has faith in what we are doing, even if some of us sound as though we do not. When we complain, it is to kill time."

Then he stops and reflects for a minute. "To be frank, I don't know what to think about our galleon. It could be a ship that was carrying gold. And it could have been captured by pirates and then sunk after the gold had been removed. Still, we know that ships of that era always carried gold and silver. Somehow, I'm inclined to believe that we will end up finding a treasure under that mountain of coral."

Gaston's case is interesting. He is an electrical engineer, and a lover of coral; indeed, almost a fanatic on the subject. His job on the *Calypso* is to maintain the minisubs — a responsibility that he meets with the greatest diligence. By avocation, or perhaps by contagion, he is also a diver and an amateur biologist. In the Red Sea and in the Indian Ocean, once his work was done, and if we were near an atoll or a coral bank, he never missed the opportunity to dive in order to inspect his beloved coral. Sometimes, quite late at night, we would see his floodlight, and that of his friend Marcellin, far out in the water. Finally, I had to insist that they no longer go out on these midnight excursions. Two men, alone in the water at night, is too much a temptation for any marauding shark in the neighborhood. Thereafter, they went out quietly, hoping that no one would notice. I could hardly be too severe with him, for in the course of one of these secret expeditions in the Maladives, Gaston discovered a veritable oasis of marine life, which we all enjoyed enormously and which we named "Gaston's Isle."

What Gaston found particularly fascinating here on the Silver Bank was the mass of coral. Even with the tons of it that we brought up every day, the supply seemed inexhaustible. It was a mine of coral; but not a mine of inanimate minerals. These bits of stonelike material are skeletons, vestiges of life, just as human bones are.

Gaston, like Raymond Coll, is a quiet person, not given to long speeches. I know, however, that he is fascinated by the endless coral of the Bank. Combined with his fascination, there is an element of regret; or rather, an element of respect for the living beings whose skeletons we handle every day until our palms are raw and our backs ache.

It is interesting to think that William Phips, who came here to plunder this galleon, found it already buried under a thick layer of limestone; and that we, who are here three centuries later, find the same layer — only much thicker.

The airlift brings up a mixture of sand, coral and debris of all kinds, which it spits into the baskets of the raft.

A Souvenir of Archimedes

There is a considerable difference between work done on the ocean floor and work done in the open air, in that it is possible to do things in the water that we would not be strong enough to do elsewhere. To give an example straight from Archimedes: the great blocks of coral that we manage to move within the work area and then hoist aboard the *Calypso*, are almost impossible to handle once they are out of the water. They double in weight, become much too heavy for our only crane. To move a block from one part of the *Calypso* to another, we put it back in the water and move it while it is submerged.

A full basket is hoisted aboard the *Calypso*.

None of this is a matter of surprise to Frédéric Dumas, who has had much experience in marine archaeology. The only thing so far that has evoked even the mildest astonishment in him is our team's devotion to their work. "I've never seen anyone work so relentlessly," he says. "I've been trying to figure out where these young people find the energy to go on and on as they do. Certainly, the gold is part of it, for they all believe that we'll find it. But I think that the most important thing for them is that they feel they are pitting their own strength against that of the coral, and they are determined to win out in the end." Didi is probably right. Certainly, an important factor is that almost all the men of the *Calypso* are very young. Albert Falco ("Bébert") is no teen-ager, certainly; nor is Canoë Kientzy; but they are special: they are the most experienced and competent men we have— but they are not on this particular expedition. What puzzles Didi is that all our young men, most of whom he does not yet know, work at the same level of efficiency, and are just as serious about their tasks, as Bébert and Canoë.

Monday, August 5. Today is the last day of work before we have to return to San Juan for supplies — water, especially, but also food and a few tools. At six-thirty, I make my usual daily inspection of the work area. The trench is going well, and now extends across the entire beam of the galleon. But there is still no trace of cannon on the portside. Several planks have been uncovered, and the direction in which they are lying seems to confirm my hypothesis about the axis of the ship; but there are not enough of them to be absolutely sure. The sight of the three craters dug by the explosives of our predecessors here reminds me of something. Two of them are connected by a long, narrow trench. Now I remember, and the vision of another place rises in my mind: the battlefield of Verdun.

Today's work plan is clearly defined. Raymond Coll and J. P. Durand will carefully remove the thick, individual planks from the crater in which we found the barrel of nails, after having numbered them. Then, with the airlift, they will try to cut an opening to the hull and the keel. All this, of course, will be done under the eye of the camera.

In practice, our plan does not work terribly well. The process of photographing and filming the work requires a great deal of time, because the water has already begun to cloud. Moreover, Raymond is disgusted. Under the planks, he found only sand, and fragile blocks of some kind that look like dead coral, or viscous sand.

At this point, Didi takes over and changes the plan somewhat. He begins by using the airlift to dispose of a twelve-inch layer of debris that covers the galleon's deck, in the forward part of the ship. Under it, he finds several square yards of large, parallel dovetailed planks. The other teams are in-

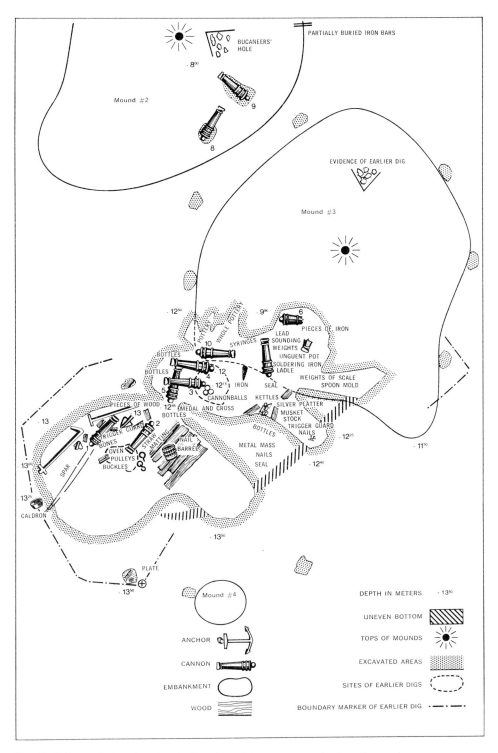

PARTIALLY BURIED IRON BARS

BUCANEERS'
HOLE

- 8⁰⁰

Mound #2

9

8

EVIDENCE OF EARLIER DIG

Mound #3

- 12⁵⁰   POTTERY   - 9⁰⁰   6   PIECES OF IRON
         WHOLE POTTERY
         SYRINGES   LEAD
    10   SOUNDING
BOTTLES   WEIGHTS
                     UNGUENT POT
BOTTLES   4   12   SOLDERING IRON
         5   3 SEAL   LADLE
    - 12¹⁵   IRON   WEIGHTS OF SCALE
                     CANNONBALLS   SPOON MOLD
PIECES OF WOOD   KETTLES
         - 12⁸⁵   SILVER PLATTER
- 13   13   BOTTLES MEDAL AND CROSS   MUSKET
         TRIGGER CURRI   2   STOCK
         BONES   MATTING BOTTLES TRIGGER GUARD
- 13⁰⁰   OVEN STRAW   NAIL   NAILS
         PULLEYS   BARREL   METAL MASS
    SPAR BUCKLES   NAILS   - 12²⁵
- 13²⁵   SEAL   - 12⁴⁰
CALDRON   - 11⁵⁰

- 13⁵⁰

PLATE

- 13⁵⁰

         Mound #4   DEPTH IN METERS   - 13⁵⁰

ANCHOR   UNEVEN BOTTOM

CANNON   TOPS OF MOUNDS

EMBANKMENT   EXCAVATED AREAS

WOOD   SITES OF EARLIER DIGS

                     BOUNDARY MARKER OF EARLIER DIG

Detail of the work site, showing the location of the cannon and other discoveries.

Left: A single day's haul of cannon balls. Behind is the compressor, whose roar deafens us all day long.

Below: At work in one section of the site. Captain Cousteau is at the center.

Above right: The divers must often work in a cloud of mud from the bottom.

Below right: A basket is dumped onto the rear deck, and the pile of debris to be broken open grows.

structed to continue working in the area where Didi has begun. By nightfall, a large section of the galleon's forward starboard has been uncovered. Not far from where the foremast should be, we find a huge iron ring, and a very large iron crock yoked to the iron straps of a winding block — all exactly where they should be. Next to these items is a well-preserved primitive pile driver, made of wood. The debris, upon examination, contains a large quantity of rather handsome bottles, all broken. These must have either been stored on the bridge, or else carried there to be used by the survivors of the wreck who remained on the reef.

By now, Dumas and I are almost sure of one thing: that the ship is in better condition than we originally thought. The fact that Raymond found only coral under the planks of the deck means that the rest of the galleon is down under that limestone. After all, Dumas and I know what happens to a wooden ship in the Mediterranean; but no one knows what effect coral has on wood over a long period of time. Far from destroying it, it may well act as a preservative.

Remy de Haenen never tires of assuring us that we are dealing with a very large galleon, of which we have so far uncovered only a small part. Didi agrees, to the extent that the size of the anchors, the weight of the cannon, and the dimensions of the hardware indicate that it was indeed large. But, so far, neither Dumas nor I have been able to uncover any evidence as to the age of this ship — which is a crucial point in determining whether or not it is *Nuestra Señora de la Concepción.*

After lunch, I telephone our Puerto Rican agent to tell him our expected time of arrival tomorrow. He informs me that my son, Jean-Michel, is in San Juan.

Shortly before dinner, I have my drawing table brought up to the wardroom, with an overlay of the galleon showing the location of the various hard objects we have found — the anchors, cannon, etc. Then, I make a situation report to the assembled crew, the point of which is to show that there is still room for hope in our quest.

After dinner, we dump another pile of coral on the rear deck and set to work. The size of the pile indicates to our satisfaction that, with the improvements we have made in the organization of our shifts and in the airlift apparatus, we have considerably increased our daily output. We work until very late that night; and find, in those tons of coral and mud, a single prize: one blackened nutshell.

Tuesday, August 6. The preparations for our run into San Juan have begun very early, and Didi, De Haenen, and I go down for the daily inspection.

The lead seal of the West Indies Company. This was used to mark all objects sold by the Company, and signified that the object had to be re-exported within six months.

One one side of the seal is the motto of the West Indies Company, *Florebo quo Ferar*, and three fleurs-de-lis. On the other side, a silver mountain. The fleurs-de-lis symbolize the sky of France, separated from the field by a band of gold. The whole is surmounted by the royal crown. On both sides of the shield, two shadowy figures represent Indians.

Yesterday's discoveries have answered many questions about the position of the sunken ship. It now seems likely that her axis lies on a line with the broken cannon on top of the mound. Before returning to the *Calypso*, we take a look at the trench on the starboard side of the galleon, and Dumas uncovers another cannon. This one is almost parallel to the two cannon near it, but faces in the opposite direction. Most important, we note that it is trapped both *in* — and *under* — the surrounding coral rock. Here is striking confirmation of the hypothesis that the mound and the galleon are one and the same. The missing two-thirds of the ship have been found.

We also uncover some pieces of rigging, and two more large, but rather slender, anchors.

Later, at lunch, Dumas, who has had experience with a sixteenth-century ship in the Mediterranean, explains that anchor rings at that time were usually very large. Interestingly enough, those on the anchors that we found this morning are of a good size. Moreover, they have very large flukes — which, according to Didi, is a good sign. An anchor manufactured in the right century would be all we need to convince us that our galleon is indeed *Nuestra Señora de la Concepción*.

During the morning's work, the divers also found a sword hilt, and a pistol — little of which is left, other than rust-colored impressions within the broken coral. It is impossible to identify the century of origin of either of these finds.

It is clear by now that there are *two* decks on the galleon, one very close to the other. Moreover, what probably happened was that the upper part of the hull settled on the bottom, while the lower part was surrounded by, and held up by and in the coral.

Before weighing anchor, we take the airlift apparatus aboard. The metal baskets, however, are left on the ocean floor, and the *James and Mary* is scuttled for safekeeping. We will raise it when we return. During the sinking, Remy remained in the water to make sure that no damage was done to his brainchild. He was so preoccupied that he did not notice a barracuda, very similar to those we have seen at Shab Rumi, swimming around him and looking at him hungrily. The divers knew this particular barricuda rather well, so to speak, and had named him Jules. Michel Deloire captured the whole sequence on film. It should be very amusing to watch.

The compressor has been taken down below, and the entire *Calypso* is scrubbed from one end to the other. And tonight we will be able to take showers. Then we get underway, maneuvering through the channel without mishap. Once out in the open water, everyone tries to sleep, but the sea is quite rough and most of us are awake. The farther we go toward the east, the rougher the water becomes.

Right: Some marvelous coral — the skeletons of which we pounded apart until our hands were raw and our backs ached.

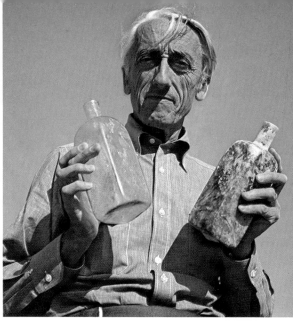

The medal of St. Francis that we found among fragments of coral brought up in a basket.

Many square bottles, some of them intact, were found in the wreck's cargo.

EIGHT

The Great Treasure

On November 28, 1686, a sleek frigate of 200 tons dropped anchor in the Bay of Samarea, off the Spanish island of Hispaniola. Like all vessels of the period, whether merchantmen or warships, the frigate was heavily armed, with twenty-two cannon projecting from its portholes. Despite this formidable armament, the frigate's mission was a peaceful one. England and Spain were no longer at war. Several decades before, in 1648, the Peace of Westphalia had brought to an end the conflict that had lasted for a hundred years. And peace had been confirmed in 1671, by a new treaty. Not even two treaties, however, were enough to safeguard the security of the Caribbean. Buccaneers and pirates did not consider themselves bound by the diplomatic amenities.

The captain of the frigate, William Phips, boarded a launch and was taken to shore, where a crowd awaited him. The people on the dock were all his friends, for he was well known and well liked in the islands. Although he had been born far to the north, in Boston, Massachusetts, he had been engaged in business in the Caribbean since he was a young man. Everyone admired his loyalty to his friends. And everyone admired his prudence, for never once had he engaged in piracy. Rather, it was his business to supply provisions to the whole of the Caribbean area, pirates or not. It was a difficult job, and one requiring precisely those qualities for which Phips was known: consummate tact, business acumen, and maritime skill.

The Spanish crown, in theory at least, still retained its monopoly on supplies for its subjects in the New World; but those subjects would have been virtually without food or clothing if they had depended upon His Most Catholic Majesty for them. They relied instead upon foreign ships — those of Phips's, in this case — who smuggled these contraband items to their shores. At the same time, of course, Phips had to furnish supplies to the enemies of the Spanish crown; that is to the privateers, pirates, and corsairs. He therefore walked a tightrope between the Spaniards and their mortal enemies.

The purpose of his present visit was to deliver some of that superior merchandise: painted tankards, fine stockings, hats, serge, buttons, swords and daggers, scissors, liquor, and gunpowder. And, everyone noted, Phips had brought these goods on a fine new ship bearing the name of the English sovereigns, *James and Mary*. The frigate itself was the object of admiration and envy; for it was an outstanding example of the work done in the shipyards of the Thames.

One of Phips's first calls ashore was to the Spanish lieutenant governor; and the next was to the captain of the local garrison. To these officials he offered valuable presents. He was then in a position to begin selling his goods. The entire cargo was liquidated in four days, in exchange for a large number of gold and silver coins. The *James and Mary* thereupon took on supplies of food and water, and sailed out of the Bay for a destination which was unknown to any of his friends on shore. For, in those days, especially in the Caribbean, one took care not to inquire too closely into the affairs of one's friends, or into their background.

A Boston Carpenter

The New England coast of North America in the middle of the seventeenth century was still untamed, and the recently installed colonists had all they could do to protect themselves against the forces of nature and the attacks of the Indians. Many of these immigrants were Puritans, who had left their native lands in order to safeguard their religious convictions. They were people known for strength of character and resoluteness of will.

A small group of these men and women settled in an especially wild spot at the mouth of the Kennebec River, in Maine. There, they built a village, which they named Pemaquid. And it was to Pemaquid, not many years later, that the shipbuilders of Boston came to buy the lumber for their ships.

William Phips was born in Pemaquid, in 1651, the twenty-first child of a Puritan family. His father, James Phips, was a blacksmith, and very poor. At an early age, therefore, William was expected to earn his keep. At first, he worked as a shepherd. Later, he took up carpentry, and went to Boston, where he was employed in a shipyard.

The shipyards of New England were highly regarded, and enjoyed a brisk trade, not only in the actual construction of ships but also in their repair and maintenance. A wooden ship did not take too long to build; but that was only the beginning of the work on it. Any storm might splinter its masts, damage its hull, and open its seams. Algae and barnacles would cover its hull and diminish its speed. It often had to have its leaks repaired, and its sides scraped and tarred. And this was the trade in which William Phips came to specialize. Meanwhile, he learned also to dive, and to see in the water by looking through a "calking glass" — a piece of glass held in a round wooden frame.

Phips built for himself, with his own hands, a cutter, which he christened the *Star of Boston*. Next, he bought and repaired a decrepit schooner. And then he was ready to undertake what had long been his ambition: trade in the Caribbean.

It is not difficult to understand how Boston, in the latter half of the seventeenth century, could awaken such thoughts in a young man. To the shipyards came vessels of every sort, and men of every kind. With them they brought tales of faraway places, of Tortuga and Jamaica, and stories of adventure and wealth beyond the imaginings of a simple Puritan boy from Maine. For by now the sun had set on Spanish supremacy, and a famous buccaneer named Henry Morgan — known to later generations simply as Morgan the Pirate — was following in the footsteps of his predecessors, Hawkins and Drake. Morgan, it was said, had attacked and plundered Porto Bello, the port of embarkation for the king of Spain's gold. He had seized Maracaibo. In 1671, he had marched across the Isthmus of Darien at the head of twelve hundred men, to pillage and burn Panama, which was then reputed to be the wealthiest city of the New World.

Such was the stuff of which the dreams of New England's youth were made. William Phips, however, the son of a poor blacksmith, did not share those dreams without reservation. He could not imagine himself as an adventurer, and he had heard too much of pirates to have any illusions about them. The wealth they ripped from the feeble grasp of Spain was spent as quickly as

Above right: Among the sea fans, sponges and coral are some Blue Chromis and a Haemulon.

Below right: A school of surgeonfish, some *Acanthurus leucosternon*, and, in the background in the grotto, an *Acanthurus guttatus*.

opportunity allowed, or was dissipated in gambling. Phips wanted to be wealthy; but he wanted wealth that was more solid, and more respectable. Besides, there were other ways in which an intelligent and enterprising young man could make his fortune in the Caribbean.

Phips was able to borrow the money necessary to buy his first cargo of merchandise; and, one morning, the; *Star of Boston*, under the command of its twenty-three-year-old owner, set sail for the fabled Caribbean. At the time, Phips was Boston's youngest ship's captain; and probably younger than any captain in the fleets of England, Holland, or Spain.

His first voyage was an unqualified success. He was able to sell his cargo at a good profit, and, with the proceeds, to buy sugar, vanilla, indigo, cochineal (a scarlet dye), and, above all, tobacco.

A Survivor

Phips, in the course of his voyages to the Caribbean, had an experience that was to affect the rest of his life. One day, while he was resting, he heard a cry for help. It seemed to be coming from a delapidated barracks nearby; and the repeated shouts were in English. Phips arrived just in time to save the life of an old man who was being beaten by two natives. He revived the old man as best he could, and then asked him why the Indians had attacked him, since the man obviously possessed nothing that thieves might have coveted.

"I have not always been as poor as you see me," the man replied. "But now I have only one treasure left: a secret. And the men who attacked me wanted to rob me even of that. I will share that secret with you, since you have saved my life. Perhaps you will help me to find enough gold to sweeten the remaining years of my life."

"Does your secret have to do with gold?"

"Listen, and I will tell you. My name is Ottavio. I am not a Spaniard, but I have sailed on the galleons of Spain. I never missed the opportunity, on each voyage, to do some trading for myself, as everyone else did. I even succeeded in putting together a modest fortune. My last voyage was as helmsman aboard the flagship of the Fleet of Tierra Ferma, a galleon called *Nuestra Señora de la Concepción*. My ship was wrecked one night on the terrible reefs of the Silver Bank. I was one of the survivors of that catastrophe, and I was able to make my way to the island of Hispaniola. But I had lost everything: gold, an emerald — the whole of my profit from the sale of my own goods, and all the money that I had been able to save.

The only known portrait of William Phips. (Mansell Collection, London.)

"I was still young at that time, and I could have returned to the sea and tried to rebuild my fortune. But I was prevented by the thought of that galleon lying on the ocean floor. I knew that she contained enormous wealth, for I had watched her being loaded: ingots from Peru and Mexico, precious stones from Colombia, and pearls from Venezuela. I could not put her out of my mind.

"I returned once, at great risk to myself, in an Indian canoe, and I saw the galleon's masts beneath the surface, in shallow water. But I was alone, and by then I was already old. All I brought back with me was a broken sword.

"I would like to lead you to the spot where the galleon lies. Look, I will draw you a map. Here is Porto Plata. From there, one must sail north-north-east. But beware of the reefs! If I should die, I will leave this map for you . . . ."

William Phips did not doubt the truth of the old man's story, but he knew the area well enough to be certain that, if he was able to find and recover the treasure of *Nuestra Señora de la Concepción*, he would become the prey of every pirate ship in the Caribbean. It would be impossible to keep such a venture secret; and the *Star of Boston* was obviously incapable of holding off three or four pirate ships. He would therefore need one or more heavily armed frigates, as well as other powerful means of protection from attack.

Wrecking

William Phips had often thought about the wealth that disappeared beneath the waves of the Caribbean almost every year. As everyone knew, there

The divers are on friendly terms with the fish of the Silver Bank. Here, a porgy is being fed by hand.

Left: The *Calypso*'s hoist brings up an old anchor covered with coral. Note the unusual width of this anchor's flukes.

were sunken Spanish ships virtually everywhere in the sea. The English had been the first to take advantage of that situation by founding a profitable business: the recovery of treasure from sunken galleons. From the beginning of the seventeenth century, Englishmen had occupied themselves in what they called "wrecking"; that is, recovering sunken cargoes. It was a career made possible by the fact that almost all of the ships lost in the New World went down in shallow water; they were washed up against rocks and reefs, where divers could reach them.* Moreover, it was well known on Hispaniola that Admiral Villavicencio, who had been absolved by the Casa de Contractación of any blame in the loss of his ship, had attempted several times, in vain, to find the wreck of *Nuestra Señora*.

By the latter half of the seventeenth century, Port Royal, on Jamaica, had become the headquarters of the wreckers who worked the Silver Bank, and elsewhere, for their own profit. Tales of sunken treasure, however, were not confined to that island, and there were many "secret maps" revealing the location of this wealth. With respect to *Nuestra Señora de la Concepción*, there was no doubt in anyone's mind that the galleon had been heavily loaded with treasure, or that she had gone down in the Silver Bank.

*Diving was an ancient art in the Caribbean. Columbus had remarked that the Indians of what is presently Venezuela were in the habit of diving for pearls. The best divers in the New World, however, were the Indians of Lucayes (The Bahamas), whose services the Spanish often employed in their attempts to salvage their cargoes.

William Phips, in pursuit of the sunken galleon, sold his *Star of Boston* and took passage on a ship to England. There, he knew, one could always find men willing to finance an expedition that promised a high return on their investment. And, in fact, he found one such man in the person of the English king, Charles II, an amiable sovereign, more French than English, who was overly fond of amusing himself and who, consequently, was always short of money. With King Charles's backing, Phips was able to obtain a frigate of eighteen cannon; the *Rose of Algiers.*

Thus outfitted, Phips returned to the Caribbean and made directly for the Silver Bank. Despite the constant threat of hurricanes, he spent days studying the bottom through his calking glass, and he sent out all of his boats to study the area. Nothing was found, however, other than marvelous coral formations, an abundance of "plumes of the sea" (which were to be known later as sea fans), the fleeting shapes of barracudas, and the dark shadows of sharks. Phips regretted not having landed at Hispaniola to take on native divers; he had been afraid of sharing his secret with too many people.

In the meantime, Phips's supplies were running low; and finally, his crew rebelled and refused to continue the search. He was forced to return to Hispaniola, where he learned that Ottavio had recently died. Now almost completely discouraged, Phips set sail for England. He was bringing back only one "treasure": a sea fan, in which was embedded a silver ingot. This had been found in the Silver Bank, and had been a source of great encouragement to Phips at first. But a thorough search had revealed that there were no more ingots, and indeed, no sunken galleon, in the area of his search. Once in London, Phips would have to explain this failure to his royal patron.

Upon docking in England, however, Phips learned that Charles II was dead. He had been succeeded by his brother, James II. The new king was as dour as his predecessor had been genial. He was suspicious by nature, vindictive, intolerant, and narrow-minded. In his name, England was currently being subjected to an orgy of hangings, torture, and public whippings. And Phips fared no better than the natives. As soon as he stepped from the deck of the *Rose of Algiers*, he was made aware that he was no longer in favor, and was denied access to the royal court.

Phips had been through too much already to lose hope at this point. He had powerful friends at court, whom he asked to intercede on his behalf. Chief among these friends was Sir John Marlborough, former First Lord of the Admiralty, who had preserved his influence with the king even though he had lost his office. Another was Henry Christopher, Duke of Albemarle, an ambitious young man and a gambler, who had need of much money. Sir John obtained Phips's release from prison; and Albemarle obtained, from the

Portrait of King Charles II of England, by Philippe de Champaigne. Charles financed Phips's first expedition. (Cleveland Museum.)

king, a "concession," dated June 18, 1686, authorizing him to seek out and recover all sunken ships lying to the north of Hispaniola. One-tenth of any treasure found was to belong to King James.

With such friends behind him, Phips had no trouble finding other backers, and he was able to buy a ship of 200 tons, armed with twenty-two cannon, which was called the *Bridgewater*. Phips, in a diplomatic gesture, renamed it the *James and Mary*. Then he bought another ship, this one smaller and carrying only ten cannon, and called it *Henry of London*. (The Christian name of the Duke of Albemarle was Henry.)

According to the terms of the contract with his associates, Phips was to receive one-sixteenth of any treasure found, after all expenses had been paid (including the cost of the ships) and the king had received his one-tenth. What remained was to be divided among Phips's partners, of whom there were six.

On this trip, Phips was carrying with him a bizarre apparatus that he intended to use in order to recover the treasure of *Nuestra Señora*. It was a large barrel-shaped device, circled with iron rings and ballasted by heavy weights. This contraption was called a "Catalan bell." It was supposed to be lowered vertically into the sea, so that the air at the top of the barrel could not escape. This air was to be the oxygen supply of the diver. The Catalan bell was known for many years before Phips's time; but few divers had been sufficiently adept in its use, or sufficiently courageous, to risk using it.

A Secret Mission

The *James and Mary* was also carrying a commercial cargo, so that there might be a profit from the expedition even if the treasure-hunting mission was unsuccessful. The cargo consisted of merchandise intended for Phips's friends: the pirates, and the colonists of Spain.

Phips's two ships sailed from England on September 12, 1686. On November 28, the *James and Mary* dropped anchor, as already noted, in the Bay of Samarea. The *Henry of London,* however, was not with it. It had gone instead to a small port on the same island of Hispaniola, called Porto Plata, on a secret mission. Its assignment was to recruit experienced divers. Phips was not going to make the same mistake twice. For the selection of these divers, he depended upon the judgment of his second-in-command, Henry Rogers, who was captain of the *Henry of London*. When Phips's own *James and Mary* left the Bay of Samana, it was to join Rogers in Porto Plata.

In order not to arouse the curiosity of the town, Phips went about his usual business; that is, he docked in the little harbor and displayed his merchandise for inspection by the Porto Plateans. Meanwhile, the *Henry of London* quietly weighed anchor and sailed northward. Rogers, following Phips's instructions, was bound for the Silver Bank to begin the search for *Nuestra*

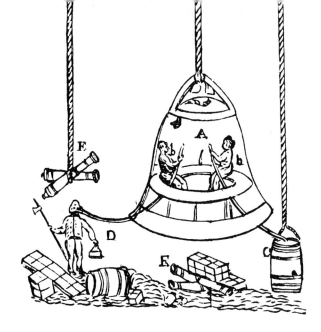

Drawing of the diving bell employed by Phips in the Silver Bank.
A - the bell
B - diver seated on a round bench
C - air tube
D - diver breathing air trapped in the bell
E - the wreck

Señora de la Concepción. With him were three divers, and his first mate was a man named William Covell. This was on January 13, 1687. For several weeks, Phips remained at Porto Plata, vending his wares; an innocuous smuggler, to all appearances. Then, on February 7, the *Henry of London* returned to Porto Plata, and Rogers made his report.

His ship had reached the Silver Bank on January 29. The search for *Nuestra Señora* had been conducted by William Covell personally, in a small canoe, similar to those used by the Indians, which had probably been designed and built by Phips, the former carpenter. The galleon they were seeking had been found, eventually, wedged among the coral, in six to eight fathoms of water. It was so covered with coral that it had been almost impossible to tell the poop from the prow. The search party had picked up an ingot, a disc of precious metal, and returned to the *Henry of London* to announce their discovery. Then, they had returned to the wreck, marked the site with a buoy, and taken other ingots, some pieces of eight, and some broken plate. For three days they had continued to work; but then the weather became threatening, and they were compelled either to leave or to face being trapped on the Silver Bank by a storm. From there, they had made their way back to Porto Plata.

The Treasure

Phips was eager to return to the Silver Bank with Rogers, but first his two ships had to be put in proper condition. Phips was an ingenious smuggler, and a determined treasure hunter; but he was first and foremost a seaman, and he knew the ways of ships and the sea. Both the *James and Mary* and the *Henry of London* were heeled, and their sides scraped thoroughly, so that they would be more maneuverable. Then food supplies — salted food, according to the Spanish custom — was taken aboard. Finally, the two ships sailed from Porto Plata on February 17. By February 22, they were riding at anchor near the Silver Bank. And immediately William Covell set to work. Before nightfall of that first day, he had brought up some pieces of eight. That night, there was great excitement aboard the ships.

The diving continued as long as the weather permitted. In the beginning, the individual pieces were registered by the ship's "scribe," as soon as they were deposited on the deck of the *James and Mary*. The register, however, contained references only to the gold coins, silver ingots, and metal plate. Later, when the sea was calm, the pieces of eight and the ingots were carefully weighed. Everything was written down in the account books maintained by Thomas Wadington, Phips's assistant, and by Charles Kelly, former page of the Duke of Albemarle. These accounts clearly showed that the divers had found the treasure room of the galleon, for they noted that silver plate had been found — which could have come only from that room — as well as sacks of pieces of eight weighing 1138 pounds.

Despite its success, the expedition was not without problems. Work had to be stopped several times because the native divers "were not feeling well," or because it was Sunday. The fact that the weather was ideal was apparently irrelevant. Then, on one occasion, the wind rose, and the *Henry of London* broke its moorings and smashed its rudder. It narrowly avoided being thrown against the reefs, but was saved at the last moment by the skill of its captain and the ability of its crew.

For two months Phips and his party remained on the Silver Bank. Long before the end of that time, sailors and divers alike were exhausted. Sometimes a diver would return to the surface, out of breath, pale, trembling, and vomiting blood. Much treasure was being recovered, but it was at the price of incredible human effort. Finally, the lack of food, the stale water, and the sight of so much wealth that would never be theirs, brought the crew to the verge of mutiny. It took all of Phips's authority to restore order; and it also took a promise that every man would receive a share in the booty before they would consent to return to work.

One morning, Phips was disagreeably surprised to see another ship, a sloop, enter the Silver Bank and drop anchor not far from the site of *Nuestra Señora*. Aboard were two men who had accompanied Phips on his first voyage to the Bank, William Davis and Abraham Adderly. The little sloop was not particularly worrisome to Phips; a single broadside from the *James and Mary*'s cannon could have sent it to the bottom in minutes; and no one in the

Above: Captain Cousteau, Surrounded by the *Calypso*'s divers, examines the ocean floor in an attempt to make out the shape of the wreck.

Right: Aboard the *Calypso*, Paul Zuéna takes inventory of the numerous ceramics brought up.

A seventeenth-century galleon. Drawing by Leon Haffner.

Caribbean would have been the wiser, or, for that matter, cared. But that was not Phips's way of doing business. Instead, the New Englander struck a bargain with the intruders. He would allow them to prospect in the vicinity of the wreck, on condition that they agreed to give him half of whatever they found. Moreover, Phips would have the use of Davis' sloop, and of a shallop, or small open boat, belonging to Adderly.

Difficulties were beginning to multiply for Phips and his crew. The Catalan bell was used several times, but it proved impossible to handle except in a calm sea. Moreover, the broken bottom and the coral heads threatened at any moment to upset it and destroy the divers' supply of air. To make matters worse, the treasure that now remained on *Nuestra Señora* was more difficult to reach, being contained in a hold deep within the ship. The divers often returned empty-handed, explaining that the galleon no longer contained anything of value that could be reached.

Phips succeeded one day in persuading the best of his divers to go down deeper than he had ever been into the broken hull. The diver stayed down for a long time, and when he returned his face was covered with blood. He was so weak that he had to be hauled aboard. When he was able to speak again, he announced that he had found a great chest, and touched it, but it was so heavy that he had been unable to move it.

For three days the divers worked, tying lines to the chest and dragging it out of the wreck. Finally, they got it aboard the *James and Mary*. It was opened, with an ax, to disclose an Arabian Nights treasure of pearls, emeralds, rubies, diamonds, golden jewelry, statues of unknown gods with hideous faces, and crystal cups so fine that they broke with the sound of cathedral chimes.

The sight of this incredible wealth restored the enthusiasm of everyone aboard. But enthusiasm was not enough. The *James and Mary* and the *Henry of London* were, by now, dangerously low on food. On March 29, therefore, Phips dispatched the shallop to Jamaica for provisions.

While waiting for the shallop's return, the diving continued. The men were now so weak, however, that they were unable to spend much time in the galleon; and no threats or blandishments were able to make them regain their strength.

By April 19, the shallop had not yet returned from Jamaica, and provisions were now almost completely exhausted. Moreover, a gathering of clouds on the horizon announced an approaching hurricane. In these circumstances, Phips had no alternative but to leave the Bank, and he ordered the ships to get under sail.

The wind had hardly moved the ships before the watch announced the sighting of a ship. It was a brigantine, carrying twenty cannon. Phips recognized it immediately as the *Gloire*, a French privateer celebrated in the Caribbean for its feats of derring-do. It was doubtful that even the combined artillery of the two ships under Phips's command — twenty-two cannon on the *James and Mary*, and ten on the *Henry of London* — could prevail. Moreover, Phips was determined to avoid a fight at any price, even a fight in which he stood a chance of being the winner. He had no wish to risk his cargo of gold, silver plate, and precious stones. Taking advantage of the wind, he changed his course. The brigantine followed suit. The wind was brisk, and for a whole day the chase continued, with the English ships being able to maintain distance between themselves and the pirate vessel. By nightfall, however, it became obvious that the pirates were gaining, and that there must soon be an encounter.

The wind continued strong all night. There was no moon, and the darkness was impenetrable. The *James and Mary* and the *Henry of London* were under full sail, and no one was able to see where they were heading. Even the French ship was scarcely visible. Taking advantage of the situation, Phips ordered that no lights be shown, not even the glow of a pipe, and that all conversation was to be in a low voice. Then, in the middle of the night, he ordered a turn to starboard — a course which would bring the ships straight to

A diver digging at the foot of a coral massif.

a dangerous reef called the Handkerchief Bank. When the sound of breakers could be heard from the bridge of the *James and Mary*, Phips ordered the sails furled and all anchors dropped. The sea became rougher, squall followed squall all night, and everyone prayed that the moorings would hold. During the night, the *James and Mary* was thrown against the reefs, but no damage was done.

The gray light of dawn revealed that the two ships were alone on the sea. The *Gloire*, thrown off the track by Phips's maneuver, had apparently continued on a straight course.

But Phips's trouble was just beginning. His ships were at the northeastern tip of the Handkerchief Bank, and the hurricane was catching up with them. The wind was mounting, and great black clouds billowed across the sky. The rain fell in torrents. The crewmen on watch at the prows of the ships could not see thirty feet in front of them.

Phips set a course toward Florida, and the ships moved out into the open sea, tossed about by giant waves. The crew, weakened by two months of backbreaking labor, were fighting for their lives. Finally, on April 20, the sea slackened somewhat, and the vessels anchored off Cotton Key. The launches made several trips to shore to fill the ships' water barrels, and to buy exotic fruits from the natives: papayas, mangoes, and pineapples.

Captain Cousteau examines a jar that a diver has just brought up. The jar was used to store shipboard provisions.

William Phips had no desire to push his luck further by calling at the ports of the Caribbean. Instead, on May 2, he set sail directly for England. The crossing was uneventful so far as the *James and Mary* was concerned. On the first day, the *Henry of London*, a slower ship, fell behind and was lost from sight. No other sail was sighted until May 31, when an English ship, the *Lisbon de Barbados,* under the command of a Captain Price, came into view. Phips took the opportunity to go aboard the *Lisbon* in order to buy supplies.

On June 4, within sight of the Scilly Isles, the two ships separated. And, on June 6, after avoiding the Barbary pirates who swarmed in the Channel, he arrived at Deptford, the port from which he had sailed nine months before.

Phips's partners had been notified of his arrival and were all on hand. His Majesty's Government had also been notified, and Sir Samuel Pepys, the celebrated secretary of the Admiralty, had sent a representative with orders to station a guard around the *James and Mary* in order to safeguard the king's one-tenth of the treasure.

Pepys was as careful as he was competent, and he took every possible precaution to see that nothing unforeseen happened to the booty from *Nuestra Señora.* He even had to satisfy himself as to the honesty of the officials of the Exchequer who boarded Phips's vessel. When the High Court of the Admiralty attempted to interfere by ordering the entire treasure to be seized, Pepys simply forbade the order to be carried out.

The foreign diplomats in London then tried their hand at despoiling the *James and Mary*. Ambassador Barillon wrote at length on the subject to his master in France, King Louis XIV. And Moreau was no less assiduous in corresponding with the king of Poland. The Ambassador of His Most Catholic Majesty of Spain registered his outrage in an interminable memorandum to James II. The treasure had been taken from *Nuestra Señora de la Concepción*, he stormed, which was a Spanish vessel; therefore, the treasure belonged to Spain. He then brought suit before the Admiralty court; but the judges, to no one's surprise, rejected his claim.

The Division of Spoils

In London, the success of William Phips, the Duke of Albemarle's good fortune, and the size of the treasure and its division, were the subject of every conversation.

Before long, three officials of the royal treasury, and Charles Duncombe, the famous goldsmith, appeared on the *James and Mary* with orders to weigh the treasure and measure out the king's tenth according to the terms of the contract of July 18, 1686. Their great scale was installed on the *Monmouth*, a royal ship docked alongside the *James and Mary*, and they proceeded to weigh an incredible quantity of silver: 35,538 pounds of it. In addition, there were 27,556 pounds of silver in bars, 347 pounds of plate in precious metals, 25 pounds of gold, and a large number of pieces of eight. Finally, there was a separate item of 3770 pounds of silver registered under the cryptic heading of "Seamen's silver" — which was the 50 per cent received by Phips from the booty found by William Davis and Abraham Adderly.

Despite the precise figures given in the inventory, it is possible that the weights were not as accurate as they might have been. But merely to have undertaken the task, and compiled a list, was an accomplishment; for the officials of the royal treasury were known for their ability to create disorder, their inefficiency, and their tendency to waste money.

The king's share easily came to 20,700 pounds, and that of the seven remaining partners was proportionately large. Their investment had amounted to £3200, and they were receiving in return thirty-four tons of precious metal worth, in 1687, £207,600.

The common seamen received a share: from £20 to £60 each; while the officers, the carpenters, etc., were each given £1000.

The portion of the Duke of Albemarle was over £43,000. It was said that

Medal commemorating William Phips's exploit. On one side of the medal are the English sovereigns, James II and Queen Mary. On the other is Phips's ship, and (in the foreground) two canoes, with sailors aboard, out hunting for treasure. (This last representation copies the sculpture from Phips's tomb.) (British Museum, Department of Coins and Medals, London.)

he had the gold melted down in his own garden; and his friends were heard to remark that His Grace would surely "spend the rest of his days near his furnaces."

William Phips, the former Boston carpenter, for his share received the one-sixteenth provided for in the contract; that is, approximately £11,000, not counting the items of less value that had been found along with the silver, jewels, and gold. The remainder of the cargo comprised six bronze cannon (which were given to the Tower of London), candlesticks, cups and plates, broken pieces of gold, buttons, pearls, collars, a great golden chain, and a hatband of braided gold. If one may believe a later deposition, given under oath, by the disgruntled cook of the *James and Mary*, the golden chain went directly to Mrs. Phips, without being entered in the official inventory; and the hatband went just as directly onto Phips's hat. Whatever the truth of the matter, it is known that the Duke of Albemarle presented to Mrs. Phips "a cup of gold, worth about £1000."

Honors

On June 28, 1687, William Phips was presented at court by the Duke of Albemarle and knighted by the king, in recognition of "his good and loyal services in the course of the expedition," as the *London Gazette* put it.

At left: Divers returning to the *Calypso* after a two-hour shift on the bottom.

Above right: The "Loch Ness Monster," with its panels and floats.

Below right: On some days, the coral fish seemed particularly numerous and bold only a few dozen yards from our work site.

In the months following, Phips — now Sir William Phips — was presented with the medals that had been specially struck in his honor. One showed the effigy of the English sovereigns on one side; on the reverse was the *James and Mary*, anchored over the wreck of *Nuestra Señora de la Concepción*. The inscription was unusual: *Semper Tibi Pendeat Hamus* — "Let your hook always hang down." It was an allusion—taken from Ovid—to the grappling irons and iron hooks by means of which Phips's divers had tried to retrieve still more treasure. The other medal showed Neptune, with his trident, watching the progress of the treasure hunt. This Neptune bore a striking resemblance to the Duke of Albemarle, with his wig and his sharp features. The motto here was more straightforward: *Ex aqua omnia* — "Everything comes from the sea."

On July 28, Phips's partners gave a banquet in his honor at the Inn of the Swan, in London, during which they presented him with still another medal, of gold, on a golden chain. Every member of the crew was also given a medal and chain, but of silver.

King James II offered Sir William a position in the English Navy, as a quartermaster. Phips, however, refused. He preferred to return to New England. In Boston, he built a handsome brick house of two stories, ornamented with a columned portico in the fashion of the day. The house, which survived into the twentieth century, stood at Greenlane and de Charter streets (a corner of present-day Salem Street).

It was not in Phips's nature to retire to comfort and obscurity. He was named governor of Massachusetts by King James, and governor general of Maine and of Nova Scotia. It was Phips, therefore, who waged England's war against France's American possessions, and who invaded and seized Acadia

(and who therefore was indirectly responsible for Longfellow's *Evangeline*). Phips's adventure ended in defeat, however, when his forces were repulsed at Quebec.

As a consequence of his gubernatorial career, Phips now found himself surrounded by enemies, deep in debt, and as poor as he had been as a boy. His fortune had lasted only eight years. Once more he decided to go to London in order to make a new start. Upon his arrival, he was immediately arrested for a debt of £20,000 and thrown into prison. Already enfeebled by attacks of tropical disease, he could not endure the dampness of the prison, and died on February 18, 1695, at the age of forty-four.

Phips was buried in London at the king's expense, in the church of St. Mary Woolnoth, in Lombard Street. His wife had a monument of marble built for the tomb, surmounted by an urn between two cupids. A bas-relief showed the *James and Mary* at anchor, with its boats out hunting for treasure. It was a reproduction of the reverse side of the medal presented to Sir William. Phips's tomb has now disappeared—and no one knows when, or why, it was demolished. The urn, the cupids and the sculptured scene no longer exist, but the epitaph has survived to our day:

> Here lies Sir William Phips, knight, who, in the year 1687, by his great effort, discovered among the rocks near the Bahamas banks, to the North of Hispaniola, a Spanish galleon that had been on the bottom for forty-four years; from which he recovered gold and silver to the value of three hundred thousand pounds sterling; and, with a fidelity equal to his conduct, he brought that entire sum to London, where it was divided between himself and the rest of his companions in adventure.

> For which great service he was knighted by His Majesty, King James II; and, at the request of the chief inhabitants of New England, he accepted the government of Massachusetts, which he retained until his death, and acquitted himself of his task with such zeal for the good of his country, and with so little regard for his own interests, that he justly won the esteem and affection of the greatest and best part of the people of that colony.

There exists an English map of the eighteenth century showing a reef situated to the north of Hispaniola, and giving the name of that reef as the Silver Bank. There is no doubt that the name came from Phips's discovery of so much silver at that place. On a map of 1680, the same reef is designated by its old name of Abreollio. In *The English Pilot*, published in London in 1706, the same reef is called Plate Wrack. But in Sloane's *Voyage to the Madeira Islands*, published a year later, it is shown as Phips's Rack.

NINE

Strange Cargo

Wednesday, August 7. It was a bad night at sea, hot and damp, and we pitched and rolled constantly. This morning is hardly better. As Puerto Rico begins to show on our radar screen, it is raining in solid sheets, and the sky is heavy with clouds. There is nothing unusual in this, for it is the hurricane season. Fortunately, we have experienced nothing like it on the Silver Bank. Not yet, at any rate; but we can hardly expect our luck to hold out forever.

My son, Jean-Michel, is waiting for us on shore. He has just returned from a reconnaissance mission in Peru. We are in the process of getting together an expedition to that country for the purpose of exploring Lake Titicaca with our minisubs. So far, his reports have been encouraging; but the expedition to Lake Titicaca, as intriguing as it sounds, will involve a good deal of schedule-juggling. The *Calypso* will have to find her Spanish treasure in short order, for she must be in Peru no later than September 25 if she is to avoid the worst of the hurricane season in the Caribbean. Jean-Michel — who, by profession, is an architect — is under pressure to return immediately to Marseilles to supervise the construction of the Center for Advanced Marine Studies; but he must also spend six weeks in Peru and Bolivia, starting on September 1. My own situation is equally impossible. I must be in France and Monaco in September, and in Hollywood in October to edit our film on whales — and, at the same time, I am supposed to be at Lake Titicaca with the *Calypso*.

Saturday, August 10. Before casting off, we take on a very heavy cargo: 42 tons of gas oil, 21 tons of water.

Left: A diver, equipped with new scuba equipment, surveys the wreck's environs.

Right: On the bottom, two divers guide the airlift and uncover wood from the wreck.

Starting at breakfast today, we are using only paper plates and cups aboard the *Calypso*. Our purpose is to save water by not having to wash dishes, and thus to be able to stay on the Silver Bank as long as possible. Our new kitchen hand can hardly believe his good luck in finding a berth aboard a ship with no dirty dishes. He sings all day long.

Sunday, August 11. There was bad weather last night, but, at dawn, the sea became more calm, and we arrived at the Silver Bank an hour before schedule. We were able to pick up a radar signal six and a half miles away. At one-thirty in the afternoon, we are in the buoyed channel leading to the site of our galleon. The launch and the *Zodiac* are lowered so that the divers may film the *Calypso*'s passage among the coral peaks. There are massifs at a level with the water's surface: an impressive sight, but not a very reassuring one.

By three-thirty we are anchored in our usual spot, and we set to work. The first task is to raise Remy de Haenen's raft, the *James and Mary*. It comes up, but reluctantly. It was lying on its side on the bottom, and we spend much time getting it upright with our hoist and then pumping it out. Then, we check our anchorage lines to make sure they are secure, and end the day by launching the airlift's raft and vertical piping. The twenty feet of single-unit rigid piping in the latter will now be replaced with two sections, one of ten feet and the other of seven feet, in order to avoid hitting against the surrounding coral. The air intake will be located at no less than forty feet.

Tonight, everyone is exhausted. I order a general ration of rum — a custom dating from the days of sailing ships.

Frédéric Dumas dived this afternoon to take a look at the work area. He touched one of the corrugated-iron baskets that we had left under the surface when leaving for Puerto Rico, and found that the basket, as well as all the others, were covered with tiny coral polyps — after only six days in the water. These waters are a veritable hothouse of coral culture.

At night here we find tranquility; and we almost find relief from the heat. The tropical night falls swiftly, and with it a breeze blows over the water and refreshes us as it passes over our bare chests. At least we are better off here than in Puerto Rico. We can almost forget the human shouts, the automobile horns, and the rest of the city noises. The roar of the air compressor has made us both oblivious to other sounds, and yet strangely aware of them.

There are meteorological signs that make us vaguely uneasy. The color of the sea has changed. It is no longer blue and green, but is now heavily flecked with gray, and beneath the surface it looks as though the water has lost its transparency. Most ominous of all are the short waves that are breaking around us. Also, the sunset was too gorgeous: a splendor of red and gold shining through huge clouds of purple and black.

I feel sure that we are in for a bad time; not tonight, but soon. This time of the year was once the nemesis of Spanish galleons, and I have no wish to follow in their footsteps. I ask Caillart what he thinks, and he assures me that we will be able to avoid the weather. He has a weather map that he keeps diligently up to date. Meteorology, he assures me, is almost an exact science today.

Ten Tons of Coral

Monday, August 12. At six-thirty this morning I take my customary inspection dive to the worksite. It is exactly as it was when we left for Puerto Rico. I position ten small colored buoys around the (presumed) forward section of the galleon so that the diving teams can locate it even in troubled waters. Back aboard the *Calypso*, I order the ship to be moved about fifteen feet southward, and the tin drums — decorated with hippie flowers — that we have been using as floaters for the airlift, are moved about twenty feet to the southwest, as is the *James and Mary*.

The first diving team to go down installs the flexible pipe that comprises the lower section of the airlift apparatus. They replace the old 90° elbow with a new one of 45°. We hope that this one will have less of a tendency to jam and become blocked with debris.

The second team installs airlines, and then begins to tie lines around coral blocks. In the process, Remy, who has decided to join one of the teams, smashes his little finger. Our doctor sews it up, without anesthesia.

The wind, from the southeast, is quite strong, but does not really bother us. We spend the rest of the day in the usual way, raising blocks of coral onto the *Calypso*'s rear deck and then breaking them apart with sledgehammers and drills. There are coral chunks everywhere, from which we pick out any metal that we see or anything else of interest. What remains — the coral pieces themselves, and debris of various kinds — is hauled to port amidships and dumped overboard. About twelve tons of coral are handled in this way every day, and a pile of fragments is beginning to grow under the keel of our ship: an artificial reef.

There are a few interesting discoveries today, particularly an enormous hinge which may have been used on a large door on a hatch cover. There are also several cannon balls. Coll and Durand, the last diving team, bring up a conical weight for a fishline, a chain net, a broken belt buckle and a whole belt buckle, a bronze uniform button, and a bone. The doctor tells us that it is a rib — the first human bone that we have found.

There are butterflies around the *Calypso* today, and a small bird came to rest for a moment before continuing on some mysterious journey. Could this southeast wind have brought them from Africa?

A Feast in the Sky and in the Water

Tuesday, August 13. At 6 A.M. Bernard Delemotte comes to awaken me. I throw a bit of water on my face; and the water is still relatively fresh, without the strong smell of potassium chloride. I quickly join the first diving team on deck for a cup of instant coffee. Then I put on my diving gear. The sun has just risen and is partly obscured by low-lying clouds on the horizon. Great beams of light cross the still-dark sky: it is the perfect dawn, I breathe deeply as Bernard helps me to put on my air bottles. The beauty of the tropical day infects even the usually taciturn Bernard, and he laughs and jokes.

The water as I dive is splendidly clear, a proper complement to the feat of light in the sky above. I lie still, my arms and legs extended, and let myself drift slowly downward. In five or ten minutes, I know, Raymond and Jean-Pierre will join me. Meanwhile, I give myself over to the joy of being alone in this magical place. Not even the local barracuda, whom we have named Jules, is in sight. But then, there is an intruder. A *snapper* is swimming about, inspecting our work area. Dumas has seen this fish before and says that it is very intelligent. As soon as it catches sight of me, it comes toward me and stays nearby, a slight distance in front of me, for the whole of my time in the water.

The appearance of the work area, particularly in its forward section, has changed considerably since we began digging. The tons of coral that we have removed have had their result, and it is a bit easier to make out the lines of the galleon. I note all this carefully, almost mechanically; for in a little while I will have to give instructions for the day's work. But my attention is really held by something else, by the sight of the area as a whole, transformed as it is by the light of dawn filtered through the crystal water. Everything seems larger than life. Some of the objects glitter with unaccustomed color. The grays take on varied hues. The planks of the old ship are no longer altogether black. The sand sparkles with ochre and mauve. Even the fauna seems to sense a change. A school of small spotted groupers appears and swims about the work area fearlessly, ignoring me. A school of snappers flashes past like a fleet of diminutive Boeings, with yellow arrows on their flanks, and a few pale red mullets turn slowly near the bottom. The anchors and cannon of our galleon are those of a ghost ship, and the long pipe of the airlift is transformed

A view of the coral wall beneath the reef. The fish with brown and white stripes is a Chaeto-dontidae — a *Heniochus*.

into a great sea serpent. It is not difficult to indulge oneself in such fantasies when one is alone, at the bottom of the sea, at the beginning of a tropical day. At such moments, time and space seem no longer to exist. How greatly my attitude toward the world, toward men and societies, and toward myself, have been influenced, or perhaps even dictated, by my thirty-two years of diving. But now, I must abandon my thoughts. Raymond Coll's silhouette can be seen near the galleon, and it is time to begin thinking of practical things.

The results of our work for today are as follows: a pulley; a sack of nuts (almost intact); the trigger-guard of a firearm; a huge nail; a few pieces of iron; a long, hooked iron tool of some kind; three pieces of a large copper caldron; some sheaves; many bones of cows and pigs; an angle made of some exotic wood; the wooden handle of a tool, with the imprint of ironwork; and some pieces of very thick jars.

Left: "It is a day of celebration in the sky and in the water. . . . Today, everything is beautiful. . . . Everything is magical."

One of the most important factors in the length of our stay here will be our water supply. We are therefore doing everything that we can to eke out our supply. Even so, we now find ourselves in the paradoxical situation of having what seems a great deal of water, for our distilling apparatus has produced four hundred liters of it. Tonight, there will be a two-hour shower period.

As it turns out, our distiller cannot keep up with us. At the end of the shower period, I discover that we have used three times the distiller's production: 1200 liters. Next time, we will have to limit ourselves to one hour.

A Hurricane Warning

Wednesday, August 14. My morning dive at six-thirty is as pleasant as yesterday's. The water is still clear, and I am pleased to see that much work was done yesterday. Even Remy, despite his smashed and still unhealed finger, insists on working.

At eight forty-five the *James and Mary* is brought near the *Calypso* and its load of coral-filled baskets is hoisted aboard under the eye of the cameras. An examination of this material, however, turned up nothing of value: an apricot seed, bone buttons, many bones of cattle, a perfume-bottle stopper of glass, a wooden handguard (used in sewing leather and sails), a belt buckle, four musket balls, pieces of a copper caldron, and a scalloped banderole of copper with three rivet holes.

Everyone is of the opinion that we must dig a transversal trench. The question is, Exactly at what point must it be dug, and how deep should it be? The reason for this opinion is that the juxtaposed planks that we have found seem to be deck planks, that is, there are no large nails visible, and no timbers. On one side, these planks seem to rest — at least in places — on large, hard blocks that Gaston calls "the terrestrial crust." After much discussion, I suggest that we continue working for another twenty-four hours before reaching a final decision; in this way, we will be able to uncover a larger section of these planks. My suggestion is adopted.

To the problems posed by our sunken ship is added that of the weather, which is getting steadily worse. Great clouds roll across the sky and seem almost to touch the sea. There are no more fresh evening breezes, and the heat is unrelenting. We often experience a feeling of vague unease and apprehension. I have witnessed this complex of signs before: in the China Sea, and in the Indian Ocean barely two years ago, just before the advent of a hurricane.

Is it reasonable for me to keep the *Calypso* at anchor here, in the most dangerous spot of the Caribbean, during the hurricane season? Even more, do I have the right to do so?

"Yes," Captain Caillart assures me. "The hurricane will pass to the north."

"I hope you are right," I reply. But, given the signs in the sky and the sea, I know that I will soon have to make a decision, either to give up our quest, or to take a chance and work as fast as possible. And, a few hours later, my personal forecast is officially confirmed: a hurricane warning is issued by the U. S. Meteorological Service.

Thursday, August 15. Today, Catholics celebrate the Feast of the Assumption, that is, the feast day of *Nuestra Señora de la Concepción.* Despite this favorable omen, my morning dive to the work area is made in cloudy water. Everything seems somber, depressing. I show Bernard Delemotte, who is with me, the direction for today's dig. Then, north of the mound, I find a battered beer can. No doubt it is a relic of our predecessors here, and possibly it was used to house one of their explosives.

I have rearranged the diving teams to make up, in addition to the four regular shifts, a "floating" team. Under Gaston's supervision, these men will dig in the center of the mound. During the afternoon, however, Gaston soon discovers that the mound contains more sand than coral, and thus cannot be excavated without the airlift. Gaston's team is then assigned a new job: to cut away the large blocks of coral so that the other teams will have more time for digging.

Frédéric Dumas went down this morning for an hour and a half. Upon his return, he announced that he had found, toward the portside of the galleon, level with the presumed deck planks, a compact black mass made up of wood, rusty nails, bottles, pottery, and barrel hoops. We brought up several blocks of this mass and carefully broke them apart, but found nothing of special interest. We had no better result with the basketload of coral fragments brought aboard from the *James and Mary.*

Late in the afternoon, however, Dumas finds a plank onto which a section of packing is attached by means of pieces of wood and four little square nails. Is it a patch? A "cork" for a leak? If so, this means that the planks are from the hull of the ship, and not from its deck. It also means that this may well be *Nuestra Señora de la Concepción* after all; for all accounts of that ship are full of stories about how it leaked like a sieve from the moment that it was launched.

And then the storm breaks, preceded by strong gusts of wind. I send divers down to make sure that our seven anchorage lines are secure, and they report that there is no sign of any loosening. Next, there is rain, and we welcome it. It is a sweet balm to our parched and cracked skins.

It turns out that Caillart was right. The hurricane has passed us to the north, and we are merely on its fringe.

Thirty or Forty Hurricanes

I have an interesting discussion with Remy de Haenen, who tells me his conclusions concerning our galleon. They are based upon a hypothesis about the aging process of a wooden hull. According to Remy, the deck and all its cannon would have slowly slid toward the starboard in less than a century if the wreck had originally had a starboard list. In Remy's theory, the planks that we have found would have come from the deck, as we first thought, rather than from the hull. The hull would then be farther southward. In support of this theory, Remy cites the fact that we have found no cannon on the portside, but only on the starboard.

In order to understand the wreck, we must take into account the recurrence of hurricanes. At least one passes over the Silver Bank every ten years, which means that the *Nuestra Señora* must have gone through thirty or forty hurricanes since the time that she sank. Moreover, Remy, and everyone else who knows this area, says that during the hurricane season, it happens occasionally that the Silver Bank is struck by breakers almost forty feet high. These "rollers" must have had considerable effect on the wreck.

This effect is a matter of particular interest to Frédéric Dumas, who had made a specialty of it in the course of his underwater digs. His position, however, is different from that of Remy de Haenen. "I have never been tempted to trespass into the area of the archaeologists," he explains. "My sole interest has been to study the way in which sunken ships are transformed, to understand what they become after they are sunk. I've spent thirty years trying to explain how and why a ship on the bottom becomes what it becomes."

So diligently has Dumas cultivated this "special interest" that he is able, at first glance, and basing his judgment only on the sight of a few water jars protruding from the sand, to say whether a wreck is large or small, where it lies, and what its state of preservation is. This ability was acquired through the study of hundreds of shipwrecks in the Mediterranean. He has supervised a large number of submarine digs, and he has developed some remarkable prospecting methods. His method is to sound the bottom with a small stainless steel triangle, or rod, about six feet long. He is a true virtuoso in the use of

One of the beautiful parrotfish common in the Silver Bank.

this instrument, and, like a blindman with his cane, he has developed almost a sixth sense in its use.

The Rising Ground Level

Dumas has also developed a general theory of wrecks with respect to their position under the bottom. "In the sea, as on land," he explains, "the ground level rises. On land, dead cities lie buried — even their highest monuments. The same thing happens to ships on the sea bottom. Ocean currents carry sand, which piles up against the wreck.

"Along the seacoasts everywhere, the bottom also rises. Part of that rise is attributable to land erosion resulting from rain; and some of it is due to the wind. In the case of sunken ships, however, there is another factor: marine life. Fauna clusters around a wreck and covers it with solid matter: crustacean shells, limestone skeletons, and encrusting algae.

"In a coral reef such as the Silver Bank, this accretion is considerable, because life flourishes here and coral grows at an accelerated rate. That is why we have found here masses of coral weighing four or five tons — blocks so heavy that we have been unable to bring them up.

"So, coral has covered the wreck. But the coral, in turn, has been eaten by parrot-fish; and the parrot-fish have excreted the coral in the form of sand. This sand falls to the bottom, from which it rises in mounds among the coral, in such a way that the ocean floor itself is rising evenly and continuously. This rise accounts for the fact that we found tableware buried at a depth of from fifteen to twenty-seven inches from the ocean bottom.

"The study of the evolution of coral over a period of three centuries is challenging, but also discouraging; for it is likely that a great many sunken ships have disappeared forever beneath the rising ocean floor and will never be found."

There is another area that we know very well in which ships have disappeared entirely: the Red Sea. Frédéric Dumas enjoys reminiscing about Shab Rumi, for the benefit of the crewmen who were not aboard the *Calypso* at that time. "When we were shooting *World Without Sun*," he said one night, "we were accompanied by a cargo ship, the *Rosaldo*. Some Greek sailors from that ship were collecting shells on the reef one day when they discovered some amphorae, or Greek vases. They told me about them, and I went immediately to inspect and photograph them. They were probably from the Island of Cos, but dating from the Roman period. It was interesting to see what two-thousand years in the sea had done to them. They were virtually mounted in coral. The vases were at surface level, and normal erosion had undercut their support, so that they looked like fairyland chimneys protruding from the reef. Or, more realistically, they seemed to be set atop small pillars of coral. There was obviously an old sunken ship somewhere in the area."

Right: According to Remy de Haenen, the wreck, over a period of two centuries, settled on its starboardside. This would explain why all the cannon were on the starboard, and none on the port side. It would also mean that all the planks discovered on the bottom were from the bridge, and not from the hull of the wreck.

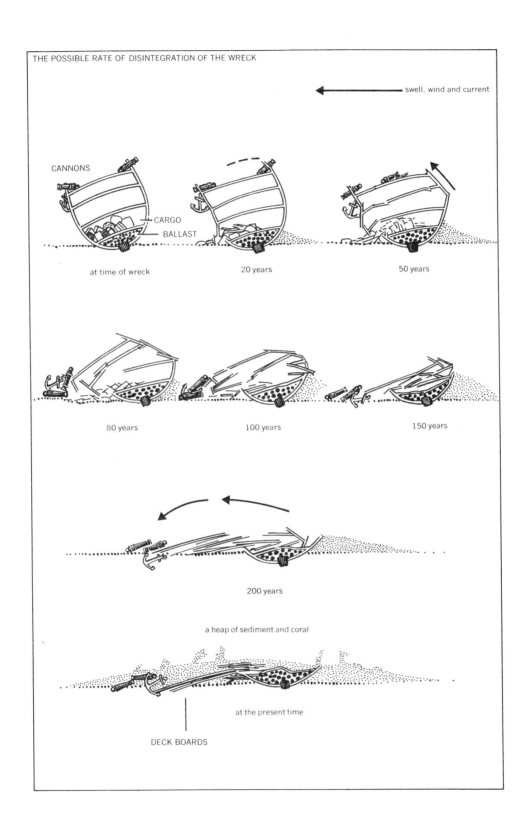

THE POSSIBLE RATE OF DISINTEGRATION OF THE WRECK

swell, wind and current

CANNONS

CARGO
BALLAST

at time of wreck   20 years   50 years

80 years   100 years   150 years

200 years

a heap of sediment and coral

at the present time

DECK BOARDS

The hurricane passes near the *Calypso.*

Such wrecks, as Dumas is quick to point out, are a mystery. We do not know what process of change they undergo in coral waters. That is why I regard our venture on the Silver Bank as being of great importance. It is the first systematic dig of its kind that makes use of the most up-to-date equipment available.

Friday, August 16. I make my customary morning dive, this time with Raymond Coll. The water, like the weather, is unpleasant, and the work area is entirely covered with "dust" — fallen from the *James and Mary*.

Raymond finds an American sledgehammer. It is ironic, since nothing that we have found shows any signs of having been worked on by any previous treasure hunters.

Our second trench across the galleon, at a level with the so-called "deck planks," is going ahead. So far, we have removed great masses of material, especially in the rear (i.e., rear port) section. At the end of the day, however, the diggers run into a hard, white substance, which indicates that they have reached the outer edge of the ship. We conclude that the galleon is not as large as we had thought, and that it does not run as far forward as shown on the map that I made up.

For the rest of us, the day was not more rewarding. Gaston, after spending the morning removing blocks of coral from the work area, began working on the mound that is even with the last cannon starboard-amidships. He hopes to find other cannon. Frédéric Dumas and Jean-Paul Bassaget explored the level reef, but the only excitement was their meeting with a shark. In sum, the day's work yielded three cannon balls (we are still wondering where the portside cannon are); a very thick piece of wood with traces of nails and pegs; two magnificent bottles, almost intact and filled with sand, that somehow survived the shipwreck; a small, shapeless plaque of a metal harder than lead — probably a lead alloy; a modern sledgehammer (American) with a broken handle; the soles of two sandals, belonging no doubt to our mysterious predecessors; and finally, a lead seal, brought up by Riant, which is in better condition than any of the seals we found earlier.

Dumas also made an interesting discovery. Near the two cannon of mound number two, he found two very old crowbars. Are they a relic of Phips and his divers? Is it possible that mound number two marks the aft section of the galleon?

On the basis of Didi's find, a new theory is formulated: the forward section of the galleon — about a third of the ship — may have broken off, and the rest of the ship would then have sunk at a 30° angle, or even a 90° angle. The hypothesis of a 30° angle would explain the presence of four cannon on mounds number two and three.

An enormous load, weighing more than a ton, was hauled aboard from the *James and Mary* today. For all our breaking and chipping, however, we found not a single object of interest.

The Stem

Saturday, August 17. It is now 7:30 P.M., and the roar of the compressor has finally come to a halt. I am exhausted, both physically and mentally. It has been a day full of incidents of all kinds, of finds, of discussions and theories.

It began early this morning, when my morning dive was delayed for fifteen minutes because of compressor trouble. When I finally went down, at six forty-five, with Serge Foulon and Riant, the water was clear, but we had to be extremely careful not to touch anything for fear of raising a cloud of dust. The work area is very dirty, and there was no current at all to carry away the dust.

Surveying the work area, it suddenly dawned on me that the ship must be at least ten feet more to the rear than we had originally thought. It was comparatively narrow in the beam on the spot where we were digging our trench; therefore, the trench must be near the stem. And the two cannon near the anchors — which have smaller bores than the others — must be the pursuit cannon. The hypothesis of the ship breaking into two parts seems verified.

I told Serge to stop working on the forward transversal trench and sent him to do as Raymond Coll had suggested; that is, to dig to a depth of two to three feet under the round pots at the base of the mound. He found seven more pots, all intact. But there was nothing else. If the mound marks the spot at which the break in the ship occurred, these pots were probably contained in a crate which fell from the broken section.

As this was going on beneath the surface, I was supervising the moving of the *Calypso*, of the airlift raft, and of the *James and Mary* to a position that would be more convenient for working on mound number three. Then, I make an overlay of a galleon layout, with the galleon broken into two parts, and I superimpose it over my map of the work area. Everything seemed to fall into place. "Our galleon must be shaped like a snake," Dumas exclaimed when he saw my overlay.

Didi had just returned from a dive, and he had several important things to tell me. In the mound, under some rocks, he had found a sort of chamber pot. It was intact, but, in trying to disengage it with his crowbar, he had unfortunately broken it. Next, he went to explore mound number two, in which he found the two crowbars yesterday. This mound, Didi reports, which is a conical limestone formation, seems to be broken at almost a right angle — at the very spot in which the crowbars were found. It was easy to conclude that it was there that Phips or his successors had tried to dig their way into the "treasure room" of *Nuestra Señora de la Concepción*. According to my new overlay, the location of this mound was precisely where the rear section of *Nuestra Señora* should be.

At ten-thirty, I dived again, this time with Michel Deloire. After visiting the work area, we went to mound number two in order to study the layout with a view to filming Didi's discovery. It was just as Dumas said. The thick crust of the mound had been broken; and it had been broken centuries ago. Then we inspected, successively, the isolated anchor (which we call the aft anchor), a stack of oven bricks which seemed undisturbed, some cast-iron pots, and a battered copper caldron. There seemed to be bits of metal scattered everywhere. It occurred to me that there was probably a second ship nearby, also very old and completely buried. According to my calculations, it lay almost against the reef, at a depth of no more than twenty or twenty-five feet.

After my return to the *Calypso* a U. S. Navy plane (a Lockheed Neptune) flew over at a low altitude and took photographs of us. Then the pilot waved, and flew away. (As it turned out, he visited us once a week for as long as we stayed on the Silver Bank, no doubt to break the routine of his patrol flights.) I wonder what he was going to make out of Remy's contraption, the *James and Mary*.

A Load of Ceramics

The plane had no sooner disappeared from sight than Raymond Coll climbed aboard in a state of great excitement. Raymond is known for his habitual calm and his quiet nature; his discovery, however, justified a momentary loss of tranquility: a cache of china, intact. He dived again, with a camera, and Michel Deloire went with him to film the digging out and the hoisting of this find. It consisted of a group of very handsome decorated bowls of small size, and some larger, and less fine, bowls, as well as several chamber pots. This was a significant discovery. It meant that we finally had begun to uncover the cargo of the galleon.

Gradually, the divers dug out other bowls and fragile cups, all unbroken. These pieces had been stacked together in such a way as to indicate that they were packed in crates. Based on this evidence, Frédéric Dumas came up with a theory: that the crates containing this tableware were stored on the deck. When the ship began to list, as it was sinking, they slid into the sea. This would account for the fact that their contents were unbroken. If they had been stored in the interior of the ship, they would surely have been smashed when the ship's timbers gave way in the wreck.

The discovery of these cups and bowls gave us all courage. They seemed

The divers found a great quantity of bowls and goblets.

Bernard Delemotte once more examines the work area, in search of the smallest clue.

to be true Chinese ceramics, and worth a small fortune. And where there was precious china, we reasoned, there must also be gold. In any case, Raymond's find is of prime importance. If this is really Chinese ceramic, its presence aboard this galleon proves that the ship took on its cargo at Veracruz, and that it was on its way back across the Atlantic to Spain. It would have been a tragedy to discover that we had been digging out a ship returning from Spain to the New World, after having unloaded its treasures at Cádiz.

The problem now is to find out whether these ceramics are really of Chinese origin; that is, whether they were brought to the New World by the galleon of the Pacific — the *Nao de China* — from the Philippines to Acapulco, and thence, by mule train, to Veracruz.

"Chinese? Chinese?" Dumas said. "I would not bet my last dollar on it. Nonetheless, it is an interesting find, and an unusual one." And then he began examining them again with the jeweler's eye that he wears on a string around his neck.

The workday ended late. Everyone was tired, and the joy of discovery was mingled, as it always is, with a certain depression. I decided that it was time for a break. Tomorrow, there will be no excavation, and the workday will start late: at 8 A.M.

After dinner, Remy de Haenen decided to use hydrochloric acid to clean off one of the ceramics. He succeeded in removing the dirt and the discoloration, and also the glaze and all the ornamentation. A disaster; but a minor one that amused everyone.

From the five or six tons of coral that we broke open today, we took a small sack of nails; four cannon balls; seven intact pots; a carved sword handle; four chamber pots (two of them broken); 88 whole goblets; 19 more goblets, unbroken but stacked one inside the other in such a way that we cannot separate them; 36 bowls, all unbroken; and another 23 bowls, also intact but inseparable from each other — for a total of 107 goblets and 59 bowls. In addition, there were numerous fragments of broken pottery.

Sunday, August 18. A relatively leisurely day. The compressor stands silent; what delicious quiet. Breakfast at seven o'clock, and then a dive, with Bernard, at eight. I give instructions to raise the airlift pipe a bit, to prevent its rubbing against the coral, and then attach an old tire in the proper spot to prevent a recurrence. Next, I inspect the hole in which our ceramics were found. It is at least six feet from Dumas' cannon. The hole was under some large rocks; and there are some of these rocks around it. They resemble Gaston's "terrestrial crust."

Bernard and I examine the old excavation of mound number two. The sight of it is striking enough; but what is even more extraordinary is that the divers of Phips's time were able to cut this hole into the hard crust of coral beachrock with their crowbars (which we have found), and also that they carefully filled in the hole that they had dug with debris and coral blocks. It was an almost perfect camouflage. I wonder whether the men who wielded those crowbars belonged to Phips's own crew, who complained about the difficulty of "digging into the crust of coral covering the hull." Or were they one of the pirate crews licensed by Phips to dig for the treasure, with the understanding that Phips would receive half of whatever they found? These pirates might well have found something — and then covered the traces of their excavation rather than give Phips his share. Something out of Robert Louis Stevenson.

Later in the day, Didi dives to clean off the planks that are visible, so that they will show up better on film. Then I go down to meet Didi, while Deloire films, in clear water, a segment on "a visit to the work area on the fourteenth day." Again I am reminded of the battlefield of Verdun: an area cut through with trenches, with abandoned cannon standing starkly about.

When the filming is completed, I lay a blue nylon line to designate the boundaries of a new digging area. This one starts from the southern base of mound number three and includes the broken cannon.

At 1:00 P.M., we begin work again, but this time without the airlift. The four teams occupy themselves by tying slings around the larger blocks of coral. By evening, almost all the blocks south of the mound have been removed. Under one of them, a new cannon is discovered; the eleventh. Only its mouth is visible.

While this was going on, Gaston was emptying out the "buccaneers' hole" in mound number two. There, he came upon a strata of debris that we will have to remove with the airlift tomorrow.

Remy de Haenen spent the day storing our ceramics in plastic bags and packing them into crates.

Our distilling apparatus has been running for twenty-four hours, and has produced a ton of fresh water. To celebrate, Remy puts together a marvelous punch. A Sunday of semirepose has restored everyone's spirits.

The Ship's Pharmacy

Monday, August 19. An inspection dive at 6:30A.M., and then Bernard turns on the airlift. About 9 A.M., while the divers are working on mound number three, Gaston gets to work on the "buccaneers' hole" with the second airlift. The Worthington compressor, supplying air to two airlifts, is running full blast, and literally roars.

The diving teams relieve one another at the airlift in the area where the ceramics were found, and soon the last of the bowls and goblets are aboard the *Calypso.*

Dumas persists in believing that we are working beyond the limits of the galleon, and that the galleon itself lies to the south and the east of the cannon. Nonetheless, the last team brings up a 20 cc. brass syringe, corroded and covered with limestone, and a small cracked bottle filled with sediment. In with the sediment, however, we can see a few drops of mercury. Does it come from the ship's pharmacy?

Under the newly discovered cannon, we find scrap iron, cannon balls, and wood — but white wood.

We can now come to certain conclusions. First, we have finished excavating the forward part of the ship, and have established the possibility — even the probability — of a breach in the ship. We do not know precisely where this break is, but we do know that it alone can explain the isolated cannon on mound number two. We also know that mound number three is full of debris, either from a galleon or from its cargo. What we do not know, however, is the exact position of that galleon. We have not yet found its keel. And we are therefore still in the dark.

Bernard finds a relatively flat and broad "path" between the two mounds. It could be the hull, flattened and covered with sand.

The present pace of work — twelve hours with the main airlift, and three hours with the auxiliary airlift — is exhausting. I wonder how long we can continue at this rate. Every day, the diggers and the breakers are visibly more tired. They are suffering numerous cuts on the coral, and the cuts are becoming infected and will not heal properly.

Nonetheless, everyone goes down for his regular shift, without complaining. Most of them use their fingernails as tools. And yet, back aboard the *Calypso* they still discuss their plans for the future and dream their dreams of a vast fortune in gold.

Remy de Haenen has never lost his confidence that we are on the right track. His face lined with fatigue, unsmiling, he works constantly and without rest. He gains strength from his passion for treasure. He is certain that our galleon is indeed *Nuestra Señora de la Concepción.* In his opinion, all that we need now is patience and more work; and, from the amount of work that we are doing, he has concluded that our efforts will be crowned with success.

A Visit from Sharks

This wreck is like none other that we have visited in the Mediterranean, or even in the Red Sea. It is entirely petrified in coral, totally broken apart and unrecognizable. No octopus or grouper finds shelter in it. But the reef fish, who scattered when we first arrived and began working, have now returned and appear untroubled by our presence. Jules, our local barracuda, is especially bold, and he never leaves the company of the divers. He has never been aggressive, even though he does swim very close to our teams. There have also been occasional visits by sand sharks; but the permanent residents seem to be groupers and parrot fish, who eat the worms and the basketstars that the airlift turns up. And there are also castagnoles, who live among the coral branches and attack the divers furiously when they break the branches.

When we first arrived, there were numerous sharks in the vicinity; gray sharks, of considerable size. But we had had more than a little experience with this species in the Red Sea, and even the youngest of our divers quickly learned to ignore these beasts. As soon as we began to use the compressor, the sharks disappeared and never returned. Sharks have a highly developed sense of hearing. They are attracted by the sounds of explosions or individual loud noises, but they dislike sustained noise as much as humans do. Yesterday, when the compressor was not running, a large blue shark — very majestic, and obviously very disdainful of us — arrived for a visit. He slowly toured the work area, and then left again, without once glancing at us.

TEN

Maritime Disasters

A change in the Spanish royal dynasty at the beginning of the eighteenth century effected a correspondingly brusque change in the structure of power in the Caribbean. In 1700, Carlos II, a mediocre king, so average as to be almost mentally retarded, and an epileptic, died without having produced a male heir.

On his deathbed, he designated as his successor the Duke d'Anjou, a French prince who was a grandson of King Louis XIV. Thus it was that a scion of the House of Bourbon mounted the throne of that most imperial of all the Hapsburgs, Charles V. The new king of Spain was known as Philip V. He is described by one historian as "compassionate, high-spirited, full of good intentions, but lacking in the ability to make decisions."

The other nations of Europe could not feel safe with a French prince on the throne of Spain — even an indecisive French prince. The virtual union of France and Spain under a single dynasty presented a very real danger to their well-being, even though the two nations over which the Bourbons ruled were far from being economically healthy. Louis XIV and Philip V therefore had to do battle against three allied powers — England, Austria, and Holland — in the conflict known as the Spanish Succession.

So far as the New World was concerned, this war served to make galleon traffic even more hazardous than it already was. Despite her three centuries of seafaring, Spain had never succeeded in becoming a maritime power, and at the time of this war she had no more than fifteen warships. France had around sixty; England, about twice that number; and Holland, as many as England.

Spain's lack of military progress on the seas was matched by her status in the field of commercial shipping. It is true that galleons were now lighter and sturdier, and that the prow and poop sections were lower and closer to the water. But they were still hopelessly outclassed by the ships of England and Holland, which were better built, better armed, and more adept in the use of sail. Such improvements as had been made in naval architecture during the centuries in which Spain ruled the Americas had been made by the English and the Dutch.

France was in a better position than her Spanish ally. Under Jean-Baptiste Colbert, the most able minister of Louis XIV's earlier years, French ships had been improved until they were a match for the best English vessels. The French, therefore, now became responsible for maintaining Spain's lines of communication with the New World and for protecting the Spanish colonies there.

But King Louis was not a man accustomed to doing favors and expecting nothing in return. In payment for the services rendered by the French Navy, France demanded, and obtained, the right to trade freely with Spain's colonies in the New World. This arrangement, of course, spelled ruin for French privateers in the Caribbean. Louis might wink at contraband activities so long as they were directed against the economy of Spain under a Hapsburg dynasty; but he would not tolerate it when its victim was a Bourbon prince — and especially not when it interfered with French profit. The privateers were therefore driven out of business and dispersed.

Their place was taken by shipowners and merchants from St. Malo, Nantes, and Bordeaux, who began trading along the coast of South America, and even (following the example of the privateers) rounded Cape Horn to do business in the Pacific. In a few years, they were selling their merchandise on the western coast, as far north as Peru.

Such enterprise was not unrewarded. In 1702, a French company obtained an exclusive franchise to the *Asiento* — that is, to the lucrative slave trade which brought blacks from Africa to the West Indies.

A Franco-Spanish Fleet

Spain was not such an ally as Frenchmen found easy to deal with, particularly in the New World. The sensibilities of viceroys had to be taken into account. The greed of the great lords had to be satisfied. And, above all, the bureaucratic tyranny of the Casa de Contractación had to be dealt with. The Casa was not merely a thorn in the side of French merchants. Its autocratic methods were to have catastrophic results for Spain as well and were to provoke one of the greatest maritime disasters of Spanish history.

On June 11, 1702, a French vice-admiral, the Marquis de Chateau-Renault, set sail from Havana for Cádiz. Under his charge were twenty-two galleons, loaded with an extremely valuable cargo consisting half of precious metals and half of merchandise. The official value of this cargo was set at thirty million piastres — an estimate which did not include, of course, the illegal cargo which every galleon carried.

Chateau-Renault's Spanish counterpart in the *flota* was Captain General Don Juan de Velasco. Between the two of them, they had taken every precaution for a safe crossing with their precious load. And, indeed, the Atlantic voyage passed without incident. It was not until the fleet was in Spanish waters that an Anglo-Dutch fleet, under Admiral Rooke, attacked the convoy. Chateau-Renault had been forewarned of Rooke's plan, and had attempted to escape by putting into a French port. The gentlemen of the Casa, however, had forbidden him to do so. They had no wish to see Spanish treasure within the reach of a French monarch. Whereupon, a Spanish captain suggested that the fleet sail into the Bay of Vigo, on Spain's northwestern coast, where, he was sure, they would be safe.

Chateau-Renault agreed, and his fleet dropped anchor in the bay a short time later. The merchant ships of the convoy were anchored within the bay itself, while the warships were positioned in such a way as to block the passageway into the bay. In addition, a bulkheading was constructed at that point. Two ruined forts were hastily repaired. Then cannon from the ships were set up in batteries along the shore.

Once this was done, there was still time to unload the ships' cargoes. But this could not be done. The captain general of the kingdom, the Prince de Barbanzon, dared not give such an order. The regulations of the Casa de Contractación specifically forbade that any merchandise be unloaded from a Spanish ship except in the presence of its representatives.

Embezzlement had been epidemic throughout the period of Spanish domination. It reached such a point that even the royal treasury could no longer count on receiving full value in the ingots carried by the royal galleons. The silver ingots, which were in the form of bars, were often found to be made of silver-plated lead or copper. And the gold ingots, which were disc-shaped, were sometimes found to be mostly platinum - which, ironically, was regarded at the time as being valueless. The chief problem in stealing the king's gold and silver was that of how to get the loot back to Spain unde-

Following page: A large shark pays a visit to our divers.

tected. In this respect, the generals, admirals and captains exercised considerable ingenuity. One high-ranking officer, it was discovered, had his gold
melted down and cast in the shape of an anchor, which was then carefully
coated with a substance resembling iron.

Over the centuries, a ceremonial had been evolved covering unloading.
As soon as word arrived that a fleet from the New World had been sighted off
Cádiz, the president of the Casa set out to meet it. He boarded the flagship,
where he asked for a copy of the general inventory. This was then verified
aboard each galleon by his agents, who checked off the gold, silver, and merchandise. It was invariably discovered that the inventory listed only about a
third or a half of the actual cargo. This discovery was the occasion for an
"arrangement," which left everyone satisfied, and much richer. No cargo
could be unloaded, nor could any ship of the fleet touch land, until this ceremony had been completed.

It remained to be seen whether the fleet in the Bay of Vigo would be
dispensed from this time-honored regulation. The Prince de Barbanzon sent a
courier to Madrid to ask for instructions. The Council of the Indies solemnly
convened and discussed the matter; then they announced that part of the
cargo might lawfully be unloaded: the precious metals belonging to the king.
A courier was dispatched to Barbanzon with this unprecedented news, and
arrived at Vigo two weeks later. But, by then, it was too late for dispensations
to be of any avail.

On October 23, Admiral Rooke had disembarked two detachments of
four thousand men each on both ends of the bay, and the forts fell to them
after a brief struggle. At the same time, he had ordered two warships of
eighty cannon to destroy the defensive bulkheading, which they did in short
order.

Behind the two warships sailed the entire Anglo-Dutch fleet, and a terrible battle had ensued, with cannon being fired at point-blank range. The
heavy merchantmen, crowded as they were into the narrow confines of the
bay, had had no room in which to maneuver, and made easy targets. Burning
rigging was carried by the wind from ship to ship, without regard to nationality; and Admiral Rooke's flagship, the *Torbay*, had to be abandoned.

Chateau-Renault, seeing that the battle was lost, had ordered his captains to destroy their vessels rather than let them fall into the hands of the
English and Dutch; and, one by one, the French ships were set afire or scuttled. The rest had already been lost through fire or by running aground.

Captain General Don Juan de Velasco had given similar orders to the
Spanish captains, and all of the galleons that had not already fallen to the

enemy were set afire; and seamen, burned and half-naked, began swimming ashore — clutching silver ingots, dishes of gold, or sacks of piastre.

The English share of the loot came to a million and a half pounds sterling. And yet, only five of the nineteen galleons of the fleet had fallen into English hands; and, of these five, only four reached England, the fifth having sunk in the Bay of Biscay.

The rest of the treasure was at the bottom of the Bay of Vigo, where it remains to this day, a source of dreams to every treasure hunter worthy of the name. (One such hunter, incidentally, found a mass of broken porcelain, from China, in the Bay.) One of the latest operators at Vigo, Robert Stenuit, estimates that there are still over forty million pieces of eight (the equivalent of about 22 million) in the sunken galleons.

An ironic note is that a great part of the cargo of this ill-fated fleet belonged, not to subjects of the king of Spain, but to English and Dutch merchants who shipped their goods through Spanish intermediaries because only Spanish subjects had the right to join a transatlantic convoy.

The Opulent Caribbean

One of the most fortunate decisions of the indecisive King Philip V of Spain was to make a Frenchman, Jean-Baptiste du Casse, his Captain General of the Sea. Du Casse was a former privateer, and, as such, he had had much experience with the English and the Dutch. Banking on this experience, he was able to inflict several defeats on the ships of England, and to lead the Fleet of New Spain safely across the Atlantic to Cádiz.

His most striking accomplishment, however, was an expedition against Jamaica, the greatest commercial center of the New World and the haven par excellence of the Caribbean buccaneers. Jamaica, like the rest of the Caribbean, had, in less than a century, become enormously wealthy. Its wealth, however, did not only come from the galleons of the Spanish king, but from the exporting of merchandise to England and to North America.

Initially, this merchandise consisted principally of sugar, rum, and molasses. To this was added cotton, tobacco, ginger — and, of course, the contraband articles sold to the Spanish colonies. Finally, slave traffic was added, and conferred enormous profits on the traders, both French and English. (The franchise on slaves passed from the hands of the French into those of the English in 1712.)

The Spanish subjects of the New World were no less wealthy than the

At left: Forward section of a seventeenth-century galleon, the *San Juan Nepomuceno*. (Drawing by Jean-Charles Roux.)

Right: A diver, accompanied by sergeant-majors, explores the plateau a short distance away from our first dig site.

Below: The sea offers us far more wealth than the gold of the Spanish galleons.

French and English merchants. They represented a large market for European goods; and the goods they demanded were no longer the necessities — tools and food — but the luxuries: the finest weapons, the most luxurious silks, and the most exquisite porcelain.

New Commercial Routes

It is difficult today to appreciate the volume of Caribbean commerce in the eighteenth century, or the immense number of ships that were engaged in it. And this, despite the dangers of trade with the New World, both from pirates and from navigational hazards. It is true that, by now, seamen were

more experienced and more knowledgeable with respect to the peculiarities of the American coastal waters, reefs, and, above all, to the winds and storms of the Caribbean. The Florida strait, for instance, was no longer regarded as the only possible point of entry into the crown of islands in that sea. Ships now sailed through the channel between Cuba and Hispaniola, and through the "Passa Mona" between Hispaniola and Puerto Rico. Another route ran north from Trinidad and passed by Martinique and Guadaloupe to lead out of the Caribbean by way of the Lesser Antilles. All of these routes converged on Bermuda, whence ships entered the Gulf Stream and caught the west winds.

The ships of this era were still incapable of tracking; but their captains had discovered a secret: along the coastlines of the New World, there was a variation of 10° (and sometimes of 20°) in the direction of the wind during the day and at night. They took advantage of this phenomenon, for example, to skirt the coasts of Venezuela from Cartagena to Trinidad.

The English, French, and Dutch seamen who developed such techniques and followed these new trade routes were now more traders than pirates. They brought to the Americas the luxury goods for which the colonials had developed such an avid need; and they returned to their home ports loaded down with rum, logwood, and sugar. And they made an enormous profit in both directions.

Luxury in the New World

In the eighteenth century, New Spain — present-day Mexico — cultivated a luxurious style of life that rivaled, or surpassed, that of the mother country. There were now "gold and silver families" — counts and marquises named Las Rayas, Otera, Valenciana, Obregon, and Ruhl, among others. These families were not content with building magnificent palaces for themselves in the formerly poverty-stricken colonies. They also aspired to live the life favored by the great lords of Europe; and for this they required silks and laces for themselves and their ladies, and sumptuous furnishings for their houses. Thus, to Mexico City (as well as Lima, Quito, and Oaxaca) came glass from Venice, mirrors from St.-Gobain, satins from Florence, and furniture from Paris. The creole ladies were not happy unless they were decked out in French finery. Everywhere, one saw the finest velvets, muslin, ivory, and painted or printed fabrics.

The wealth to support these tastes came not only from the gold and silver mines of the New World, but also from other, more exotic sources. At Oaxaca, for example, great fortunes were made by means of an insect, the cochineal, which, when dried and powdered, became a dyestuff highly prized in Europe. The cochineal alone brought, revenues to New Spain of some eight million pounds a year. Cocoa, ipecac, and vanilla also brought in huge sums. Quinine — known as Peruvian bark or Jesuit powder — was greatly sought after in Europe. And tortoise shell and mother-of-pearl were the objects of a flourishing traffic.

A Pitiful Fleet

Given the intense commercial activity of the English, Dutch, and French in the New World, it was inevitable that the role of the Spanish galleon should decline in importance. And, indeed, by the beginning of the eighteenth century, they were at the sunset of their long, and sometimes heroic, history. The Spanish flotas had at one time counted as many as a hundred ships. But, after the disaster at Vigo, they seldom could gather more than ten or twelve vessels for a transatlantic convoy.

By the end of 1712, the best that Spain could do was to assemble a fleet comprising two warships, two cutters, and an ancient merchantman called the *Urca de Lima.*

This pitiful Fleet of New Spain gathered at Veracruz, under the command of Captain General Juan Esteban Ubilla. At the same time, the Fleet of Tierra Ferma, commanded by General Don Antonio de Echeverz y Zubira — who was more a speculator than a general — arrived at Cartagena.

The fact that the two fleets had assembled in their respective ports did not mean that they were about to set sail on the first leg of their crossing to Spain; for the Spaniards had very few ships that were in any condition for a transatlantic journey.

Indeed, Spain had few ships of any description. The best of Ubilla's vessels, for instance, was a former English warship, the *Hampton Court*, captured by the French and presented by Louis XIV to Philip V. It had been built in London in 1678 and modernized in 1701. And as for the ships of Don Antonio de Echeverz y Zubira, two of them were French, and two were Dutch. All of them had this in common, however, that they were in need of extensive repairs, their hulls all had to be scraped and painted, and their riggings had to be replaced with hemp from Manila. This work proceeded at the languid pace customary in tropical lands.

This gold collar was the badge of rank of Captain General Juan Esteban Ubilla. From it hangs a whistle — which does double-duty as a toothpick and an earpick. The collar was found in the wreck of a galleon that went down off present-day Cape Kennedy, in 1715. (Photo, Taylor and Dull, Inc.)

Porcelain from China

As soon as the repairs had been completed, the cargoes of the two fleets were loaded. On this occasion, these cargoes were of particularly great value, for, because of pirates and the continuing war with England and Holland, there had been no convoy for the preceding two years. A heavily guarded convoy had just arrived with a large quantity of silver bars and gold pieces struck at the Mexican mint.

The loading took a considerable amount of time; but, even when it was completed, the fleets were still not ready to sail. The *Nao de China* had not yet arrived at Acapulco with its load of marvelous Chinese products, brought to Manila by junks.

Manila at that time was the market place of Spanish and Chinese merchants. To that city were brought the masterpieces of Asiatic workmanship, and especially the exquisite K'ang Hai porcelains that were so highly prized in Europe. This commerce between the East and the West had long been the exclusive province of the Portuguese and the Arabs, who had access to the Moluques (Indonesia) through the Indian Ocean. The Spaniards, however, had discovered another route, that of the Pacific; and, thanks to their possession of the Philippines, they also had a key to the fabled world that Columbus had only dreamed of reaching. That dream had been realized, but not by Columbus. A Jesuit missionary from Spain, St. Francis Xavier, named papal legate to Goa, in India, had evangelized that country, visited Malacca, Indonesia, and Japan, and died in China, near Canton. Now, galleons in the ports of the New World took on spices, and the silks and translucent bowls and cups that the manufacturers of France, Germany, and Holland were attempting to imitate.

Don Juan Esteban de Ubilla therefore had no choice but to wait for the mule train from Acapulco to arrive with the merchandise brought by the *Nao de China*. And he waited almost a year; for mules are notoriously slow animals, and the Spaniards relied heavily upon them for inland traffic. In 1712 alone, one hundred thousand of these animals had been imported into the New World.

Meanwhile, at Cartagena, Don Antonio de Echeverz y Zubira was waiting for other caravans. These crossed the Isthmus of Darien, carrying to the Atlantic coast the cargoes brought to the ports of the Pacific, and especially to Callao, the port of Lima.

Finally, in March 1715, the Fleet of Tierra Ferma and that of New Spain were ready to sail for Havana, where, according to custom, they were to meet for the transatlantic crossing. At Havana, however, there were new delays. There were feasts and celebrations to be attended, as there always were when the fleets assembled in port.

It had been three years since the Cubans had seen a fleet, and they would not be deprived of the opportunity for merrymaking. And the most insistent celebrant of all was the governor of Havana, Casa Torres, a man of ninety years.

The number of ships in the combined fleets was increased to eleven at Havana by the addition of a French vessel, the *Grifon*, commanded by one Captain Daré, with a precious cargo. Daré, fearing a pirate attack, asked permission to join the convoy, and, despite Ubilla's opposition, was finally allowed to do so. The cargo of the fleet as a whole was also increased in value by the addition of merchandise that Cuban businessmen were shipping to Spain.

Finally, on July 24, 1715, the fleet weighed anchor. Despite the small number of ships, the sight of the fleet filing past the fortress of El Moro under full sail, hulls bristling with cannon, must have been an imposing sight. If so, it was only superficially so. The truth of the matter was that, of the eleven ships, only the *Grifon* was truly seaworthy. The others were overloaded, and their seams leaked outrageously. It was to these sieves that Spain entrusted her treasure.

To make matters worse, the fleet had delayed its departure until late in July, the beginning of the hurricane season. For delapidated ships that were loaded to the decks with heavy cargo, and were too high out of the water and too clumsy to be able to maneuver, it was almost a sentence of death to the two thousand men aboard the vessels of the fleet.

A Hurricane Breaks

For the first day of the voyage, the sea was calm, the sky clear, as the convoy sailed northward toward the Bahamas. After two days, the clouds gathered, and visibility was reduced to almost nothing. It was an ominous sign for those who knew the waters in that region.

The following night, the wind rose, and the ships began to roll, and passengers and cargo were tossed about. By morning, black clouds were rolling across the heavens, and the heat had become unbearable. On the horizon, squalls could be seen, purple in the distance. By the time the fleet reached the Florida canal, the wind had doubled in force. The ships were now caught between a coastline bordered with murderous coral on one side, and the Bahamas Bank, with its reefs, on the other. But no one knew for certain what was the position of the fleet, nor how far it was to shore. The sea was so rough that it was impossible to take soundings. Twice, a man had been installed on the prow with a sounding line; and twice the line had been ripped from his hand by waves.

On July 27, the hurricane broke with full fury over the ships, smashing their masts and shredding their rigging. The vessels were incapable of withstanding such a storm. With their square sails, their short rudders, and their heavy hulls, they could not maneuver to escape from the wind that was driving them toward the Florida coast. The crews and passengers, convinced that their hour had come, fell on their knees and prayed, and resigned themselves to death. Many of them were washed overboard by the waves and disappeared into the sea.

The end came shortly thereafter. A lookout on Captain General Ubilla's flagship sighted the breakers and gave the alarm, but his voice was drowned in the wind. A few minutes later, the galleon struck the reef barrier and disintegrated almost instantly. At the last moment, Captain General Don Juan Esteban Ubilla was glimpsed on the poop, dressed in silk, his hand resting on his sword, with the great gold collar of his rank hanging from his neck. Then he and several hundred of his crewmen were thrown into the sea and disappeared forever.

Two goblets found intact in the wreck.

A short distance to the south, the ship of Don Antonio de Echeverz y Zubira met the same fate, as did eight other ships of the fleet. Only one vessel managed to escape the reefs; Captain Daré's *Grifon*.

Daré had disobeyed orders and, rather than follow the course established for the convoy, had sailed northeastward, and was thus able to flee before the storm.

Over a thousand men perished in the disaster. The survivors were those who were washed up onto the shore. And, in the sea, was the treasure, valued at 14 million.

Of the survivors, some took all that they could find of gold and jewels and made their way into the interior. Others made rafts and floated to the city of St. Augustine, a journey of several days' duration.

Shortly thereafter, rescue teams were sent out, along with a company of Spanish soldiers and a group of native divers, in an attempt to bring up the

Two bowls that were part of the wreck's cargo. They probably came from the pottery works of Samadet.

treasure in the flagship of the fleet. But the news of the disaster had, by now, also reached Jamaica, the haven and home of the Caribbean's English adventurers. One of the most famous of these, Captain Edward Teach — better known as Blackbeard — and Captain Henry Jennings, launched several attacks against the Spanish camp and managed to reach the sunken ship. Jennings alone was able to bring back 350,000 pieces of eight from this adventure.

Then, the ships of Don Juan Esteban Ubilla and Don Antonio de Echeverz y Zubira, or at least what was left of them, remained undisturbed in their sand and coral graves for 250 years. It was not until 1965 that an American, Kip Wagner, having read an account of the destruction of the fleet, decided to locate the sunken ships.* On the east coast of Florida, not far from Cape Canaveral, he located the site of the Spanish camp from which the Spaniards had attempted to salvage their treasure; and in the ground there he found several pieces of silver, a gold ring, and thirteen pieces of eight. The real treasure, however, was in the sea, and Wagner brought up a fortune in pieces of eight and gold escudos — and also the magnificent gold collar of the Captain General of the Fleet.

This insignia of rank is made of a chain over twelve feet in length and comprising 2176 links. From it hangs a gold whistle, in the form of a dragon; and the dragon is shaped in such a way that one end is able to be used as a toothpick, and the other as an earpick.

The Seafaring Dutch

During the first half of the eighteenth century, the Dutch, more than the English, were the true rulers of the sea. For fifty years, they were the greatest maritime power of the world. They had the best ships, the best men, and the best merchants. And they also had the best financing, from the Bank of Amsterdam. The Dutch were strictly traders, and their ships, only lightly armed, were on every sea. They flourished in the Far East, and traded with China

---

*Wagner wrote an account of his adventure in *National Geographic*, and then in a fascinating book, *Pieces of Eight* (New York, Dutton, 1967), on which the above narrative is based. The most beautiful of the treasures he removed from the ships were sold by Parke-Bernet in New York, who have allowed us to reproduce several of the photographs from the catalogue issued on that occasion. The reader will find additional information in a booklet issued by Parke-Bernet for the exposition that preceded the sale, entitled *Treasure of the Spanish Main*.

and the East Indies. From their colony of Batavia, they imported spices and porcelain for European use. Under the influence of China, the Dutch began making their own chinaware in more than thirty factories, most of which were located in the town of Delft; and they exported their product to the whole world.

As the center of this intense activity, Amsterdam became the banking center of Europe, and it was to that city, in one way or another, that half of the silver from Mexico found its way.

Dutch interests in the Caribbean area, which went back to the sixteenth century, made it necessary for them to have a local base of operations. And that is why, since 1648, they have shared with France the little island of St. Martin, which is near Remy de Haenen's own St. Barthélemy.

The Company of the Indies

French maritime interests had begun to share in commerce with the New World at the beginning of the eighteenth century, when trade had begun to replace piracy in the Caribbean. The creation by Jean-Baptiste Colbert of a trading company, the Company of the Indies, had contributed greatly to that involvement. Its headquarters were in Paris, but it had offices in five port cities: Bordeaux, Le Havre, Nantes, Rouen, and Lyon.

By 1750, the Company of the Indies had thirty ships, of which it lost three or four each year. From France, these ships carried wine, liquor, mirrors, and musical instruments. If they were bound for China, they brought back porcelain, tea, spices, and fabrics. The merchandise they brought back was sold, first, at Nantes; then, after 1733, at Lorient. A strict inventory preceded every sale, for certain kinds of merchandise could not be offered in France: calico, cotton prints, and silks. The reason for this regulation was to protect French manufacturers of these goods. Calico, for instance, was being manufactured at Nantes itself. Muslin and white cotton would be sold, but only if they were clearly "marked," and if they were intended for export.* Whoever bought such merchandise was required to sell it abroad in no more

---

*The "mark" consisted of attaching a piece of parchment to the fabric, by means of lead seals. These seals showed the fleur-de-lis, and the motto, *Florebo quo ferar* — which was the motto of the Company of the Indies. The fact that the company was dissolved in 1770 enabled us to fix a terminal date with respect to the seals we found on the Silver Bank.

than six months and to have that sale verified by the nearest French consul. No doubt, such regulations were more honored in the breach than in reality; but the shipowners of Nantes, and the merchants of Bordeaux who traded with the Indies, certainly took advantage of them to effect a quick turnover of merchandise in the Caribbean.

Nantes did not languish when it was deprived of its position as the market place for the goods of the Company of the Indies. To the contrary, it turned its attention to the Antilles, to which it sold calico, porcelain, and ebony taken from the coasts of Africa.

On the return trip, the ships from Nantes carried rum, sugar, and tobacco, among other things. It is estimated that forty shipowners outfitted a hundred ships a year for this commerce — although it is true that ships were no larger than three hundred tons.

Coral — which turned out to be our worst enemy on this expedition.

ELEVEN

Finally: a Date

Tuesday, August 20. The days are getting shorter. When I go for my morning dive at six twenty-five, it is daylight, but the sun is not yet over the horizon. The water is clear, and there is no current.

I am going to place a buoy marking a spot for Gaston to make an exploratory sounding, behind the third mound and on the axis of the galleon's forward section. Nonetheless, I am reluctant to let Gaston work in that spot, because the ocean floor is a thick crust of limestone.

I look at the spot where Gaston was working yesterday, around the cannon with the chain on it. The hole is still small. There is more work to be done here.

The "buccaneers' hole" is not much bigger than Gaston's. Here, I pause for a remarkable sight: two huge, superb parrot fish, black with blue bands, are suspended motionless in the water, in a vertical position with their heads straight up. They are being "cleaned"; not by the little blue wrasses — the *Labridae dimidiatus* — who usually do that job, but by bright yellow wrasses.

Upon my return to the *Calypso*, we begin breaking open the pieces of coral brought up by the baskets last night. There are a few pieces of iron; and there is a pistol, encrusted with coral, but with its carved butt and its firing mechanism still intact. The barrel is very pitted and scarred.

Throughout the day, the diving teams relieve one another in the usual fashion over a twelve-hour period. At the third mound, the exploration team (Gaston), spends the morning deepening the hole around the cannon, and, in the afternoon, begins a hole in the sand between the second and third mounds. Under the cannon, we discover a piece of black petrified wood, a lead ball, a few pottery shards, a sheet of lead like those used between a cannon and its carriage or mounting, and a pulley sheave made of guaiacum. But there is absolutely nothing in the hole between the two mounds.

During the afternoon, I dive with Bernard for a while, and then with Gaston. I ask Bernard to work on a bias toward the east. I watch the airlift at work. On a level with the breach of the new cannon, I see that there is still much wood. It is only a thin layer, however, and has splintered visibly over rocks in some places, while in other spots the rocks seem to be on top of the wood.

Our auxiliary airlift is hard at work, looking for all the world like a miniature volcano in eruption. It is almost comical; but it does an effective job.

At 11 P.M., when we are about to go to bed, a squall comes up from the south and the water becomes very choppy. The *James and Mary*, loaded down as it is with its baskets, begins to fill with water. In another half hour, it will sink. The divers are immediately in the water, and, working under our floodlights, they bring the raft near the *Calypso* and we remove the two baskets. One of them contains about a ton of material, and the other half as much. Then the raft's floats are pumped and bailed, and the *James and Mary* is saved.

By the time we get to bed, the barometer is climbing.

A Century Too Soon

Wednesday, August 21. The day begins late: at 8 A.M. The reason is that we want to test some of our new theories. In order to do this, three teams will be assigned to dig systematically around the mound, while two other teams will work at taking apart the mound.

My dive this morning reveals nothing new. I place four buoys to show the teams where to dig today.

Late in the morning, Serge brings aboard a few items taken from the area to the southeast of the mound: a large, deep earthenware plate, intact; two items that look like bronze spoons, but with their patterns reversed. These, we surmise, are the two parts of a mold for casting small spoons, probably of pewter or silver. There is also a large piece of bronze, which we assume to be a pestle, or a bell hammer. But as soon as Frédéric Dumas catches sight of it he identifies it as the movable weight of a large Roman scale, with its iron hook missing.

Top left: A diver uncovers still another cannon in a coral crevice.

Top right: One of the largest cannons we found.

Bottom left: The cannon is lowered to the rear deck.

Bottom right: Paul Zuéna uses a sledgehammer to rid the cannon of its coral covering.

Frédéric Dumas holds a cannon ball in front of the cannon to determine its caliber.

This weight, as it turns out, is the occasion of a terrible disappointment. On one side of it, there is the remnant of an inscription: *DC*. It is what remains of a date, in Roman numerals. Taken alone, they may mean 1500. On the other side, however, there is another inscription, this one reading originally 1700, but with the two zeroes almost obliterated and two rather fuzzy threes inscribed over them. It is probably the last date on which the weights of the scale were inspected and verified. Still, the figures are difficult to make out, and there is still room for doubt. But then, Raymond Coll brings up another weight, this one smaller and much lighter. This one, we soak in acid while we are having dinner. And now, we read, very clearly and in several places, a series of dates: 1722, 1730. Then, another date which could be 1723 or 1755 or 1766. And, finally — and with irrevocable clarity — *1756*. It is likely that the questionable date on the large weight, which we optimistically interpreted as 1733 is also 1766. This means that our galleon sank after *1756*.

It means, therefore, that our galleon is not *Nuestra Señora de la Concepción.*

This is difficult to swallow, and our disappointment expresses itself in a bitter rechristening of the wreck; *Nuestra Señora de la Decepción.*

During the afternoon, Michel Deloire — always the sharp-eyed one — finds two new cannon near the small anchor, about two hundred feet to the north of the galleon's forward section, and also two pieces of mounting from the rudder and the stern post. It seems that the pintle is in the reef above the small anchor, and the gudgeons are farther away.

I decide that we must make an exhaustive search for other pieces, and then make a new map of the work area, which now seems to be getting larger, so that we may start working in other reefs at the same latitude as the present one.

The problem is this: along this reef, there are either two sunken ships, or one ship that has scattered its parts all over the bottom. If there is only one, it is not *Nuestra Señora*, as demonstrated by the dates that we have just discovered. But if there are two, the second one may be *Nuestra Señora*.

I put myself to sleep tonight by reading a book on whales.

A Large Cannon.

Thursday, August 22. A disorganized day — which shows how deeply we have been shaken by yesterday's discoveries.

Bernard and I juggle the diving teams and have the new assignments approved by Captain Caillart, and then I post the day's work schedule in the wardroom. This schedule, however, is not followed to the letter. Altogether, we work for nine hours on the mound. Gaston digs hole number six but finds nothing; and then he finds a few pieces of metal and pottery behind mound number four. Late in the day, Philippe Sirot and I work in the same spot with the auxiliary airlift for a half-hour or so, which is as much time as I have air for. We will continue digging here tomorrow.

Among the other things accomplished today was the finding of a third cannon near the north anchor. This one is completely covered by a cone of coral. Caillart and Sirot have completed a map of the northwestern sector of the work area, and this should give us some clue to the solution of our problem.

Also this morning we brought aboard one of the two forward cannon of the galleon. This is that cannon whose mouth was protruding from the oven's hole when we first arrived. We cleaned it off with sledgehammers and brushes and found a number, crudely written and split in two parts by the touchhole, on the rearmost part of the cannon: H 2250 A. And that was all.

I did not expect to learn much from this cannon. Galleons did not always carry Spanish artillery. They often had French, Dutch, or Italian cannon, for Spain bought her weapons from almost every country in Europe. The fact that our cannon bore no date was not particularly significant, for a date would not have told us much about the year of the ship's sinking. After all, cannons made in the sixteenth century were in use as late as 1820.

Even so, an examination of the cannon did reveal one thing: that, at the time of the wreck, this ship's cannon were loaded and ready for battle. We

Facing page: The forward and rear sections of the wreck, lying about 150 feet from one another. The sketch also shows the *Calypso*'s two anchorages.

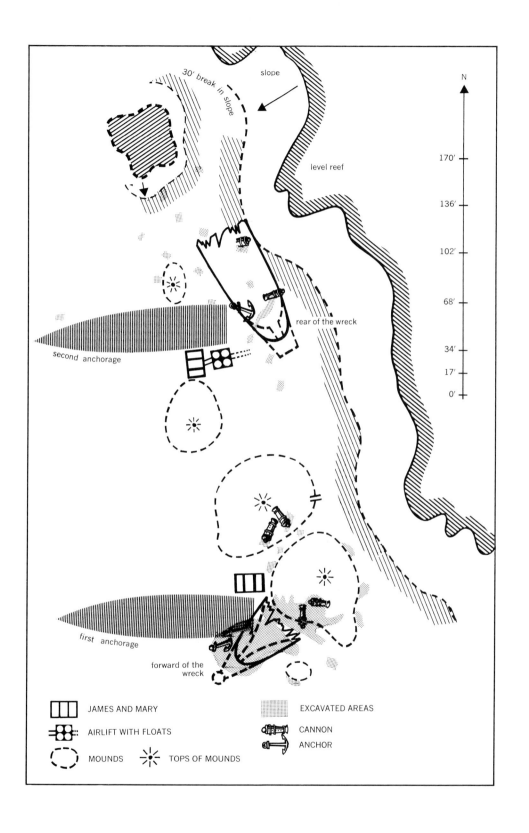

30' break in slope

slope

level reef

N

170'

136'

102'

68'

34'

17'

0'

rear of the wreck

second anchorage

first anchorage

forward of the
wreck

JAMES AND MARY

EXCAVATED AREAS

AIRLIFT WITH FLOATS

CANNON

ANCHOR

MOUNDS

TOPS OF MOUNDS

An eighteenth-century glass boat. The standard shown is that of Leghorn (Livorno), a city that carried on a brisk trade with the Antilles. (Musée des Arts Décoratifs, Paris.)

Captain Cousteau, on the bridge of the *Calypso*, holding the ship's mascot, Ulysses.

found the cannon ball in place; and no doubt the powder was also there. In an age of pirates, few ships carrying rich cargoes dared sail without being ready for immediate combat.

We weighed the cannon, and found that it was 2500 pounds. Then we oiled it down and stored it temporarily on the rear deck.

The only other find of interest was a broken plate, decorated with an obviously Indian motif in blue.

All day long there have been impassioned discussions about yesterday's find. This is our seventeenth consecutive day of work since returning from Puerto Rico; and they have been seventeen exhausting days, working with the incessant roar of the compressor, spending hour after hour breaking coral

A diver goes on a final search in the dig area.

Above: The fish of the reef, now that man has left them in peace, resume their tranquil lives. Here are two specimens of *Pomacanthus paru*.

Right: We scuttle the *James and Mary*.

— almost 300 tons of it so far, we estimate. And, to date, our reward has been some ceramics of dubious value, a cannon, and a few cannon balls. From a financial viewpoint, we have spent without counting the cost; and, from the standpoint of human effort, there has been an incalculable expenditure of energy. To make matters worse, we do not even know the identity of the sunken ship on which we have spent all this time, effort, and money. All we know is that it dates from the eighteenth century, and that it is not *Nuestra Señora de la Concepción*. It is probably not even a galleon.

Despite all this, the divers have not lost hope. Why shouldn't an eighteenth-century ship contain a treasure? And who knows for sure that *Nuestra Señora* is not actually somewhere in this area? Such is their reasoning.

A Find

Friday, August 23. What a day filled with contradiction! It is not bad enough to have discovered that our wreck is not what we thought it was. Now we are finding less and less in the third mound. There is less wood, and the holes all around the mound show no trace of a galleon. We have indeed found the forward section of a large ship; but the rear section, and even the middle, seem to have disappeared without a trace. The cannon are the only basis we have for weaving our theories.

At 8 A.M., I dived with Raymond. In the southern sector of the work area, we seem to have laid bare the skeleton of the mound. The faults, filled with mud and debris between the coral, have been emptied out by the airlift. I pointed out to Raymond a place to dig around the broken cannon; then I went to look at the new cannon discovered by Michel at a distance from there, near the north anchor. By some extraordinary chance, we had passed that spot twenty times, without seeing them. They were all covered by a large mass of coral which, as in the case of the cannon we discovered earlier, was in the form of a pagoda. Deloire and Dumas call this formation "cannon coral." Somehow, I have the feeling that there is something in this area; but something that is entirely covered. It may be another ship, or it may simply be the rear of the ship on which we have been working.

On our ship we have found two sizes of cannon. The two pursuit cannon were seven feet four inches long; and the others were eight feet. And now, the cannon we are finding are eight and a half feet. "Yes," says Dumas, "but we have found cannon balls in three sizes."

So, we have decided to expand our activities. De Haenen, Coll, and Durand took the launch and went to explore a reef about a mile to the east of our anchorage. There, they found an anchor, smaller than those we found here.

Sirot and Caillart, meanwhile, were working with picks about fifteen feet from the reef we dynamited on July 28, and Gaston was using the auxiliary airlift on holes six and seven. The results: zero. The rear section of the ship has obviously disappeared, and the theory of a total break in the wreck has been confirmed.

During the morning, Bassaget and Foulon brought up an unguent container, or a kitchen vessel of some kind, which was probably at one time finished in the same sort of glaze as the ceramics we found earlier. It is hard to tell, because the glaze is rather fragile, and has been mostly obliterated by the coral. This pot had a large inscription, in black lettering: J. WYN. Is it a Dutch ship? Or Swedish? Or is it a pirate ship, with loot from a Dutch or Swedish ship?

During the afternoon, Gaston took the auxiliary airlift — with an air hose extension of almost three hundred feet — to the location of the isolated anchor and the three cannon, which we now call the rear work area. His first hole, dug near the cannon which is buried under the coral "pagodas," brings up some pieces of square bottle. But another hole, dug by Dumas and Deloire near the most exposed cannon — the largest one on the reef — turns up things that can only be from a ship. In forty-five minutes, they find a handsome square bottle, virtually intact, six bowls, four goblets, a water pitcher with a spout, and many fragments. Moreover, they saw wood in the hole. *We have found the rear section of our ship.*

This presents problems of a practical nature. Since this new find is a good distance from the old work area, we will have to change the *Calypso*'s anchorage and moorings, move the *James and Mary*, and lengthen the airlift hose. I lay awake turning over these things in my mind. The most difficult thing will be to move the *Calypso* to this new spot, for there is no way to it through the coral. It seems that we will have to dynamite a passageway.

The reason we took so long to discover the rear section of the wreck is that it is not on the same axis as the forward section. During the wreck, the two pieces of the ship not only settled to the bottom at a good distance from one another, but they sank at a right angle to each other.

In the second work area we found things very similar to what we found in the first: bricks, pottery, jars, pieces of rigging, and many bottles. These square bottles are almost all broken, and very pitted and worn, since glass slowly dissolves in seawater. The glass is therefore very thin, and in some of the pieces one can see air bubbles and cracks. Others are rainbow-colored, and very beautiful. There are so many of these bottles that I conclude they are part of a cargo, and that the ship took on, somewhere in the Caribbean, a shipment of rum destined for Europe.

More Bottles

Saturday, August 24. Today, for a change, I am not diving. In the forward work area, two teams are at work with the airlift. Deloire is filming a series of shots and long shots that I drew up. On the reef that we dynamited on July 28, six teams are relieving one another every two hours in the work of removing some 200 tons of coral, at a depth of three to fourteen feet, as an added safety factor for the *Calypso*. In the western work area, Raymond Col has dug several holes, but without finding a sign of the ship except for some whole bottles, and some thick wood, that he turned up near the anchor. But no one is discouraged. We do not yet know the exact direction of the rear section that we have just discovered.

The evening is spent in meetings with the divers; with Caillart, to discuss the mooring plan of the *Calypso*; and with Deloire, to draw up our filming schedule.

Sunday, August 25. Everyone is up at 6 A.M. At 6:30, Deloire films my dive in the light of dawn; and, at 7:00, he is still filming my inspection of the work area in an attempt to capture the atmosphere of the dive of August 13. Unfortunately, the water is not as clear today as it was then.

During the morning, two teams of four men each work at demolishing the coral reef that we dynamited. And two teams of two men each film the activity in the work area, the raising of a basket, the jettisoning of the debris from the portside amidships, and the resultant increase in the size of our heap of waste coral.

Raymond continues digging new holes, this time near cannons 12, 13, and 14. He brings back a piece of flat metal — perhaps a saber blade, or a barrel ring.

In the afternoon, Deloire films Gaston working with John Soh's magnetic detector, looking for — but not finding — the missing cannon.

The main airlift breaks down, and we have to waste precious time repairing it.

Work continues on the dynamited reef. And Raymond Coll tries out, under the ship and outside the work area, our high-pressure hoses, which I hope to use tomorrow in the search for the hull of the rear section of our pseudogalleon.

We have done our best to do as little damage as possible to the spectacular marine "countryside" of the Silver Bank.

Monday, August 26. At seven o'clock. Deloire and I are in the water for the retakes of some of yesterday's shots. The water is clearer this morning, and visibility is better. The film, I think, will capture the desired atmosphere as much as is possible — taking into consideration that a man's state of mind is a matter for poets rather than for cinematographers.

As soon as we are out of the water, De Haenen and Foulon set off two charges of TNT on the reef that is still endangering the *Calypso*. They then go to the other side of the reef, and, with a very small charge, disengage a large piece of metal caught in the coral near the so-called "pump" marked on our map. It is a piece of forged steel and is one of the two pieces that supported the massive rear sections of galleons by bracing against the sternpost.

Michel, Didi, and Bernard go down to film some of the objects we missed earlier, while Gaston and Bassaget begin working to remove the dynamited blocks from the reef.

Raymond Coll, meanwhile, is working with the flame thrower to dig a trench near the north anchor. It is hard work — as it always is with a Galezaai — and it raises such a cloud that he can barely see what he is doing. Moreover, the water jet pushes mire and sand back into the hole as quickly as he can dig it.

Two Sites

Tuesday, August 27. I am not diving this morning, even though the water is still clear. De Haenen and Foulon are setting off six explosions on the reef. That is a great deal; but then, this is the last day for this kind of work. We have decided that if, by the end of the day, the *Calypso* still cannot pass over the reef in safety, then we will give it up.

Actually, we face several possibilities. We can abandon the entire project right now; but I am unwilling to do that. Or we can start a new search for *Nuestra Señora* — which I am willing to do, but only in the immediate vicinity of our present location. Or, we can stay here and continue to work so as to film the operation; but that would be worth while only if we were certain of the direction in which the rear section lies on the bottom. This is not a very inspiring list of alternatives; but then, despite our cry of victory on August 23, all of our soundings with the auxiliary airlift since then have had either negative or unintelligible results.

Today, our accomplishments have been to lower a dangerous reef by at least fourteen feet, to dig two new holes on the north site, and to work with the airlift near the block of four cannon.

In the evening, we hang our finest treasures on the port bulkhead: our bowls, bottles, and cannonballs. It looks like a flea market. Robino has cleaned out the cannon and its touchhole.

Later, an unusual mood in the wardroom. Everyone is devouring books on sunken treasure while drinking Remy's rum. And Remy is sitting alone, silently, thinking.

Wednesday, August 28. This morning, Dumas, Deloire, De Haenen and I went over the area between the "forward anchor" and the caldrons inch by inch for two hours. It seems impossible that we could have missed anything. Beginning from the last cannon found on our ship, and for a distance of about two hundred feet, there was absolutely nothing. Then, in an area of some one hundred feet, we found six huge caldrons (one of them of copper), and two stretches of stones and brick.

As soon as we were aboard, we appraised our findings. The stones from the two sites are not the same, and neither are the bricks. There is a stretch two hundred feet between the two sites, with nothing in it. Therefore, we have found not one ship, but two.

The eastern section of our first ship's forward has not yet been explored, and Didi, Michel, and Remy undertake this task. Then, during the afternoon, they inspect the "pump site" on the west side. There, they find a piece of metal similar to that found on August 26; and we conclude that our "pump" is actually the elbow of a large cast-iron pipe. It seems that now there are three wrecks.

Didi is struck by the vast coral formations — the Gothic columns, the caves, the deep, narrow vertical holes. Given this mass of limestone, there can be no question of digging out a sunken ship. "It would be insane to try," Didi says in disgust.

We have found two sets of cannon balls designed to destroy the masts and rigging of an enemy ship. They are roughly in the shape of a dumbbell, two cannon balls joined by a large metal bar. There is also a sort of vase with a round bottom, broken, but with all the pieces present; many cannon balls; and two new seals, just like the ones found earlier.

The Second Work Area

Thursday, August 29. Dumas, Deloire and De Haenen are exploring the region around the anchor found by Coll, on the reef situated a mile to the east. It is a relatively modern anchor, and rather small.

The rest of us spend the morning moving the *James and Mary* and the airlift two hundred feet to the north. It is a huge job. The vertical section of the airlift has now been reduced by ten feet, which means that the air jet is at a depth of thirty feet.

During the afternoon, there are two work sessions with the airlift near the north anchor. After the first of these, Caillart and Gaston bring back some pottery, some bottles, and some pieces of lead and wood. They report that a long piece of wood runs from their hole (ten feet to the east of the anchor) toward the anchor. The area is full of coral rocks, which means that we will have to move the *Calypso* very soon.

Robino tells me that the *Calypso* has now beaten its previous record for remaining at sea without putting into port for supplies. If we do not return to San Juan before September 6 — as we plan — we will have been at sea for twenty-seven days. This would have been impossible without our distilling apparatus, which we use only at night and which gives us some four hundred liters of water a day, and without using our paper plates and cups in order to conserve our fresh-water supply.

Friday, August 30. By 7 A.M., the diving teams are at work in the new area. At nine o'clock, I go down to see what is happening. The first thing I find is that the seven-foot length of flexible tubing, which runs from the lower end of the airlift's elbow, has been crushed and is blocking the suction. Also, the fifty-foot length of flexible tubing is rubbing against a coral growth and becoming frayed. I tell Gaston to take care of this. Then I draw a map of the excavations and correct the direction on the bottom of the three north cannon with respect to the anchor. This is very hard to do because the whole area is covered with coral, and even more so because the pieces of the ship are from twenty-four to thirty inches beneath the ocean floor. It would be difficult for anyone to guess that a ship sank here only two hundred years ago.

During the morning, an exploration team consisting of Deloire, Dumas, and De Haenen go to film the massive coral banks to the east and west of the reef. There is no sign of the *Nuestra Señora* in the vicinity of the metal piece found on August 26.

During the afternoon, Dumas changes the direction of his trench, and finds an amalgam of metal that seems to increase in density as he works away from the north anchor and toward mound number two.

At night, after the second dinner service, we try, without success, to assemble some of our friends in the wardroom in order to film an attempt to use hydrochloric acid on some of our finds. When we did this earlier, and spontaneously, everyone laughed a great deal. But now, it seems that no one can forget the overpowering stench of acid working on metal, and everyone asks to be excused. Of course, everyone is tired; and it is 9:30 P.M.

Tomorrow, if the weather is good, we will move the *Calypso*.

Saturday, August 31. Today has been a day of doubt and discouragement.

First of all, at the practical level, we are wasting our time. Since August 21, we have known that our wreck is not *Nuestra Señora de la Concepción*. At the same time, we discovered that the eighteenth-century vessel on which we have been working was broken into two sections, and that only the forward section is here. Where is the rear? On August 23, we thought we had found it; but now we are not so sure. Of its cargo, we have found only some square bottles and some pieces of pottery, some of it very handsome and the rest of dubious quality. The only reason we really have for staying here any longer is that we have found eleven lead seals, of which ten are marked with the fleur-de-lis — which means that they were not used to seal sacks containing ordinary merchandise. Of course, we are filming everything, and we are getting some beautiful footage. Until now, I personally had never covered a subject like this one. So, we have an extraordinary film.

So for the practical aspect. That, however, is not the most important consideration. The theme of my disenchantment today is the same that, more or less secretly, has been with me for thirty-eight years, since October 1930, when I joined the French Navy without knowing precisely what it was all about. From 1930 to 1937, my doubts were centered on the meaning of military life, and on my "vocation" — for I had always hesitated between three very different kinds of work. There is nothing unusual in that, of course. I have since learned that most Navy men, in every country, have the same doubts.

Since 1937, however — that is, for thirty-one years — I have given myself over, body and soul, carefully burning all bridges behind me, to the sea. I have renounced my ambitions in all other areas, even though, at times, I have been sorely tempted by the attractions of a different kind of life. And I have been loyal to the sea, with a fierce loyalty that springs, in part, from the knowledge that I am not really suited for the life that I lead, either physically or mentally.

From the very first, my sense of wonder at the sea has alternated with a sense of revulsion. My joys have been interlaced with pain and disappointment. For every pleasure that I have derived, I have had to scale a mountain of aversion. I was the only one who knew this; and even I refused to admit it completely to myself. My motive in seeking out new sites to explore, in diving ever deeper, in staying below ever longer, in filming, in fighting, was, certainly, the satisfaction of my curiosity about the sea. But it was also an emotional, almost a sexual need. I had to possess the sea, to dominate it, to conquer it. I was biologically drawn to the sea; and I knew very well that I would never succeed in possessing it totally. Every time that I manage to make a small discovery in the sea, to find a spot of beauty or a moment of ecstasy, my satisfaction is that of a man who succeeds, at least momentarily, in having his way with the woman he loves. And, as in a love affair, the story of my romance with the sea is the story of temptation, disappointments, betrayals, misunderstandings, quarrels, and rages. Underneath it all, there has always been a sense of being trapped. And today, resentment at the trap dominates my emotions; resentment, and almost hate, toward the unceasingly evasive and artful love of my life. And so, today, I will sulk. I will not dive. I will remain alone on this little ship, bitter, with accusations of infidelity running through my mind.

On the New Site

It has taken the whole morning to move the *Calypso* to the new position. There were lines and cables to be shifted, mooring points to be found, and the hundred other tasks that make the displacement of a vessel a more complicated job than one might think. We are now anchored against the wind and against the swell that turns about the southern point of the reef. The rear deck is about fifteen feet to the north of the *James and Mary*.

During the afternoon, three teams work the airlift in relays. The total result: a lump of small nails, found to the south of the trench dug southeast of the anchor. There is nothing more, it seems.

The only notable find of the day has been a small cannon that we found early this morning, on top of mound number three, before displacing the *Calypso*. It is a culverin — very graceful in form, but very rusty.

Sunday, September 1. This is our first day in the new work area. In order to allow for a bit of rest, the day begins only at 8 A.M., with teams of four men each working with both airlifts. The large airlift, following the ditch running toward the cannon, turns up a fair quantity of pottery; but, the nearer it gets to the cannon, the less it finds and the nearer the pottery is to the surface of the ocean floor.

The auxiliary airlift is digging two holes between mound number three and the dynamited reef, and two more between the mound and the reef's slope. Finally, another hole is dug on a spot suggested by Michel Deloire, about three hundred feet from the anchor. There, Coll finds a large lead sheet, some wood, and some iron benches.

The afternoon is spent clearing the work area; that is, in removing the larger blocks of coral and staghorn with which the site is literally covered.

The cameras are at work the whole while, filming every step of the operation.

Dumas and De Haenen are very excited over some new pottery that we have just found. These seem to be of the same kind that we found in our first work area. If it turns out that the cargo in this area is the same as in the first one, it seems that we have finally found the location of our ship's rear section.

Monday, September 2. Our supplies are running low. Our chef has not yet begun serving us leftovers, but his pantry is almost empty.

Morale, to all outward appearances, is still high, but I can feel that the men are keeping up their spirits out of a sense of regard for the *Calypso*'s reputation, and by an effort of the will. There is no doubt that everyone is tired, and disappointed, and has lost his drive.

I go down, as usual, at six-thirty, and carefully inspect the holes. There are vestiges of a ship, bottles, pottery, metal, wood, barrel hoops — all caught in blocks of dead coral, and sometimes under three to five feet of dust and pebbles. There is no trace of ballast, nor of a keel. I return to the *Calypso*, convinced that the rear two-thirds of the ship, after breaking away from the forward section, was smashed to bits against the reef, and that the pieces were carried away by the swell before they could be buried. Then, I reach a decision: we will dig a large hole, for the sake of principle, in the most likely spot. If we find nothing, we will give it up and leave.

The job of clearing the work area continues all morning, with four teams of two men each working in shifts. The *Calypso*'s windlass manages to tear free a "cannon pagoda" with its cannon, but then drops it under the *Calypso*.

Tuesday, September 3. Today, we try to find the maximum number of significant objects — an effort that does not bear much result except for a few new kinds of pottery. Nonetheless, Dumas comes up to tell me that the hole dug by Raymond Coll, to Michel's specifications, is beginning to turn up wood from a hull at a depth of about four feet beneath the bottom, at the foot of a giant meandrine. The planks found so far are all parallel to the reef — which allows me finally to make an approximate overlay of the rear section of the ship and to attach it to our map of August 24.

The Last Dive

Wednesday, September 4. I am going to make a last dive before giving the order to abandon our work in the Silver Bank. I want to make a final visit to our dig, while everyone else is still asleep. Paul Zuéna, who is on watch on deck, gives me an accomplice's smile. I suit up as quietly as possible and slide softly into the cool water of dawn.

I feel strangely alone, and my equipment seems to weigh less than usual. I let myself sink slowly. I can see the whole work area in a single glance. I

The reef fish once again begin grazing on coral. Here is a *Chaetodon falcula*.

know that, in a short while, we will give up our treasure hunt for good. And I know that, in fifteen minutes or so, Raymond and Jean-Pierre will begin their work. But, for the moment, I am alone in the sea; and, as before at such moments, success and failure blend together, and neither one seems of much importance.

We see, surrounded by coral, sponges and algae, a Chromis (foreground) and some specimens of midnight-blue triggerfish.

The Division of Spoils

We are getting ready to leave. This morning, in order to set their minds at rest, the divers set to work once more, but without result.

Early in the afternoon, I organize a film-showing on the rear deck. Everyone is there, watching. There are three cannon, a two-ton coral pagoda, the north anchor, a basketful of staghorn, pottery and bottles, the wheelbarrow in action, Gaston and his tape recorder, four divers suiting up, a bit of horseplay between Michel Deloire and Bernard Delemotte. During this last scene, I had Laban's violincello placed against the giant pagoda. Michel turned, saw the violincello, and registered an expression that is priceless.

The showing was a great success, and morale was marvelously high — at the very moment of our failure. Everyone was in fine humor. There was no nervous laughter, and not a trace of bitterness.

Then, as soon as the film is over, work begins again. But, this time, it is the work of clearing the decks of the *Calypso* of our tools — the sledgehammers, markers, crowbars, picks. The coral fragments and the baskets are thrown overboard. The compressor is lowered into the hole. And finally, the hoses and the brushes are put into action. The *Calypso* is still dirty, but at least it is clear, and her old self again.

In the evening, after dinner, we distribute souvenirs of our quest, three per person. Whatever is left will go to Remy de Haenen — except what, by common accord, we have decided should be given to museums.

The division of spoils is at once cordial, solemn, and disappointing. These are, after all, rather dingy treasures. I myself have no complaints. My souvenirs are what I like best: some collages of blackened pottery, glass and shells, cemented together by coral. Mounted on a socle, they will become instant surrealistic art objects, or abstract sculptures. And I find this form of art much more enjoyable than pieces of eight.

TWELVE

A Lesson from the Sea

Alone in my cabin at night, I reflect on the frantic activity of the past weeks and on the unexpected denouement of our treasure hunt. I know that, in my heart, I am strongly relieved that we found no gold, no silver, no pearls, no emeralds. Only rusted iron, a few pieces of porcelain, and a medal of St. Francis.

If things had turned out differently, if we had found the treasure that we sought, it would have been the first time in my life that I gained material wealth from the sea; and that fact would have changed something in my relationship with the sea. I think that, as a result, I would have been the loser rather than the winner — even though, in the opinion of many, money in the bank is the only measure of success.

I cannot speak for other men. For myself, however, for my wife, and for my friends aboard the *Calypso*, I can say now that our investment in the sea is too large to risk losing merely for the sake of a few dollars. That investment consists of what we have sacrificed to lead the life that we do: money, of course; but also time, family ties, and almost everything else that people generally regard as most precious in life. I do not mean to imply that we are martyrs, or ascetics. Certainly, our investment has already been repaid a thousandfold, in happiness, in satisfaction, in the joy of discovery, in the knowledge that we have been able to contribute something to man's understanding of his world and that we have succeeded in opening, however slightly, a door through which other men will follow. I cannot help feeling that this reward was that which came also to the men of the Renaissance, and to the seamen of the Age of Discovery whose ship we sought so diligently and so vainly. This tradition of non-material compensation on the sea is a very old one and is reflected both in history and in fiction. Captain Nemo, Jules Verne's protagonist, took gold from sunken ships — but only to turn it over to support causes that he considered just. There is undoubtedly a morality, an ethic, of the sea; and, even more, an ethic of diving. And, like every ethic, it implies sanctions. In my own case, I am certain that if we had found our sunken treasure, I would inevitably have lived to regret it; for it would have spoiled our Adventure.

These thoughts run through my mind as the *Calypso* cruises through rough gray water. The waves wash over the deck, returning to the sea the last of its coral that we took from it at the Silver Bank. And so it ends. Our work, the tons of limestone that we hauled aboard and broke open with our hammers and picks until our hands bled and our backs ached — all this is now no more than an episode in our lives, a chapter of marine treasure hunting in the story of the *Calypso*. It is good to be on the open sea again, to hear the sweet sound of our engines instead of the compressor's hateful roar. And, above all, it is good to be together, to have survived the gold fever that might have destroyed our team, and to be on our way to more rewarding adventures. I have before me a long list of future projects: an observation, at close quarters, of sea elephants, of walruses, of sea cows; an expedition to investigate the Blue Holes of the Bahamas; another to film the salmon and the otters of Alaska; another to dive on the Great Barrier Reef off the Australian coast; another to dive in New Caledonia and in the Sonde archipelago . . .

The men of the *Calypso* have returned to the open sea, to do the work for which they are best suited by temperament and training. But what are their thoughts? Are they bitter at the realization that their dreams of wealth have, once and for all, gone up in smoke? I know that they are not. At no time did our project on the Silver Bank, for all its psychological dangers, compromise the spirit of our team, its solidarity, or its good humor. I have the proof of this here, within reach of my hand: the interviews taped by Michel Deloire once it became certain that our sunken ship was not *Nuestra Señora de la Concepción*. Everyone aboard, from the galley hand to the captain, had made plans on how he was to spend his fortune; for everyone had believed in the treasure, in the same way that men believe they may win a lottery. Some had planned to

Facing page: Michel Deloire takes a final swim along the coral wall of the Silver Bank before the *Calypso* weighs anchor.

buy houses and boats; some, fur coats for their wives; and others, stores or other businesses for their parents. Morgan, an inveterate bettor, planned to buy race horses. But not a single man expressed either regret or rancor at having worked so hard without material gain. Their reward is the adventure that they lived, and the sense of accomplishment that they have gained, a feeling not unlike that of a man who climbs a mountain.

I know that they are not merely concealing their disappointment for my sake, for I have exactly the same feelings as they; the same conviction that true wealth consists in living and in working. It consists of diving to a sunken ship — even if that ship turns out to be empty of treasure.

A sunken ship, for that matter, is never really empty. It contains history. It tells us about men who lived and suffered in a land that was, at that time, at the very edge of the world. While we were diving to what we thought was *Nuestra Señora de la Concepción*, we often would experience a feeling of sympathy and solidarity with the men of that ship; for they, like ourselves, had traveled over the world in search of adventure, even though their motives may have been somewhat different from our own. These were the men who had dared to be *first*, to venture into the unknown; just as we ourselves were the first to venture into the sea to the outer limits of human survival.

Some of the benefit drawn from our experience at the Silver Bank is of a practical nature. We carried out, for the first time, a systematic dig in a coral bank, and we have learned something very important: that we must not expect too much from archaeological research in tropical seas. Coral grows too rapidly, and buries too deeply the vestiges of man and human artifacts, from hulls of ships to cannon balls. Even so, our dig turned up several objects that are precious to me because of the difficulties involved in obtaining them. They are objects made familiar by daily use, by man's touch: pots, plates, belt buckles. Sometimes, they are things that a man carried around with him. I still smoke, with great pride, a clay pipe that we found, intact, near the mizzenmast.

Frédéric Dumas told me a story that illustrates the sense of human continuity that one gets from such objects. He was diving to a large sixteenth-century ship in the Mediterranean, probably a Genoese warship, a few years before our adventure on the Silver Bank. Dumas was able to establish the age of the ship by means of coins — 127 of them — that he found on the bottom. He did not find the coins, however, in a treasure chest, but at a distance from the wreck, in the sand. They were in a clump, all joined together by coral. And next to them was a rapier, covered with rust; and a skull and other bones. The soldier to whom the coins had belonged had been apparently drowned in the wreck. Three centuries after his death, he was discovered by a diver, to whom he gave his money, and the means of ascertaining the date of his ship. It was a face-to-face meeting, says Dumas, that was worth all the gold in the world.

We have much to learn from the experience of the conquistadors in the New World. And not the least lesson, by far, is this: that they were ruined by their determination to accumulate as much wealth as they possibly could. This lust for gold did not enrich them; it destroyed them and the economy of their country, and compromised, for several centuries, the quality of human life in Spain. "Here is the God of the Spaniards," the Indians used to say, holding up a piece of gold.

All activity on land and in the sea should have as its inspiration, and as its rule of conduct, respect for man and respect for all life forms.

Epilogue

Thursday, September 5. Early this morning we loosen our moorings, take the airlift aboard, and scuttle the *James and Mary*. Then, we pass through our channel, away from the work area, and drop anchor in the open water, while the *Zodiac* returns to pick up the lighted buoys — and smashes against a reef and almost sinks. Finally, at twelve-thirty, the *Calypso* leaves the Silver Bank, where we spent a total of forty-four days, in addition to the time we spent going to and from San Juan for supplies. Two months out of our lives. Gaston's summing up is as follows: "It was monotonous."

Friday, September 6. We arrive at San Juan an hour ahead of schedule. The weather is beautiful; and, in fact, we have been exceptionally lucky in that respect during our whole stay on the Silver Bank. The hurricanes are late this year, it seems.

Immediately, I plunge into my work. There are telegrams to be sent, a schedule of leave-time to be worked out for the men, and the next project to be organized: the expedition to Lake Titicaca, in Peru.

In my mail, there is an ironic piece: a letter from my lawyers, explaining the laws of France on the subject of sunken treasure. I bring the letter into the wardroom and we all read it together in fascination. It seems that if a French citizen finds a treasure — on the Silver Bank or anywhere else — either he must declare it, and then he is reimbursed for his expenses, while the whole of the treasure goes to the French government; or, he can risk not declaring it, and go to prison for theft and fraud.

And that is a fitting epilogue, and a moral, to the story of the *Calypso*'s quest for sunken treasure.

ACKNOWLEDGMENTS

The authors would like to express their gratitude to the following for their generous counsel:

Mme. Nadine Gasc, Curator, Musée des Arts Décoratifs.

M. H. P. Fourest, Curator, Musée Céramique de Sevres.

M. Metman, Curator, Service de Sigillographie des Archives Nationales.

Mlle. Perrenx, Curator, Musée de Samadet.

M. Y. Plessis, Deputy Director, Laboratoire des Pêches Outre-Mer, Musée d'Histoire Naturelle.

APPENDIX I

AMERICA BEFORE COLUMBUS

The New World to which Columbus came was not, as we are tempted to believe, a wholly savage and untamed place. The People lacked some of the basics of European civilization, it is true; for instance, horses were unknown to them, and they had never discovered the use of the wheel. But there were many accomplishments to offset such handicaps. In the political domain, these original Americans, as early as the tenth century, were building mighty empires; and, in the realm of intellectual achievement, they developed a science of cosmography that was far superior to that of Europe.

It would be a mistake, however, to believe that the New World, as a whole, was an oasis of civilization in the European sense of that term. America had many faces, and to its conquerors it offered a variety of aspects. Christopher Columbus, when he went ashore on the island of San Salvador — one of the Bahamas — was greeted by the Lucayas, an agricultural and artistic people who typified the "noble savage" of popular legend. The Spaniards, on the other hand, were shortly to meet a completely different sort of native: the ferocious cannibals of the Caribbean. Such diversity is reflected in the history of the pre-Columbian New World, a history so complex that it has taken historians almost five centuries of study in order to disengage its main lines.

We know that two great empires, both of them tightly organized, dominated the Americas. The Aztec Empire, which had absorbed the ancient Mayan civilization, had its seat in Mexico. Mexico had been the site of a succession of civilizations, the social, artistic, religious and agricultural organization of which had, in its totality, produced a complex of sciences, artists and institutions which equalled, and sometimes surpassed, those of Europe.

Portrait of the King of Texcoco, from an Aztec manuscript. (Bibliothèque Nationale, Paris.)

The Inca with a llama, according to Huaman Poma de Ayala. (Bibliothèque Nationale, Paris.)

The Inca making a libation to the Sun, by Huaman Poma de Ayala. (Bibliothèque Nationale, Paris.)

The Olmecas who lived along the Gulf of Mexico, the Mayas of Central America and the Yucatan, the Toltecs in the heart of Mexico, and the Zapotecs at Oaxaca had each contributed to an "American civilization." The seventh century of the Christian era, one historian of pre-Columbian America tells us, was the time of a dozen golden ages in the New World. The Aztecs whom the Spaniards found in Mexico were not the originators of this civilization, but merely its beneficiaries. They were warlike invaders from the north, whose own culture was inferior to that of the people whom they conquered, but whose arts and sciences they had the good judgment to adopt as their own.

The Aztecs built their capital on pilings in a section of the Tetzcoco lagoon, and called it Tenochtitlán. This city grew and became a great center of industry, commerce, and wealth. There were magnificent temples, and palaces, and a great aqueduct; and each home had its own bath — for the Mexicans were a much cleaner people than their European conquerors.

The people of this thriving empire, strangely enough, had no alphabet. But this did not keep them from progressing far beyond Europeans in the fields of medicine, surgery, botany, astronomy, and mathematics. Cortez himself received the benefit of such scientific skills. A serious head wound he had suffered was treated successfully by an Aztec surgeon, by trepanation.

Cortez' enthusiasm, however, was reserved for the more tangible accomplishments of the Aztecs. He wrote to the Emperor Charles V:

"In addition to a great mass of gold and silver, I was given works of the jeweler's art so precious that, being unwilling to allow them to be melted down, I had a hundred thousand ducats' worth set aside for Your Imperial Highness. These are objects of the greatest beauty, and I have no doubt that

no other prince in the world has anything like them. And lest Your Highness think that I am weaving fairy tales, let me add this: Montezuma has had reproduced, in gold and silver, in precious stones and the plumes of birds, a copy of everything he knows that grows on land or in the water. And everything is so perfectly wrought that one would believe he was seeing the object itself rather than a copy."

As administrators, the Aztecs achieved an economic stability that spared them the years of famine that, during this same era, periodically devastated Europe. It was as soldiers, however, that they prided themselves; for they were a warrior race. Every man was reckoned a soldier from the time he reached his fifteenth year. Their chief weapons were clubs studded with obsidian points, spears, slings, and bows and arrows. They used these arms with more efficacy than one might think. A mare belonging to one of Cortez' men, for instance, had its head cut off by a single blow from a wooden Aztec sword, the blade of which was inset with points of obsidian. The aim of the Aztec warrior, however, was not to kill his enemy in battle, but to take him prisoner so that he might be used later in sacrificial rites — a fact which, no doubt, explains the small number of casualties among the conquistadors. For these imperial Aztecs, for all their high degree of civilization, practiced human sacrifice. In certain of their religious ceremonies, a priest, standing at the pinnacle of a stone pyramid, would cut open the chest of a human victim, tear out the heart, and present it to the crowd of worshipers.

The Aztecs, as has already been noted, had no horses (at their first encounters with the Spaniards, they believed that the horse and the rider were a single monstrous being); they also knew nothing of firearms, or of armor, for they had never learned how to work in iron. They were therefore at a decided disadvantage in battling the invaders from across the sea. Even so, the victory of the conquistadors was due as much to psychological and political factors as to technical superiority. Some of the peoples subject to Aztec domination took advantage of the arrival of the Spaniards to attempt to regain their liberty, a situation which contributed to the rapid conquest of so mighty an empire by a mere handful of Europeans. For, to the 1200 men under Cortez' command were added a force of some 35,000 natives, most of them Chichimecs.

If Cortez benefited from the political unrest of the conquered peoples, he took no less advantage of the religious beliefs of the Mexicans. According to various ancient religious prophecies, the old god of the Toltecs, Quetzalcoatl, was to reappear in a bloody upheaval which was to signal the beginning of a new age. Cortez thus appeared as an emissary of heaven; and the bloodshed and death which accompanied his advent were interpreted as nothing less than the catastrophic events long foretold by the wise men and priests of the Aztecs.

All these things, no doubt, explain the apparent apathy of the Aztec emperor, Montezuma, in the fact of the invaders, and the feeble resistance of his officers and his warriors.

The Mayas

For fifteen hundred years before the coming of Europeans to the New World, the civilization of the Mayas had covered Yucatan, Honduras and Guatemala with splendid cities and monuments. Under Aztec domination, however, the Mayan people had gone into a fatal decline; and, by the time of Cortez' arrival, their once thriving empire had been reduced to eight small principalities, constantly at war among themselves.

The social organization of the Mayas was very similar to that of the Aztecs, and was structured according to a hierarchical arrangement of king, priests, nobles, commoners, and slaves. The land was held in common, and every man cultivated the plot assigned to him.

The Mayas, like the Aztecs, had never discovered the uses of iron. They did not know the wheel, or the arch, and they had no alphabet. Nonetheless, they attained a high degree of expertise in mathematics and in astronomy.

The disappearance of the Mayan empire remains one of the great mysteries of history. Their cities, many of which had contained several hundred thousand inhabitants, were deserted, abandoned to the encroachments of the tropical jungle; and no one knows why. It is possible that the empire collapsed after a social revolution directed against the power of the priests.

The Incas

On the other coast of the New World, that which looked out over the Pacific, there was another empire; and this one was even more vast and more powerful than that of the Aztecs. It is known to us as the empire of the Incas, and covered present-day Bolivia, Peru, Equador — the Andes region. (The word "Inca" is used today to designate both the inhabitants of that empire, and their civilization. In its original meaning, however, it was used to designate only the sovereign, and, by extension, his family and the greatest nobles of his court.)

The Incas, like the Aztecs, were late-comers. When, in the fourteenth century of the Christian era, they established themselves in the Cuzco valley, at an altitude of over ten thousand feet, they were the last in a line of cultures, numbering at least ten, that had flourished in the preceding four millenia. And some of the antecedent civilizations had been more refined and more artistic than the Incan; the Chimu, the Tiahuanaco, the Mochica, the Chavin — which were Peru's first great civilizations. In the opinion of some authorities, the ceramics of the latter — some of which have survived to our own time — were unsurpassed by those of any other people.

The empire of the Incas was an uncompromisingly authoritarian institution, more tyrannical, and more strictly hierarchical, even than that of the Aztecs. Among the things forbidden were doors — so that government agents might not be inconvenienced in their surveillance of the people. The Incas imposed, on the peoples they ruled, a total conformity. There was one economic system: socialism. There was one religious cult, that of the sun. And even the language spoken by the people was determined by imperial edict, so that Quichua became the mandatory medium of expression.

Architecture flourished, as did the metallurgical arts, and the people of the empire were accomplished workers in gold, silver, copper and bronze. One of the most famous products of this skill was the image of the sun, in the Temple of Cuzco, which was an enormous plaque of massive gold, encrusted with emeralds and other precious stones.

The people were largely agricultural, and they raised corn, cacao and cotton. And, although they were also ignorant of the horse and the wheel, they, at least, had a beast of burden: the llama.

The priests and the caciques — nobles known for their severity — ruled the people by keeping them in fear both of their own authority and of the gods. These gods required human sacrifices even more numerous and more bloody than those in the land of the Aztecs; and, to appease them, young men, women and children were immolated, as well as prisoners of war.

The last Inca, Atahuallpa, allowed himself to be conquered and killed by Pizarro even more submissively than Montezuma had by Cortez. Pizarro was undoubtedly one of the most brutal of all the adventurers of history; and it was to his brutality, no doubt, that was due his incredibly easy victory, for his entire army consisted of some two hundred Spaniards. It would have seemed the easiest thing in the world for the natives to have ambushed and destroyed this small troop of soldiers in their mountainous and well-fortified — and therefore easily defensible — empire. But they did not do so. And it does not seem that either the horses of the Spaniards, or their beards — which were the occasion of great astonishment to the natives — were important factors in the downfall of the Incas. Rather, the chief cause seems to have been that the empire was divided by internal struggle.

One of Atahuallpa's brothers, Huascar, had rebelled against the authority of his brother, and had proclaimed himself Inca. In the course of a battle at Cuzco, Huascar was taken prisoner. His supporters, however, refused to submit; and it seems that Atahuallpa intended to make use of the Spaniards to put down these rebels. For this reason, he allowed Pizarro and his men to march through his empire, and to reach his own palace, without offering resistance. Thus, the empire of the Incas fell as quickly as that of the Aztecs.

The riddle of why these two mighty empires fell so quickly and so quietly, of how a mere handful of men from Spain were able to conquer the New World, remains unintelligible so long as one does not take into consideration the psychological differences between the men of the New World and the European invaders. They were two different races, each with their own mentalities, their own ways of living and thinking; and there had been no contact between the two worlds for thousands of years. Then, the Spaniards arrived. They were imbued with the knowledge of their own superiority. Theirs was the only true faith, Catholicism, and they were prepared to impose that faith, by any means, on natives abandoned by their gods and their kings alike.

From this attitude, as well as from the astonishment of the "Indians" and from their own lack of knowledge and understanding, the Spaniards were able quickly to turn to violence and cruelty. A few intermediaries tried to bridge the chasm between the two races. The apathetic resignation of Montezuma was offset by the stoic nobility of Netzahualcoyotl, the king of Texcoco. Bartolomeo de Las Casas, a Dominican friar, fought long and hard against the Spanish practices of enslavement, forced conversion to Catholicism, torture and massacre. Fray Juan de Zumárraga became the protector of the Indians. Some of the Spanish missionaries established "dialogues" with Aztec priests in an effort to learn their religious practices and understand their beliefs. Some of them even managed to save the sacred writings of the Aztecs from the flames of Cortez' bonfires. But all this was too little to have any appreciable effect upon the over-all story of the conquest of the New World, which is an almost unbroken tale of horror, violence, and greed.

APPENDIX II

THE CONQUISTADORS AND THE CONQUEST

It would be a mistake to think of the conquest of the New World as a sort of primitive ancestor of the colonial wars of the nineteenth century. First of all, the conquest was not a state enterprise. It was a private undertaking, organized by adventurers with the financial support of private speculators and merchants.

The conquistadors themselves generally were drawn from poverty-stricken families of the petty nobility, and sometimes from even lower in the social hierarchy of Europe. Pizarro, for example, was a swineherd by profession. Many of them were not of Spanish birth; they were Genoese, Venetians, Germans, Englishmen and Frenchmen. And the troops they organized for their expeditions to the New World were largely drawn from the flotsam and jetsam of the ports of Europe.

The ends of the conquistadors were often no more glorious than their beginnings. After their first popular triumphs, they usually ended ignominously, beginning with Columbus, who was imprisoned. Cortez was reduced to poverty. Balboa was beheaded. And Gonzalo Pizarro was ordered beaten and then executed by the envoy of the Emperor Charles V.

The sole interest of the Spanish kings in the conquest was to ensure that they received their share of the booty, the King's Quintal. For this purpose, they appointed a royal functionary, the *contador*, whose responsibility it was to see that the Quintal was forthcoming.

But even the religious welfare of the inhabitants of the New World appeared sufficient reason for the intervention of the Spanish crown. Charles V, and, after him, Philip II, already had their hands full in Europe, where they were busily attempting to put down both the Protestants and the Turks. Philip II prided himself on defending the Catholic faith against the Turks at the Battle of Lepanto, and of championing the cause of the true religion against Queen Elizabeth, the defender of the "supposedly reformed" religion (as Philip called it), in the affair of the Invincible Armada. But it never occurred to him, certainly, that the holy war that he was waging in the Mediterranean and in the Channel would soon continue to be fought out on the battlefield of the Caribbean, for the various "conquests" of the New World had a deeply religious foundation.

Pope Alexander VI, in 1493, had established his famous "demarcation line," which virtually divided up the world between the Spanish and the Portuguese. Then, in a series of four papal bulls, he had commissioned Spain to evangelize the newly discovered lands to the west. This was the juridical and religious basis for Spain's conquest of the Americas.

In the New World, this commission was put into practice by means of a bizarre formality known as the Banns of Conquest. Before taking up arms against the natives, the Spaniards sent a friar or a priest to read a summons, or *requerimiento* to them, which was supposed to be translated by an interpreter. This document had been written by a Doctor of Theology, Palacios Rubios, and its purpose was to demand that the Indians reject their own religion in favor of the true faith. It began as follows:

"Caciques and Indians, you must know that there is a God, a Pope, and a King of Castille who is the master of this land because the Pope, who is the almighty vicar of God and in whose hand the whole world rests, has given it to the King of Castille on condition that he convert to Christianity its inhabitants so that they may be eternally happy in celestial glory after their deaths."

Isabella, Queen of Castille, had declared that all Indians were free. Yet, in practice, the Indians were made into slaves from the very beginning of the conquest, and those who tried to resist were slaughtered. In a few years, the Caribbean area was virtually depopulated, and the whole New World lived under a regime of terror.

Two almost legendary figures embody the era of the seekers after gold: Hernando Cortez, the conqueror of Mexico, and Francisco Pizarro, the conqueror of Peru. Cortez was a *hidalgo*, the scion of a noble, but poor, family of Medellin, in Estremadura. He went to the New World to make his fortune, was imprisoned in Cuba, escaped, placed himself at the head of an expedition of six ships and three hundred men, disembarked at Vera Cruz, and, after a siege of ninety-three days, took Mexico City (August, 1521) at the cost of thousands of the inhabitants' lives. To an emissary from Montezuma who came to ask him to withdraw from the land of the Aztecs, Cortez spoke candidly enough: "Tell your master," he said, "that he must send us gold, much gold. For my friends and I are suffering from a disease of the heart which can

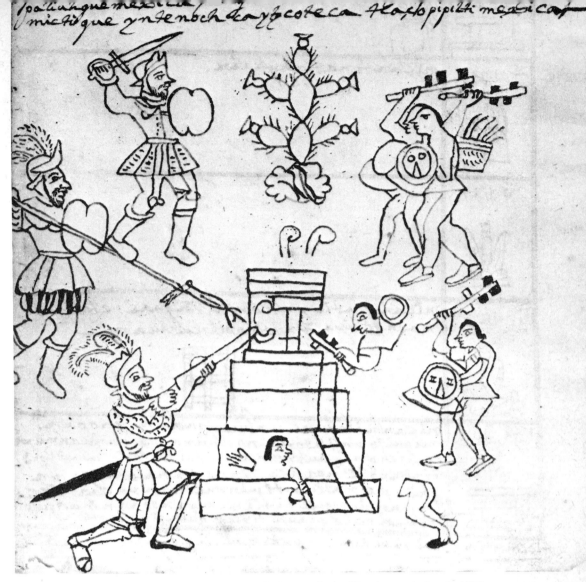

A battle between the Spaniards and the Indians. (Codex mexicain. Histoire mexicaine de 1221 a 1594, Bibliothèque Nationale, Paris.)

only be cured by gold."

After the conquest of Mexico, honors were heaped upon Cortez. He was named Captain General of New Spain — a vast country of which he knew nothing and the extent of whose resources he ignored. Charles V created him Marqués del Vallee de Oaxaca, and named him a Knight of Saint James. There seemed to be no end of glory for this scion of an impoverished family. But Cortez did not rest on his laurels. He busied himself with projects which reflected a view of the future of surprising breadth by trying to assure for Spain the route across the Pacific, to the Far East — the spice route leading to the East Indies and China. And, in a letter of October 15, 1524, to Charles V, he writes of four ships that he had ordered to be built at Zacatula, on the Pacific shore, destined for trade with the Philippines. These accomplishments

A view of Mexico City in the seventeenth century.

and ambitions might seem to guarantee his power and to ensure future honors. Cortez himself seems to have shared his view. On one occasion, at the royal court in Madrid, Charles V caught sight of him, and asked loudly, "Who is this man?" To which Cortez answered, "Sire, it is he who has given you more provinces than your royal father left you cities." But princes are notoriously ungrateful; and Cortez was destined to die in disgrace, forgotten by the Emperor, in 1547, near Madrid.

Francisco Pizarro, brutal conqueror of the Incas, was the bastard son of a petty nobleman of Trujillo. He was unlettered, and he earned his living by tending pigs. It was this uninspiring vocation that led Pizarro to the New World; for he allowed one of his employer's pigs to escape and, rather than face the punishment that was sure to follow, he fled and signed onto a galleon bound for the Americas. There, he began a new career at the age of fifty — at a time when most "Captains" were no older than their mid-twenties. He accompanied Núñez de Balboa in his trek across the Isthmus of Darien and his discovery of the Pacific Ocean. Allied to another adventurer, a man named Almagro, he attacked the vast empire of the Incas and, with 168 men and 37 horses, he conquered a land four times the size of his native Spain.

On November 15, 1532, the Spanish force reached the city of Caxamarca, to which the Inca incautiously accepted an invitation for a meeting. He arrived under a shimmering canopy, dressed in gold and sparkling with jewels. Valverde, a Dominican friar, then read the Banns of Conquest,

Forced labor by black slaves in the mines of the New World. (Engraving by Théodore de Bry. Bibliothèque Nationale, Paris.)

summoning the Inca to renounce his idolatrous cult and submit to the authority of the Castilian crown. He held out a Bible — which the Inca pushed away. The friar then raised his crucifix; and, at that signal, the Spaniards fell upon the Indians and massacred more than two thousand of them. Pizarro himself seized the Inca by the hair and ordered him to be confined to a room 22 feet long and 17 feet wide.

The Inca offered to buy his freedom by filling his cell with gold to the height of the ceiling. Pizarro accepted, and the Inca kept his word. But then Pizarro accused his prisoner of "rebellion against His Most Catholic Majesty" and the Inca was condemned to death for this crime, and strangled.

Pizarro then made a solemn entry into Cuzco. His first act was to pillage the Temple of the Sun and the royal palace, where all the furnishings, decorations and works of art were of massive gold.

Dissension soon broke out among the conquerors; that is, between Pizarro and his partner, Almagro. Thereupon, Pizarro left Cuzco to found his own capital at Lima. The battle between the two men continued for the next eleven years. Finally, Francisco Pizarro's brother, Hernando, captured Almagro at Cuzco (1538) and executed him. Three years later, Francisco was killed at Lima by Juan de Rada, one of Almagro's supporters.

Another of the Pizarro brothers, this one named Gonzalo, then chased the new Viceroy of Peru from Lima and had him executed at Anaquito. Thereafter, he governed his dead brother's lands despotically until 1548,

Forward section of a ship (from the *Encyclopèdie*).

when Pedro de la Gasca, ambassador of Charles V, had him executed.

The Emperor had made Francisco Pizarro a Knight of Saint James; and, despite the crimes of Gonzalo and Hernando, his descendants for generations bore the proud title of Marqués de la Conquista.

If it is true, as Lope de Vega has written, that Cortez gave to God "souls without number," it is also true that he gave to Spain the silver mines of Mexico. And Francisco Pizarro did even better. He gave the legendary El Dorado to the Spanish crown: the gold and silver of Potosí, the "fabulous metal" of which all Europe dreamed.

But the vast golden treasure that poured into the kingdom of Spain bore a curse and was stained with blood; and it was to bring nothing of peace or prosperity to the princes and people of that land.

APPENDIX III

SAILING SHIPS

By present-day standards, the ships that, in 1492, carried Columbus to the New World, were no more than nutshells. The *Santa Maria*, Columbus' caravel, was less than 75 feet in length; and it took her thirty-five days to cross the Atlantic. Subsequently, however, caravels proved to be too small to carry the precious cargoes of Spain and to mount the artillery that was necessary for the defense of this treasure. Larger and heavier ships were then used. These were a modified form of the Genoese and Portuguese carrack, with square sails and four masts, and were known as galleons. From fifty to sixty days were required for the transatlantic voyage.

The galleons were characterized by a very high poop — a holdover from the vessels used in the Mediterranean. Gradually, these poops, which were originally four or five stories in height, were lowered. The forecastle was replaced by a covered shelter.

These relatively simple modifications took almost four centuries to accomplish, and they followed a tendency which was to be finally realized only in the nineteenth century: to raise the forward section of a ship and to lower the aft, so as to show almost a horizontal line above the water. The length of galleons increased steadily. In the seventeenth century, there were ships of 150 to 175 feet, while merchantmen were sometimes 125 feet long.

It was due to the influence of English and Dutch shipbuilders that naval construction improved and the lines of the hull were improved. The length of the keel, which had been roughly twice the beam of a ship, was now triple the beam. And a ship's length at its waterline was four times its beam, while the depth of the hole was approximately half the beam.

Portrait of Sir Francis Drake (1540-1596) by Tarmessin. (Bibliothèque Nationale, Cabinet des Estampes, Paris.)

The Golden Hind, Drake's ship. Drawing by Leon Haffner

In 1668, half of the English fleet was composed of four-masters. From that date, they all carried topsails. The two rear masts carried triangular sails. The forward section was lengthened and reinforced by the addition of a pointed spur and decorated with a prow figure. In the seventeenth century, the spur was reduced in size and became the cutwater, on which were the prow and the prow figure.

The bowsprit carried a triangular sail, and, on a vertical spar, a square sail which was first used between 1611 and 1618. This sort of rigging, fragile though it was, was to persist until the middle of the eighteenth century, when it was replaced by the jib, or staysail.

Corsairs such as Hawkins and Drake sailed in fast, light ships. Drake's own *Golden Hind* circled the globe, and crossed the Pacific in eighty-nine days. This ship, which weighed 100 tons, was about 75 feet long overall, with a waterline length of 61 feet and a keel length of 47 feet.

The vessels used by pirates — the brigantine and the sloop — had only two masts, and used triangular sails. They were able to sail very close into the wind, and so they could easily overtake square-rigged ships which were obliged to tack.

From 1656 on, all English ships had rounded sterns; but, among the ships of other nations, the squared stern survived for many years.

To the rear, the mizzenmast carried, in the seventeenth century, a triangular sail and, above it, a square sail: the topgallant sail. In the second half of the same century, the stays and the jibs appeared, along with the reefs; while

A sixteenth-century ship, according to an engraving by Théodore de Bry. (Bibliothèque Nationale, Paris.)

the reefs themselves were in regular use starting in 1690.

The progress in naval architecture achieved by the English and Dutch resulted in important modifications: the poop was lowered even further, and reduced to two stories.

During the eighteenth century, a better understanding was acquired of the masting and use of sail. Four masts were finally abandoned, but the masts then used gradually increased in height until they sometimes reached 125 feet and were thus able to present a larger surface of sail to the wind. Smaller and more numerous square sails now allowed a ship to sail more closely into the wind. These sails were rigged at first in three, then in four stages. The main mast, for instance, had the mainsail, the lower main topsail, the upper main topsail, and, at the end of the eighteenth century, the main-topgallant sail.

During the sixteenth and seventeenth centuries, the rudder was controlled by means of a vertical level, or tiller, which turned on a level with the deck. This arangement allowed for only limited control: five degrees to either side. More complicated turns were accomplished by maneuvering the sails — particularly the lateen mizzenmast sail. It was not until the beginning of the eighteenth century that the tiller was replaced by a wheel which was mounted on a drum and which was wired to the rudder in such a way as to allow for much more maneuverability.

Navigational problems

As a matter of fairness to seamen in centuries past, we should emphasize the extent to which they lacked instruments capable of indicating their positions. At the end of the fifteenth century, there was no device for measuring the altitude of the stars. It was only beginning in 1530 that it was possible to arrive at an approximate determination of latitude by the passage of the sun at the meridian. So far as longitude was concerned, which is measured by the difference of hours between one's actual position and the meridian of origin, there was simply no way of calculating it.

In the sixteenth century, the astrolabe — the invention of which is attributed to the Greek astronomer, Hipparchus, in the sixth century before Christ — was replaced on ships by an instrument known as Jacob's staff, or a cross-staff. It consisted of two pieces of wood, the cross of which was at right angles to, and sliding on, the staff. A small hole was drilled at the end of the cross, and a sight was fixed at the end of the staff. To measure the altitude of a star, the cross-staff was sighted in that direction and the cross was moved forward or backward until the star could be seen through the upper hole and the horizon through the sight. The altitude was then read from a scale marked on the staff.

Until modern times, "dead reckoning" (figuring one's position from a landmark and the distance one had traveled) was the only possible method of navigation. The helmsman entered in the ship's log the course as he read it on the compass; and the course was expressed not in degrees, but in "quarters" which were equal to about eleven degrees. The compass, however, reflected magnetic north rather than true north — which complicated somewhat the job of the pilots, whose expertise was more a matter of experience than of scientific knowledge.

The use of the log, which allows one to measure in knots the speed of a ship, was introduced only at the beginning of the seventeenth century.

The length of the nautical mile, which was the basis for computing a course, varied. At the end of the sixteenth century it was 1620 meters; and, in the middle of the seventeenth, 1866 meters.

Shipboard time was calculated by means of an hourglass, which had to be turned every half-hour. This turning was the duty of an apprentice. It was only at the beginning of the eighteenth century that there were ship's clocks of sufficient accuracy to keep time according to the Greenwich or Paris meridian. And, with the advent of such clocks, it became possible to determine one's longitude with a certain degree of accuracy. At the same time, the oc-

A Spanish galleon of the seventeenth century. (Drawing by Gustave Alaux.)

tant — an ancestor of the sextant — began to replace the cross-staff; by the use of one mirror, at first, and then of two, mariners were able more easily to compute the altitude of sun and determine their latitude.

Despite all these improvements, however, seamen long continued to make serious mistakes and to be unaware of their position on the sea. There is no lack of examples of such cases, some of them involving even warships. A. Tomazi, an authority on the subject, tells us that, in 1778, a squadron under the command of Admiral de Grasse sailed past Bermuda to the west — while the ships of the squadron thought they were actually sailing to the east. Another squadron, under Admiral Suffren, in 1782 computed its position by dead reckoning and found that, somehow, they were fifty kilometers in the interior of Africa; and, at the same time, the frigates which were sailing in front of the squadron were not yet in sight of land.

ILLUSTRATED GLOSSARY

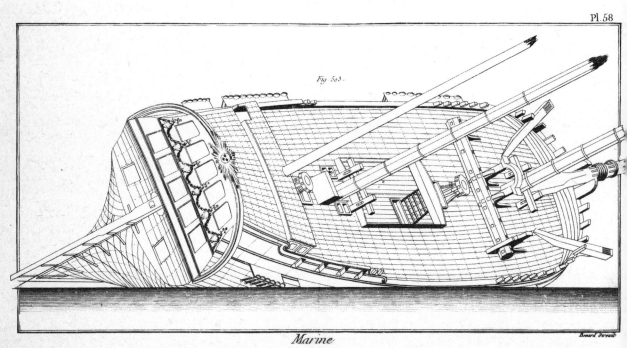

Pl. 58

Fig. 503.

Marine

Benard direxit

The careening of a ship (from the *Encyclopèdie*).

GLOSSARY

Acropora

A colonial Scleractinaria invertebrate, usually yellow, brown, green, mauve or blue, which developed in the shape of large branches or "parasols." It is a madreporarian, and extremely common in various forms in warm waters.

Afterpiece

The afterpiece of a rudder is that part which is attached to the axis, and which, according to its direction, controls the course of the ship.

Albemarle, Henry Christopher, Duke of

The son of Gen. George Monck who, after the death of Cromwell, played a large part in the recall of Charles II to the throne of England. Henry Christopher (1653–88) inherited the title, and the enormous fortune, of his father, and became William Phips's protector. At the end of his short life, he was governor of Jamaica. With his death, the title of Duke of Albemarle was extinguished.

The Antilles

Also called the West Indies, the Antilles comprise the Bahama Islands, the Greater Antilles (Cuba, Jamaica, Hispaniola — i.e., Haiti and Santo Domingo — and Puerto Rico), and the Lesser Antilles (the Leeward and Windward islands, Trinidad, Barbados, and the Dutch and Venezuelan islands). They stretch from Florida to the Venezuelan coast, and separate the Caribbean from the Atlantic.

The waters of the Antilles have a strong current which, crossing the Yucatan strait, runs into the Gulf of Mexico. There are some very deep areas, especially between Cuba and Jamaica, where there is a chasm some 25,000 feet deep. To the north of Venezuela there are depths of almost 20,000 feet.

In the eighteenth century, the Antilles comprised a flourishing economic community. Indigo and sugar cane were the main products, and tobacco and cotton were also cultivated in abundance. The Antilles were Europe's chief source of supply for sugar and rum. The center of all this commercial activity was Santo Domingo.

Asiento

A Spanish word meaning "contract" and "purchase," it designated the agreement between the Spanish government and a foreign company regarding the delivery of black slaves to Spanish America.

Since Spain herself had no trading post on Africa's west coast, and since her fleet was inadequate even to supply the necessities to her colonists in the New World, in exchange for a large sum of money she usually granted this franchise to foreign countries such as France or England.

The first *asiento* was signed in 1517, with a Genoese company. Then, the Portuguese had the monopoly until they were replaced by the Dutch in 1640. The Dutch continued the slave trade until 1695. In 1701, the monopoly was given to the French Company of Guinea, and this transfer was thus concomitant with the War of the Spanish Succession. After the Treaty of Utrecht in 1713, an English firm, the South Sea Company, obtained the monopoly for a thirty-year period, but continued to exercise it until 1759.

All of these companies were obliged, under the terms of the *asiento*, to supply between three and four thousand black slaves a year to the Spanish colonies.

Barracuda

A flesh-eating fish of the tropics, similar in appearance to the pike. It has a large mouth and razor-sharp teeth, and an elongated body the color of polished steel.

The largest of the barracudas sometimes attain a length of over six feet. They travel in schools of three or four. Smaller specimens, of the same size and the same generation, also travel in schools.

Barracudas have a bad reputation. In some areas, they are more feared even than sharks. In part, this is due to their ferocious appearance, their small hard eyes, to their formidable teeth, and to their behavior. They will follow a diver stubbornly; and, if he moves toward them, they will swim away — only to return a moment later. Even so, the barracuda's fearsome reputation is, to some extent, unmerited.

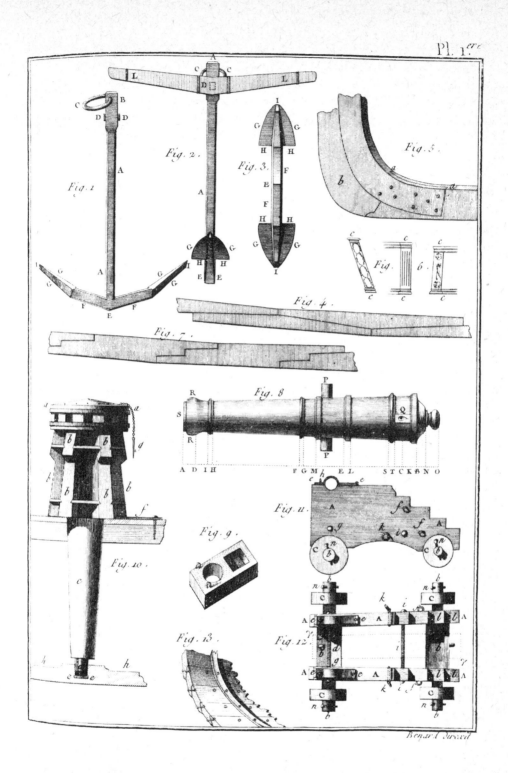

Pl. 1.ere

Seventeenth-century anchors and cannon (from the *Encyclopèdie*).

Bowsprit

A mast positioned obliquely or horizontally on the forward section of sailing ships. In the sixteenth century, there was a smaller mast at the extremity of the bowsprit, called the lesser bowsprit, or the topgallant bowsprit. At its base was a small round top, and it carried a square sail. The fragility of this mast, however (because of its position), caused it to be abandoned. On the other hand, the square sail of the bowsprit survived into the nineteenth century.

Brain Coral

This is the name divers give to certain massive, rounded madreporarian formations which resemble — because of their convolutions — the brain. Brain coral belongs to two suborders of Scleractinaria: the *Fungiina* or Porites, and the *Faviina* or maeandrinas.

Brigantine

Pirates, from the beginning of their activity in the sixteenth and seventeenth centuries, showed a decided preference for small, light ships, and particularly for the brigantine. The word "brigantine" is used generally to designate a vessel about sixty-five feet long, rigged with two masts and triangular sails. It was Mediterranean in origin, and was the vessel commonly used by the Barbary pirates. ("Brigantine," like "brig," has an obvious connection with the word "brigand.")

The brigantine was a fast ship, with very little draught, and it was thus capable of eluding pursuers by sailing in shallow waters where heavier ships could not follow. Moreover their rigging permitted them to sail close into the wind, while other ships, with their square sails, were obliged to tack.

The pirates also made use of the *barque*, or bark, which was larger than the brigantine, but had only one mast and carried only one sail. The single mast was very high, and slightly inclined toward the rear. The sail, which was triangular, could propel the bark at a considerable speed, and it was complemented by a large jib, which, at that time, was called a *trinquenin*.

By the end of the seventeenth century, pirates were also using an even larger ship, the corvette, a two-master, capable of carrying heavier armament. The corvette carried square sails on the mizzenmast, and, on the mainmast, the large triangular sail of the bark. There was, in addition, a large jib rigged to the mainmast. The whole represented a comparatively "modern" rigging.

Buccaneer

The word "buccaneer" is derived from a Tupi word, *mocaem*, which, in the Caribbean, designates meat which has been smoked according to a very old Indian recipe. It was originally used in reference to certain adventurers who made their living by hunting wild oxen and boar in the Antilles, and then smoked the meat in this fashion and sold the skins of their kill.

These adventurers were of European origin — Dutch, English and French; but, like the natives, they lived off the land. Oexmelin describes them: "As clothing, they had nothing more than a small cloth jacket, and a sort of loincloth that reached only to mid-thigh. One had to look at them closely to discover that the material from which this apparel was made was indeed cloth; for it was usually covered with the blood of animals. Moreover, these men were blackened by the sun; and some of them wore their hair short and bristling, while others wore it long, and tied in knots. They all wore long beards, and wore a sort of scabbard of crocodile leather on their belts, in which they carried four knives and a bayonet." Their usual weapon, however, was a long-barreled rifle, which they used so effectively that they became known as the best shots in the Caribbean.

These buccaneers hunted at first in the Bahamas, but the English expelled them in 1629. They then took refuge on the island of St. Christopher, but in 1630 they were chased out by the Spaniards. At that point, they formed an alliance with the French pirates on the island of Tortuga, and, in a short time, took to piracy themselves.

In 1665, four or five thousand of them occupied the western part of Santo Domingo in the name of the King of France.

Careen

The careening of a ship was an operation which, in the absence of a graving dock, allowed the hull to be repaired. The ship's cargo, ballast and cannon were all moved to one side of the ship, and the ship was then laid on that same side so that its keel was exposed. Careening was used particularly in bodies of water not subject to tides; elsewhere, a ship was simply moored in such a way that its lower sections would be exposed at low tide.

Cochineal

A species of insect — a parasite of cactus — the female of which contains a fatty substance valuable in the manufacture of scarlet dye. Cochineal, a Mexican product, was used for centuries, and was only replaced with the advent of chemical coloring agents.

Conquistadores a lo Divino

This was the name given to the friars and priests who, from the beginning of the Conquest, undertook the conversion to Catholicism of the American natives. Some of these missionaries, such as Peter de Gand, claimed 200,000 converts; and the Franciscan friars are said to have baptized seven million Indians.

The *Conquistadores a lo Divino* had their share of adventurers, and their share of martyrs and apostles. One of them, Bartolomeo de Las Casas, was the natives' greatest defender against violence, slavery, and forced labor in the mines.

Filibuster, or Freebooter

The freebooter or filibuster was an Antilles pirate during the seventeenth and eighteenth centuries. Both terms are derived from a Dutch word, *vrijbuiter*, which means "one who takes booty freely."

The golden age of freebooting was the first half of the seventeenth century, when the freebooters were the lords and masters of the Antilles waters and the Venezuelan coast.

Freebooter expeditions were highly organized enterprises, and the object of alliances between various pirate ships. The freebooters, most of whom were French or English, would meet on the open sea among the small islands between Tortuga and Jamaica, plan the operation, decide on the division of the spoils, and elect a commander in chief of the expedition.

The War of the Spanish Succession, (1701-14), which made allies of the French and the Spanish, and which led Louis XIV to forbid attacks on Spanish shipping, was an important factor in the subsequent decline of freebooting.

Foremast

The vertical mast nearest the bow of a sailing ship.

French Company of the West Indies

This company was founded by Colbert, minister of Louis XIV, in 1664, with its seat at Le Havre and a capitalization of six million *livres*. It was granted a forty-year monopoly on the development of all African territory from Cape Verde to the Cape of Good Hope, and of territory in the New World including Louisiana, Acadia, the Guianas and the Antilles.

Colbert's hope that this company would assure Nantes, Saint-Malo and Bordeaux of becoming the centers of a sugar-refining industry was not realized. The company was unable to fulfill its mission, and was dissolved in 1674.

Fungia

A form of coral which resembles, because of its lamella, a mushroom. It belongs to the order Scleractinaria, suborder Fungiina.

Guaiacum

An American tree of very hard, resinous wood. The trunk may attain a diameter of more than three feet, but its rate of growth is so slow that it may take centuries for it to reach that size.

The wood of the guaiacum was particularly prized, and used, at Santo Domingo and in Cuba. Because of its hardness, it was used to make mortars, pulleys and pestles in the age of sailing ships.

English flagship of the seventeenth century.

Gambling

What games did pirates play in their dens on Tortuga and Jamaica? Dice, certainly; and also such now old-fashioned card games as tarot and lansquenet. Their cards were more complicated than our own, and the face cards were more numerous. There was an emperor, for instance, and a conjurer, and an empress, and a lover. There was a pope — and even a popess.

One of the memoirs of the age of pirates speaks of a Frenchman who, after having won 1200 escudos, 100,000 pounds of sugar, a sugar mill, and sixty slaves, continued playing until he had lost everything — even his clothing. He was then forced to sign onto a pirate ship as an ordinary seaman.

Giant Clam

The giant clam is the largest of the bivalve mollusks, and its shell is sometimes over three feet in diameter. This shell is opened and closed by extremely powerful muscles. There are stories of accidents to divers who, according to the legend, are caught by a hand or foot in a closing shell and are unable to escape.

The giant clam is able to sense the approach of a strange object at a distance, and this perception triggers the closing valves while the intruder is still relatively far away. These valves work with comparative slowness.

Grand Congloué

The Grand Congloué is an island in the Mediterranean off Marseilles. There, at a depth of about 125 feet, the *Calypso*'s divers spent five years (1952 to 1957) digging out an old Roman ship loaded with amphoras and pottery. The vessel had belonged to a certain Marcus Sestius, who lived on Delos in the second half of the third century B.C.

Gudgeons

A piece of double-branched hardware installed on the sternpost. The pintles, by means of which the rudder pivots, are attached to the gudgeons.

Halyard

A line, running from a pulley, which is used to hoist an arm, a sail, or a standard.

Hispaniola

On October 4, 1492, Columbus had first caught sight of land in the New World at the Lucayas, and on December 5 landed on an island that the natives called Haiti. The Spaniards were so enchanted by its beauty that they christened it Hispaniola — little Spain. And then they proceeded to slaughter its inhabitants.

The local chieftains, or *caciques*, were all killed, but the people were in a constant state of revolt, which led to a gradual depopulation of the islands. Eventually, it became necessary to import slaves from Africa to work the plantations.

Beginning in 1664, the French sent colonists to a portion of the island — Santo Domingo — which was soon thriving. The Peace of Ryswick (1697) recognized French sovereignty over Santo Domingo.

Under the governership of Bernard d'Ogeron (1661), Port au Prince developed rapidly; and the entire colony began to prosper shortly thereafter, from both industrial and agricultural production. The three chief products were tobacco, sugar cane (which was the chief crop, but which exhausted the soil) and indigo. In 1688, there were fifteen indigo manufacturers; in 1730, there were twenty-nine.

Coffee was introduced on the island in 1726, and thereafter increased in importance until it attained its peak around 1770.

Indigo

The indigo plant — *indigofera tinctoria* — is cultivated in China, the Indies, Java and Central America, where it reaches a height of from four to five feet.

Indigo dye comes from the leaves of this shrub. It was known and used in the Orient for many centuries before it was imported into Europe toward the sixteenth century. Its cultivation in the islands and colonies of Spain resulted in its becoming one of the chief products exported to Europe from the New World.

In its natural state, indigo is dark blue, with reddish and purple lights; and its color is not affected by exposure to air.

The name "indigo" is taken from the Spanish, and means "Indian."

Inner Planking

In wooden ships, inner planking is the term used to designate the planks placed between the frame timbers inside the hull, while those on the exterior of the hull are called "the planking." The inner planking and the planking together form the "sides" of a ship.

Jacks

Jacks belong to the Carangidae family, which is related to the Scombridae (tuna, mackerels, etc.). They are pelagic fish and live near the shoreline, but are often found in the open sea. There are numerous species, especially in tropical waters.

Jacks are handsome creatures, with blue or sea-green backs, and gold or silvery flanks resembling polished metal. They have a well-defined lateral line which usually curves toward the rear, and they have forked tails joined to the body by a very narrow peduncle. This latter characteristic is very striking and makes Jacks instantly recognizable even when they are seen swimming in schools in the transparent waters of tropical lagoons.

Level Reef

In shallow waters, coral in tropical seas form relatively long and unbroken plateaus along coastlines and on top of reefs in the open sea (such as in the Silver Bank). These are called level reefs.

Mayflower

The *Mayflower* is one of the most famous ships ever built, and it is mentioned here as typical of its period. And yet, we know comparatively little about it. We know that it was a very old ship before its celebrated voyage to America. As early as 1588, it served as a merchantman between England and France, calling at the ports of La Rochelle and Bordeaux.

The *Mayflower* sailed for America in September 1620, from Southampton. Upon reaching the American coast, it was beset by bad weather and landed at Provincetown, on Cape Cod. It was not until December 26, 1620, that it reached Plymouth and put its passengers ashore.

The reconstruction executed by R. C. Anderson (published in the *Mariners Mirror*) and reproduced here is as exact as possible, given the lack of documents. It was a ship of some 180 tons, measuring about 100 feet from stem to stern, and carrying fifteen cannon. It was, in other words, a typical merchantman of the time.

The *Mayflower*, after disembarking its 102 passengers in the New World,

The probable reconstruction of a merchantman, closely resembling the *Mayflower.*. Drawing by L. Pritchard, according to the plan of Dr. R. C. Anderson.

set sail for England in April 1621. We know that it arrived safely there, and that it was still in service in 1624. Nothing, however, is known of its history beyond that date.

Mizzenmast

The mast furthest to the rear of a ship, and the smallest mast on a three-master. On a four- or five-master, it is the one nearest the poop. The yards used on this mast are called mizzen yards; and the sails are mizzen sails.

Morgan, Henry John

A celebrated English pirate captain, born in Wales in 1637. He died at Jamaica in 1690.

Black slaves being taken aboard the slave ship *Marie Séraphique*, along the African coast. This ship's home port was Nantes, and it plied its trade in the eighteenth century, (Drawing by Jean-Charles Roux.)

Morgan was famous for such exploits as his taking of the Spanish city of Porto Bello, in Panama. He destroyed the port of Maracaibo, burned part of the Spanish fleet, and regained Jamaica loaded with enormous wealth.

In 1670, at the head of a fleet of thirty-seven ships and twenty-two hundred men — the largest ever assembled under the pirate flag — he attacked Panama City, which was defended by a force of eight thousand men. He took the city by assault, looted and burned it, and tortured the most prominent citizens. His booty, on that occasion, amounted to some 440,000 pounds.

When the English king made peace with Spain and was thenceforth opposed to attacks by English pirates on Spanish shipping, Morgan settled down at Jamaica, married, became an Admiralty official and was knighted by Charles II. He ended his days at peace on that island.

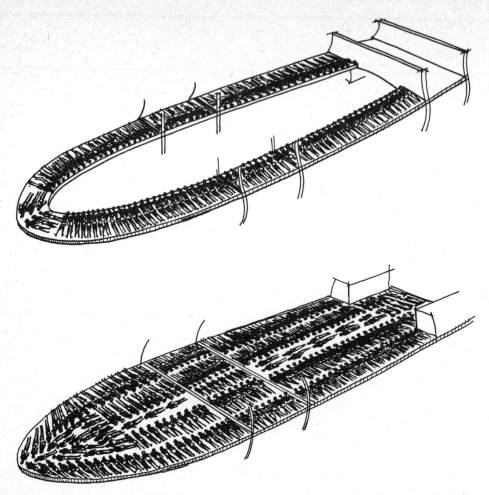

On slave ships, the blacks were jammed together so that traders were able to transport the greatest possible number of them.

Oexmelin, Alexandre Olivier

This adventurer was an employee of the West Indies Company, and was shipwrecked on Tortuga Island where he was sold for thirty escudos. From 1669 to 1674, he served as a medical officer on a pirate ship. He took part in the taking of Cartagena in 1697. He is best remembered, however, for his *History of Outstanding Adventurers in the Indies, with the Life, Customs and Morals of the Buccaneers,* which is a rich sourcebook on pirates and piracy.

Pintle

The nautical term for a pivot pin. In a rudder mechanism, pintles are used in the gudgeons of the sternpost, and this assembly, as a whole, assures the operation of the rudder.

There are also mast pintles and boom pintles.

Planking

Planking, in wooden vessels, is the whole of the planks that form the exterior facing of the ship. These planks are either tongue-in-groove, or placed side by side, and they are cut in such a way as to follow the curved lines of the ship. The joints between them are calked.

Porgy

The porgy — *Pagellus erythrinus* — is a member of the Sparidae family. It is of a pinkish color, and darker on the back, with a bright red marking next to its gills. Its teeth are pointed, and it lives on organic waste.

Privateers

Privateers, also known as corsairs, were sea captains, who had received letters patent from their governments authorizing them to attack enemy shipping.

Thus, many of these official pirates, particularly among the French, were members of their country's navy, such as Jean Bart, Duguay Trouin, and Forbin. The legality of the attacks made, and the booty taken, by the corsairs was generally established by a special tribunal, which, in France, was called the *Cour des Prises*. So respectable did privateering become that, under Louis XIV and Louis XV, ministers of state and great nobles invested freely in this sort of enterprise and reaped handsome profits from it.

Rum

Rum is made by combining syrup, sugar, and the foam from crushed sugar cane. Fermentation is spontaneous, and takes place in the barrels in which this mixture is stored. After a week or eight days, when fermentation has taken place, the liquor is distilled by means of a still.

Scuba

The SCUBA (Self-Contained Underwater Breathing Apparatus) was conceived in 1943 by Jacques-Yves Cousteau and Émile Gagnan, an engineer, as the *scaphandre autonome*. It is a simple apparatus and a safe one. It is entirely automatic, and its use is easily mastered. It has made possible underwater exploration and opened the sea to a vast public. The SCUBA allows a diver to go down to a depth of about 150 feet.

The apparatus consists of one or more cylinders of compressed air which are attached to the diver's back. A special device assures that, whenever the diver inhales, air will be delivered at a pressure equal to that of the depth at which he is swimming. The used air is expelled through a "duck's beak" contained in a metallic box behind the neck. The mouthpiece is attached to the air-intake device by two flexible tubes, one for inhalation and the other for exhalation.

Sea Anemone

An Anthozoan, the sea anemone has no skeleton and spends its life attached to the ocean floor or to rocks. It is able, however, to move about in a small area.

Its body is muscled and cylindrical. At the upper extremity, there is a mouth surrounded by retractable tentacles. These tentacles number six, or a multiple of six, and contain numerous venomous cells (called nematoblasts) which the anemone uses to paralyze its prey. The prey is then carried to the mouth.

Sea Fans

Sea fans are Cnidaria, and belong to the subclass Octocorallia and the order of Gorgonacea. It takes its popular name from its fan-shaped branches, and is found in yellow, mauve and rose-pink. These branches are actually animal colonies composed of polyps spread over a flexible limestone skeleton. Sea fans are fixed to the ocean floor or to rocks by branches, or tufts, and are sometimes found in tight groups. They have an encrusting base, which allows them to remain attached to their support.

Sea fans are found in all warm or temperate seas. In many tropical regions, they attain a height of over three feet and are one of the most beautiful objects of the underwater decor.

The abundance and diversity of sea fans was first revealed with the advent of scuba diving.

Sheave

The wheel of a pulley, containing a groove to hold the pulley rope in place.

Slave Trading

Slave ships customarily left European ports loaded with cheap merchandise and bound for the coasts of Guinea as far south as Angola — a distance of some 2200 miles. The West African coast was divided up into various sectors, each containing a trading post. At these posts, the slave ships traded their merchandise for between three and four hundred black slaves — natives who had been taken prisoner in intertribal wars and who were regarded as negotiable merchandise by the native chieftains. These men were then loaded aboard the ships, in indescribably crowded conditions, and the ships set sail for the New World. On the voyage, conditions aboard ship usually killed between 12 and 15 per cent of the slaves.

Upon arrival in America, the blacks were put up for sale in exchange either for merchandise or letters of credit. No actual cash was realized until the slave ship returned to Europe and either sold the colonial merchandise or redeemed its letters of credit.

By the end of the eighteenth century, several million blacks had been

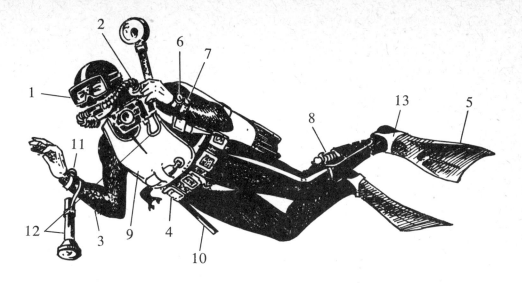

INDISPENSABLE	NECESSARY	USEFUL
1 Mask	6 Depth gauge	11 Compass
2 Regulator and Tank	7 Watch	12 Flashlight and Camera
3 Wet suit	8 Knife	13 Heel strap
4 Weight belt	9 Flotation vest	
5 Fins	10 Snorkel	

The lastest model of scuba equipment, including a helmet light and a built-in telephone. The diver is holding a shark stick.

brought to America in this way, where they were used to develop the economy of tropical America in accordance with the needs of Europe and to assure the prosperity of the great slave-trading ports of Europe — especially Nantes.

During the French Revolution, and at the Congress of Vienna (1815) and the Congress of Verona (1822), slave-trading was condemned — under the euphemism, "trading in ebony wood."

Sling

A length of cable or chain used to raise a heavy object that cannot be hooked to a hoist or pulley block. At one of its extremities, the sling has an eye through which the other end is passed, thus forming a loop to encircle the object to be raised. The sling is then pulled tight by the weight of the object when it is raised by a hoist.

Snappers

Snappers, which are numerous in warm waters, are the coastal predators of

Reconstruction of the *Vasa* (1628) by Nils Stodberg. Reproduced by the kind permission of Nils Stodberg and P. O. Norstedt Forlag.

tropical and subtropical seas. They are recognizable by their three-spined anal fins, and their heads, which are partially free of scales.

Spirographis

The Spirographis, or Feather-Duster Worm, is an Annelida, class Polychaeta. It is a worm, and lives in a vertical tube from which a colored crest emerges. The function of this crest is to serve as gills, and also to stir up the water so that food may be brought to the Spirograph. In case of danger, the crest is retracted.

Sternpost

A large piece of lumber, of the same width as the keel, at the stern of a ship. The rudder is attached to the sternpost.

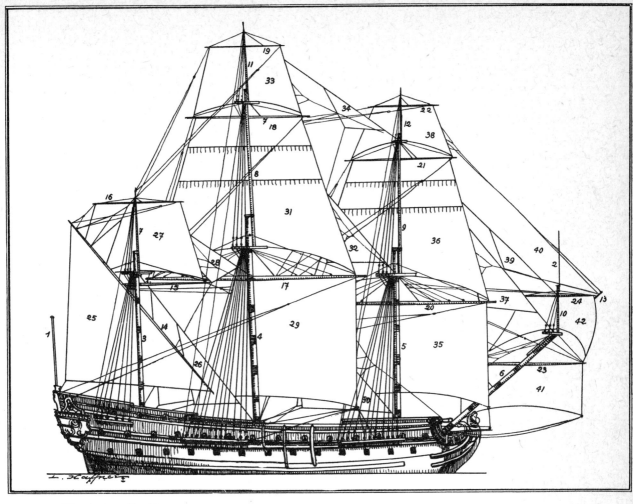

The rigging of a ship
in 1719 (by Leon Haffner):

1. Standard staff	15. Mizzen-top yard	29. Mainsail
2. Bowsprit staff	16. Mizzen-topgallant yard	30. Mainsail stay
3. Mizzenmast	17. Mainsail yard	31. Main-topsail
4. Mainmast	18. Main-topsail yard	32. Main-staysail
5. Foremast	19. Main-topgallant yard	33. Main-topgallant
6. Bowsprit mast	20. Foresail yard	34. Main-topgallant stay
7. Mizzen-topgallant mast	21. Fore-topsail yard	35. Foremast
8. Main-topsail mast	22. Fore-topgallant yard	36. Fore-topsail
9. Fore-topsail mast	23. Bowsprit yard	37. Fore-topsail stay
10. Bowsprit-topgallant mast	24. Bowsprit-topgallant yard	38. Fore-topgallant
11. Main-topgallant mast	25. Mizzen sail	39. Fore-topgallant stay
12. Fore-topgallant mast	26. Mizzen stay	40. Jib
13. Jib boom	27. Mizzen-topgallant	41. Civadiere
14. Mizzen yard	28. Mizzen-topgallant stay	42. Civadiere topgallant

Stinging Coral

These fixed, stinging animals are Cnidaria, Hydrozoa, and Milleporina. They live in colonies in warm waters, and are polyps enveloped in limestone. They are not Madreporaria, or true coral, but, like Madreporaria, they contribute to the building of reefs.

Sugar Cane

The cultivation of sugar cane is of ancient origin in India. The name itself comes from an old Sanskrit word, *sakhara*. The Chinese knew the plant in the second century before Christ. It was introduced by the Arabs into Egypt, and then into Sicily and into the south of Spain. (In the Middle Ages, sugar was considered a medicine, and was sold by the ounce, at apothecary shops.)

There was no sugar cane in the New World before Columbus. It was introduced into the Madeira and the Canary islands in 1503, and then into Brazil during the sixteenth century. It was brought to Guadeloupe in 1644, and then to Martinique in 1650.

Swinging Room

Swinging room, or berth, is the space that is necessary for a ship at anchor to swing around its anchor in the wind, or because of the current or tide.

Tafia

A Creole word used to designate a liquor which is obtained by mixing the juice of sugar cane, molasses, and the by-products of sugar cane.

In the French Antilles, tafia is a sugar-cane liqueur, as distinguished from rum.

Tonnage

The tonnage of a ship is a measure of its capacity, and not of its weight. An added factor of confusion is the considerable difference between the modern ton (2.83 meters) and that used in past centuries.

This measurement has its origin in the Middle Ages. At that time, in the ports of Bordeaux and La Rochelle, the capacity of a ship was calculated according to the number of tons that it could carry; and a "ton" was equal to the volume of four barrels of the period.

Tortuga Island

Tortuga was the headquarters of buccaneers in the Antilles after their expulsion from St. Christopher by the Spaniards. In 1638, the Spaniards seized Tortuga also, but it was retaken by the buccaneers, with the help of pirates, in the same year. From that time on, the buccaneers became indistinguishable from the pirates.

The island was taken again by the Spaniards, and held from 1655 to 1659. It lost its prominence as a pirate base when it was colonized by the French.

Touchhole

The touchhole, or vent, of a cannon was the hole through which fire was applied to the charge.

Undersea Houses

Captain Cousteau's first experiment with undersea houses took place in the Mediterranean, off Marseilles, in 1962, where two divers remained at a depth of thirty-five feet for eight days.

The second experiment was in the Red Sea, at Shab Rumi, in 1963. There, two oceanauts lived for a week at eighty feet; and eight others lived for a month at thirty-seven feet.

The latest experiment was in 1965, and was called Precontinent III. On that occasion, six divers remained at over three hundred feet for three weeks in an undersea house built in the open sea off Cape Ferrat.

The Vasa

In the Port of Stockholm, on August 10, 1628, immediately after Vespers, the *Vasa* was launched. It was a magnificent ship, built upon the orders of King Gustavus II Adolphus, and carrying sixty-four cannon.

On its maiden voyage across the Stockholm archipelago, a sudden squall capsized the ship. Water rushed aboard; and, only 350 yards south of Beckholmen, the mightiest three-master of its time sank in a hundred feet of water. The exact number of dead is not known, but the sinking of the *Vasa* was regarded as a national disaster.

In the years following the sinking, numerous attempts at salvage were made, but they all failed because of the inadequate techniques of the time.

In 1958, however, Anders Franzen, a Swedish specialist in marine archaeology, undertook to raise the *Vasa*. He found the ship surprisingly well preserved; for Swedish waters are too cold for teredos to live there. As the first step, the *Vasa*, stripped of its ornamentation, its cannon and its cargo, was raised to forty-five feet and then reinforced by divers. Then, on April 24, 1961, the *Vasa* was brought to the surface after 333 years on the ocean floor.

Today, it is a precious source of information on the construction and armament of seventeenth-century warships. The dishes, chests, clothing, weapons, and thousands of other objects found in the officers' wardroom and in the crew's quarters make it possible for us to have a detailed knowledge of shipboard life at that time. And, today, the *Vasa*, a ship that made not a single voyage, is the most celebrated of all sailing ships.

BIBLIOGRAPHY

Claude Artaud, François Hébert-Stevens, François Cali, *L'art des Conquistadors,* 1960.

Jean Babelon, *Les monnaies racontent l'Histoire*, 1963.

Georges Blond, *Histoire de la flibuste*, 1969.

Commandant Charcot, *Christophe Colomb vu par un marin*, 1938.

G. Charpentier, *Les relations èconomiques entre Bordeaux et les Antilles au XVIIIe siècle*, 1937.

Jacques Chastenet, de l'Académie Française, *Elisabeth Ière*, 1953.

Cuzacq, *Les faiences de Samadet*, 1940.

Jean Descola, *Histoire d'Espagne*, 1967.

Philippe Diolé, Le trésor du Banc d'Argent, 1956.

Victor Forbin, *L'or dans le monde*, 1941.

Anders Franzén, *The Warship Vasa*, Stockholm 1960.

Marcel Griaule, *Les grands explorateurs*, 1948.

Robert Gruss, *Petit dictionnaire de marine*, 1952.

Jal, *Glossaire nautique*, 1848.

Pierre Jeannin, *Les marchands au XVIe siècle*, 1967.

Julien Le Clère, *Glossaire des termes de marine*, 1960.

Léon Lemonnier, *Sir Francis Drake*, 1932.

Salvador de Madariaga, *Hernan Cortès*, 1953.

Salvador de Madariaga, *Christophe Colomb*, 1952.

Th. Malvezin, *Histoire dú commerce de Bordeaux*, 1892.

Alfred Métraux, *Les Incas*, 1968.

F. Michel, *Histoire du Commerce et de la navigation à Bordeaux*, 1870.

A. Oexmelin, *Histoire des aventuriers flibustiers*, 1744.

R. Picard, J. P. Kerneis, Y. Bruneau, *Les Compagnies des Indes*, 1966.

Charles de la Roncière, *Histoire de la Marine francaise*, 1933.

Guieux La Roerie, *Navires et marins*, 1946.

Robert Stenuit, *La chasse aux galions*.

A. Thomazi, *Histoire de la navigation*, 1947.

A. Thomazi, *Les Flottes de l'or*, 1937.

Kip Wagner and L. B. Taylor, Jr., *Pieces of Eight*, New York, 1966.

Index

Agostini, Yves, of *Calypso* team, 62, 71, 107

Air compressor, use of, on *Calypso*, 105, 116, 117, 166, 211

Airlift, use of, in *Calypso*'s excavating work, 105, 107, 114, 116, 117, 120, 149, 154, 155, 157, 160, 233, 242, 245, 248

Amaddio, Raymond, of *Calypso* team, 123-24

Animal colonies in sea in area around *Calypso* at Silver Bank, 29-30, 60, 111

Aztecs, in Mexico, 259-62

Balboa, Vasco Núñez de, 265, 268

Basket-carrying raft of *Calypso*, 108, 109, 110, 114, 149, 166, 192, 239

Bassaget, Jean-Paul, of *Calypso* team, 13, 24, 104, 205, 241, 244

Bonnici, Christian, of *Calypso* team, 28

Caillart, Claude, of *Calypso* team, 28, 69, 70, 74, 79, 83, 107, 112, 113, 145, 156, 194, 199, 236, 241, 242, 245

Calypso, on Project Sunken Treasure: arrival of, at Silver Bank, 12-13; previous underwater "digs" of men of, 19; motivation in present expedition, 19, 62; plan of action for handling coral at exploration work areas, 28; beginning of explorations by diving teams (July 15), 58-59; sunken ship located by diving teams, 59, 62-63; gold fever takes hold of, 63-64; secret ballot unanimous for continuation of expedition, 67-69; in the heart of Silver Bank, 71-74; Treasure Committee, and agreement on division of spoils, 74-77; in San Juan, for buying of equipment and supplies, 104-5, 164, 191; beginning work again at Silver Bank (July 26), 108-11; the pieces begin to fall into place (July 28), 111-13; fresh-water shortage on, 148, 156, 157, 164, 192, 198; morale of team, 148, 249; how evenings are spent after day's back-breaking labor, 152, 157; retaining confidence in expedition, 157; devotion of men to their work, 160; detail of work site of, showing location of cannon and other discoveries, 161; this expedition as first dig of its kind using available up-to-date equipment, 204, 256; assessment of results, as of August 19, 211; sketch showing two anchorages of, at area of sunken ship, 237; assessment of reward, as of August 22, 238, 240; practical assessment of expedition situation, as of August 31, 246-47; end of expedition, and division of spoils, 251-52; lesson learned from the sea, 253-57; attitude of men of, on failure of realization of dreams of wealth, 254, 256; epilogue, and a moral, to story of, 257

Caribbean: diversity of life forms on ocean floor of, 60; the opulent Caribbean, 219-20; volume of Caribbean commerce in 18th century, and immense number of ships engaged in, 220-22

Coll, Raymond, of *Calypso* team, 24, 70, 77, 78, 79, 80, 108, 116, 117, 158, 160, 194, 195, 197, 204-5, 206, 235, 240, 242, 244, 248, 249

Conquistadors in New World, 88-89, 100, 265-70; lesson to be learned from, 257

Coral: of the Caribbean, 11, 19-22, 23, 193, 231; secrets of, and sunken ships, 26-28; fairyland of, in area around *Calypso* at Silver Bank, 28-30, 158; breaking up of blocks of, hoisted onto *Calypso*, 82, 146, 149, 166; sifting and examining coral debris on rear deck of

Calypso, 148; hoisting of blocks of, to deck of *Calypso*, 159; amount of, handled daily by men of *Calypso*, 194

Cortez, Hernando, 260, 262, 265, 266-68, 270

Cousteau, Captain J.-Y., 10, 22*n*., 123, 162, 181, 185, 238; on his life of devotion to the sea, 247-48; 253; last dive of, at Silver Bank (Sept. 4), 249-51

Cousteau, Jean-Michel, 164, 191

Cousteau, Simone, 63

Cuba, position of, during Spanish domination of Latin America, 41

Debris brought up from the bottom: Hauling aboard *Calypso*, 121, 123; sifting of, on rear deck, 147; accumulation of, below *Calypso*'s stem, 156

De Haenen, Remy, of *Calypso* team, 12-13, 16, 22, 23-24, 26, 58, 61, 62, 64, 66, 67, 70, 71, 76, 77, 80, 81, 104, 107, 108, 144, 145, 152, 156, 164, 166, 194, 200, 202, 211, 240, 243, 244, 245, 246, 248; as moving spirit of the *Calypso*'s treasure hunt in Silver Bay, 16-19

Delemotte, Bernard, of *Calypso* team, 24, 29, 58, 59, 61, 62, 67, 70, 71, 74, 78, 79, 80, 104, 109, 112, 116, 117, 120, 152, 153, 156, 195, 199, 208, 209, 211, 233, 244

Deloire, Michel, of *Calypso* team, 22-23, 24, 46, 58, 59, 60, 62, 64 67, 70, 71, 74, 78, 80, 81, 107, 109, 112, 116, 121, 123, 166, 206, 207, 235, 241, 242, 244, 245, 246, 254, 255

Drake, Sir Francis, 92-100, 272

Dufrêche, Roger, of *Calypso* team, 117

Dumas, Frédéric (Didi), of *Calypso* team, 67, 68-69, 71, 76, 83, 105, 106, 109, 111, 112, 113, 117, 120, 121, 145, 148, 149, 152, 153, 156, 157, 159-60, 164, 165, 193, 195, 199, 00, 201, 202, 204, 205, 206, 207, 211, 233, 235, 240, 241, 244, 245, 246, 248, 249, 256

Durand, J. P., of *Calypso* team, 160, 194, 240-41

Dutch: as smugglers and privateers in Caribbean, 102, 137; as rulers of the sea in first half of 18th century, 228-29; island of St. Martin shared with France as base of operations in Caribbean, 229

England: English pirates and privateers in Caribbean, 41, 92, 97, 102, 132, 134; increase in sea power of, in New World, in 16th century, 92; development of recovery of treasure from sunken galleons as profitable business, 175

Filming by *Calypso* men, 23, 24, 116, 198, 207, 210, 242, 243, 244, 246, 247, 248

Fleet of New Spain: sailing of, from Veracruz, to become part of combined fleet sailing for Spain, 44-45, 88; capture of, in 1628, by Dutch privateers, 102; sunk by hurricane off coast of Florida (1712), 226-28

Fleet of Terra Firma, of Spain: annual return journey to Spain, with treasures from New World, 31-32; at Porto Bello, bartering goods from Spain, and loading New World treasure for Spain, 31-34, 40; departure from Porto Bello, 36-37; shipboard Mass, 40-41; stop at Cuba, on way to Spain, 41; as part of combined fleet sailing to Spain, 45; joined by fleet, with *Nuestra Señora de la Concepción* at its head, for voyage to Spain (1641), 139; combined fleet (1641) wrecked by hurricane, 142-44; sunk by hurricane off coast of Florida (1712), 226-28

Fleets of Terra Firma and of New Spain in combined fleet sailing for Spain: eighty vessels of, 45; itinerary of return trip to Spain, 46-48; dangers and uncertainties of Atlantic crossings, 48; perils of navigation, 48-51; shipboard life on voyage, 51-52; pastimes on voyage, 52-54; arrival at Azores, 54-55; arrival in Spain, 55

Fleets of Terra Firma and of New Spain in 1712 combined fleet-sailing for Spain, 224-26; valuable cargoes of, 224-25; wrecked by hurricane off coast of Florida, 226-28; Kip Wagner retrieves fortune from the sunken ships (1965), 228

Forcherie, Marcel, of *Calypso* team, 24, 70

Foulon, Serge, of *Calypso* team, 58, 70, 71, 79, 108, 153, 206, 233, 241, 243, 244

France: French pirates in Caribbean, 41, 132-34; and commerce with New

World, 223; Company of the Indies, 229-30; laws of, on sunken treasure, 257

Franco-Spanish fleet with valuable cargo from New World destroyed in Bay of Vigo by Anglo-Dutch fleet (1702), 215-19

Gaston, of *Calypso* team, 82, 108, 152, 156, 157-58, 199, 205, 211, 232, 233, 236, 241, 242, 244, 245, 246, 257

Hurricanes: season of, in the Caribbean, 13-14; apprehension felt about *Calypso* because of possibility of, 83, 109, 114; hurricane passes near *Calypso*, 200, 204

Incas, of Andes region, 86, 87, 90, 263-64, 268-69

Items found by *Calypso* diving teams: first "treasures" brought aboard *Calypso*, 24; caldrons, 61, 207, 245; miscellaneous objects, 79, 81-82, 111-12, 149, 153, 164, 166, 194, 197, 198, 205, 206, 207, 209, 211, 232, 233, 241-42, 245; St. Francis medal and cross, 146, 167, 253; lead seals, 149, 152, 154-55, 205, 245; cannon balls, 152, 162, 194, 205, 209, 245; round jars and fragments of them, 156; anchors, 164, 165, 175, 207; china, 207-10, 211; weights from Roman scale, showing dates later than *Nuestra Señora*, 233, 235

Jamaica, island of: as haven for English pirates, 41, 132, 134; wealth of, 219

James and Mary: basket-carrying raft of *Calypso*, 108, 109, 110, 114, 149, 166, 192, 239; treasure-hunting ship of William Phips, 109, 169, 178

Lead weights, to increase stability of *Calypso* divers, 117, 121

Life and Death in the Coral Sea (Cousteau and Diolé), 22n.

Mayas, in Yucatan, Honduras, and Guatemala, 259, 262

Morgan, as cook on *Calypso*, 109

New Spain (present-day Mexico) of 18th century, luxurious style of life in, 222-23

Nuestra Señora de la Concepción: sunken wreck of, as object of De Haenen's interest and of treasure hunt of *Calypso*, 18; treasure hunt of William Phips on (1686), 18, 26, 61, 109, 112, 158, 168-87; building of, at Veracruz, 138; joins fleet of Terra Firma in combined fleet voyage to Spain (1641), 139; story of death agony of, in Caribbean hurricane (1641), 142-44; survivor of, 172-73; wreck of, not located by *Calypso* expedition, 235

Omer, Yves, of *Calypso* team, 28, 116

Parke-Bernet booklet, *Treasure of the Spanish Main*, 228n.

Phips, William, 18, 26, 61, 109, 112, 158; treasure hunt of, on *Nuestra Señora* at Silver Bank (1686), 168-87; background of, 169-73; honors conferred on, 187-90

Pieces of Eight (Wagner), 228n.

Pirates of the Caribbean, 41, 91, 102, 125-32, 133-37; island of Jamaica as haven for English pirates, 41, 132, 134; island of Tortuga as haven for French pirates, 41, 132-34

Pizarro, Francisco, 87, 264, 265, 266, 268-69, 270

Porto Bello, as port of call for ships of Spain, 31-32

Pre-Columbian New World, peoples of, 259-64

Privateers of the Caribbean, 41; English, 92, 97, 102; Dutch, 102, 137

Red diving gloves of *Calypso* divers, 116, 121

Riant, Jean-Clair, of *Calypso* team, 24, 58, 61, 62, 70, 78, 153, 205, 206

Robino, René, of *Calypso* team, 77, 156, 246

Sailing ships, 271-75; structural characteristics of, 271-74; navigational problems, 274-75

Silver Bank: coral and treacherous coral reefs of, 11, 12, 23; arrival of *Calypso* at, 12-13, 22; as graveyard of many ships, 13, 23; as warehouse of treasures on ships wrecked during 16th to 18th centuries, 14-15; preliminary reconnaissance of *Calypso* at, 22-23; structure of, charted, 23; reconnoitering of area, and first "treasures" brought aboard *Calypso*, 24; overview of, 27; garden of marvels around *Calypso* at, 28-30; beginning of explorations by *Calypso* diving teams (July 15), 58-59; locating of cannon by *Calypso* diving team, 59-61; sunken ship at, located by *Calypso* diving teams, 59, 62-63; detailed map of, showing location of wreck, 71

Sirot, Philippe, of *Calypso* team, 104, 109, 112, 149, 236, 241

Soh, John, of *Calypso* team, 69, 71, 113, 148, 242

Spain and the New World: candles, commerce, and colonies, 32-33; the golden mule train across Panama, 33-34; The king's quintal, 37, 265; *La Casa de Contratación*, 38-40, 45, 55; the king's debts, and distribution of Spanish gold throughout Europe, 55-57; effects of New World treasure on Spain, 56-57; search for El Dorado, 85-88, 270; spread of Spanish conquest to shores of Pacific, 87; Spain and trade in Far East from western shore of New World, 87-88; conquest of the conquistadors, 88-89, 100, 257, 265-70; Spain's minting of coins in the New World, 90-91; Spain's deteriorating situation by middle of 16th century, 92; ambush at Panama, 92-94; increasingly difficult relations between Spanish colonies and mother country, 102; dangers to Spain's lines of communication with her colonies from pirates, hurricanes, and coral, 134-35; failure of Spain to organize naval headquarters in the Caribbean, 137; accelerating decline of Spanish maritime power in Caribbean, 138; effects of War of Spanish Succession, 213-14

Spanish galleon *Almirante de Honduras* attacked and captured by Caribbean pirates, 125-32

Spanish sea power, deathblow to, with destruction of Invincible Armada (1588), 100, 102, 103

Sunken ship, located by *Calypso* diving teams, 59, 62-63; question as to its identity as *Nuestra Señora*, 62, 64, 67, 153, 164, 165, 211; beginning work at area of (July 17), 70; the four "mounds" of work area at, 75, 80; preliminary balance sheet of first work on, 82-83; real excavating work begins at (July 31), 117-18; inventory of results of first excavation work at, 148; finding of missing two-thirds of, 165; marine life in area as divers work, 212, 232; proof that it is not *Nuestra Señora*, 235; sketch showing forward and rear sections of, 237; second ship found by divers, 245; working in second work area, 245-48

Sunken vessels, process of demolition of, over the centuries, 202-3

Tassy, Dr., as doctor on *Calypso*, 78, 109, 113, 121, 149

Television, use of, underwater by *Calypso* at excavation area, 152

Treasure of the Spanish Main, booklet issued by Parke-Bernet, 228*n*

Underwater explosions, for clearing anchorage of *Calypso*, 112-13

U. S. Navy plane photographs *Calypso* at Silver Bank, 207

Veracruz, as port of call for ships of Spain, 44, 88

Wagner, Kip, retrieves fortune from sunken ships of fleets of Terra Firma and of New Spain (1965), 228

Zuéna, Paul, of *Calypso* team, 63, 66, 70, 77, 104, 145, 181, 234, 250